If adventure is defined as "unusual [...] faith is defined as "...the evidence of things not seen," then this book is appropriately titled because Dr. Steve Wheeler's missions experiences have indeed been adventures of faith.

As you read through each chapter, his life unfolds, and the curtain is opened, revealing the prayer life of a modern-day disciple. From the moment he was born again, God was renaming him as loved, chosen, and having a purpose. He had a plethora of reasons to not follow the plan of God for his life and even more to not fulfill it once he yielded. But he persevered; he stayed the course, and he learned to live life trusting the Lord.

As you read this book, you'll be surprised as you experience with him the unearned favor of God. You'll feel the excitement from the Amazon River to the hills of Thailand to the villages of Tanzania. But you'll also empathize with him as you see the disappointments of feeling "stuck" when he feels the urgency to go. The stories of the family he loves and the sacrifices he made as he spent years on the mission field will inspire you. After reading this book, I'm convinced God has a calendar, and Steve's education, short-term mission trips, and missionary training were all on that calendar. This is a story of a life encountered by God, a life redeemed by Jesus, and a life led by the Holy Spirit.

This is a book I recommend anyone who feels a call on their life as a "sent missionary" to another people group and perhaps another nation to read. It will motivate you to a life of prayer and inspire you to find your part in the great commission. May you trust His leading as you walk out God's plan for your life.

Dr. Tim and Barbara Odom
Foursquare Missionaries, St. Lucia, West Indies

Adventures of Faith is the real story of a real person just trusting God with the next step. I remember Steve joining our team in Manila in 1996 and all the questions that followed. Steve has told his story in all its raw, honest truth, in which I believe he has given us a valuable picture of the reality of serving God, and especially of being a missionary. Serving God does not always come with a five-year plan laid out neatly before you. Serving God is a faith walk of trusting Him and acting on step one before He gives you step two. Steve is one of those people who typically needs answers to his questions, but God called him to follow despite unanswered questions. In walking that road, Steve has overcome his personal constraints to enjoy a thrilling journey of adventure, glorious ministry, and nation-changing impact. What made the difference is Steve chose God's plans every time.

Steve has become more than a fellow missionary to Eric and I; he has become our brother. I remember so many of the highs and lows, the talking it out, and searching together for the next step. I remember deep conversations, simple encouraging words, and times of just having fun together. Serving God is for real people, and God works through real people. That's what this story is about—just a regular guy who said yes to God and then went on to have an extraordinary journey with Him.

Eric and Therese Nehrt
Staff pastors, Christ Community Church
Camp Hill, Pennsylvania, United States

It is an honor for me to endorse and recommend Steve Wheeler's life story, *Adventures of Faith*. My late husband, Dr. George Meyers, and I have known Steve since he first came to Calvary International in 1995. We were pleased to offer counsel at his request at various stages of his ministry. He has done an amazing job of recounting his adventures and experiences as he walked with the Lord in multiple settings, mostly in Asia and Africa. I admire his transparency as he shares trials and challenges as well as victories along the way. Until the last few chapters when a wonderful helpmeet joined him on the journey, Steve served alone in various roles as a servant of the Most High God. Some of his stories are hilarious, some are heartrending, and he has faithfully given the praise and glory to the Lord for the triumphs and achievements that extended the kingdom of God. You will be edified and challenged in service to the King by reading Steve's autobiography.

Janet Meyers
Special Assistant to Mobilization, Go To Nations, United States

Steve's life is an inspirational story of a young man who went from a drug addict who could barely string words together to make a coherent sentence to earning a doctorate in theology. As you read this book, you will be challenged to believe for the impossible and attempt the impossible. I found myself laughing, crying, and being convicted to examine my own commitment to Jesus. You will not be bored as you read this exciting journey of faith as Steve literally goes to "the uttermost parts of the earth" with the gospel. I highly recommend this book to any believer!

Hal Boehm
Lead Pastor, Summit Church, Elkins, West Virginia, United States

If you ever thought that being a believer in Jesus Christ is a boring life, get ready to be surprised. Steve's book will give you glimpses into what is possible for the person who is all in for God!

His adventures as a modern-day pilgrim who follows Holy Spirit into the nations of this world will thrill and challenge you at multiple levels of your faith.

Thank you, Steve, for writing such a transparent and God-honoring account to inspire all of us as we journey with God.

Mike D. Robertson
Lead Pastor, Visalia First, Visalia, California, United States

Adventures of Faith is an in-depth story of a life filled with trials and triumphs. Steve Wheeler has written a true depiction of his journey through life with the ups and downs commonly experienced by missionaries throughout the world. This is a must-read for anyone considering full-time global mission work and those who love a good story. Steve shows us what an adventure life can be when we follow the Lord in obedience.

Sharon M Williams
Founder/Executive Director, Act 4 the Nations
Women Alive The DAWN Program, Florida, United States

Every believer struggles with hearing God's voice and leading the Spirit-led life. Steve is real, vulnerable, and funny as he tells his story of following God's leading. Be prepared to have your faith challenged as you read about his conversion as a drug addict, being discipled, to his missionary work through Southeast Asia and East Africa, to the pandemic. You will find encouragement in your own life as you journey through Steve's fears, personal struggles, and present dangers, and then rising to the challenge over and over again. There will come a point when you begin to see the brushstroke of Steve's life—a life of obedience and the rewards that come. Sometimes, we think our lives are too simple to make an impact on humanity. Steve's humble life of obedience shows us just the contrary.

Nancy Lovelace
Executive Director, Go To Nations, United States

Obedience usually requires some type of sacrifice which presents an opportunity for us to live by faith. Steve's journey is a beautiful example of living by faith. Learning to trust God through all circumstances. Life seldom goes according to our plans, but Steve's personal stories remind us that ultimately God is in control.

I had the privilege of serving with Steve in Las Vegas, Nevada. It's been a wonderful experience to watch God work in and through his life. I pray this book will bring encouragement and hope to your journey and remind you that living by faith will be an experience that brings both fulfillment and joy.

Tom Westerfield
Pastor, South Coast Christian
San Juan Capistrano, California, United States

Adventures of Faith by Steve Wheeler, opens to every passionate believer how God can take a willing heart and demonstrate His own will upon and through their lives. Steve's journey chronicles the challenges of faith, the choices and cost of obedience, the manifestation of God's abundant grace, and the open reward for those who respond to the missions mandate of the gospel.

Adventures of Faith speaks loudly of the capacity for the hungry soul to seek God's voice and hand in every situation great and small, the stretching of our humanity that redefines one's understanding of personal faith on behalf of others, and the capacity to stand resolutely upon the unshakable Word of God despite the circumstances.

I thank God for my time and fellowship with Steve over the years on the mission field and for this greatly encouraging book and the real life, warts and all recounting of Steve's journey this far and I look forward to the yet to be lived and written chapters of a life well spent and fully for God!

My prayer is many who read this inspirational journey and life will answer the call of Isaiah 6:8, "Then I heard the voice of the Lord saying, 'Whom shall I send? And who will go for us?' And I said, 'Here am I. Send me!'" (NIV).

Reverend Jonathan Vickers
Founder of Christian Outreach Centre, The Haven Foundations, and House of Praise International, Thailand

ADVENTURES
of
FAITH

ADVENTURES
of
FAITH

DR. STEVE E. WHEELER

An Imprint of Go To Nations
Jacksonville, Florida 32207

ISBN: 978-1-7361605-5-8 (Paperback)

ISBN: 978-1-7361605-6-5 (Hardcover)

Printed in the United States of America.

Cover Design: Nathan Atwood

Published by Go To Nations Publishing
3771 Spring Park Road
Jacksonville, Florida 32207

DEDICATION

This book is lovingly dedicated to my wife Veronica, my best friend. You believed in this book, even when I didn't. You have been a constant source of encouragement. Most events I wrote about in this book happened before we met, and yet you laughed and cried at my story.

My children, Grace and Sarah. My desire is you will always have this written record of how the Lord used your mom and I. May it always be a source of comfort and encouragement to you as you seek to do the will of our Father.

My brother Glen. We never talked about my mission's career, and I thought if I could put a book in your hands to read, you would gain a better understanding of what God was doing in and through me. Sadly, Glen passed away before this book was completed.

CONTENTS

FOREWORD

In 1995, as the Regional Director for Asia, based in Manila, Philippines, we were looking at over twenty nations in Asia, more than three billion souls, and more than 60 percent of those had NEVER heard the gospel. We needed manpower. We needed leaders. So I sat down with our International Field Director at that time, now our President, Dr. Jerry Williamson. We recognized leaders are not recruited; they are raised. So together, we laid out a framework for a Timothy Internship Program (TIP) that would apprentice fledgling missionaries as they discovered and established their call to missions.

Steve was in that first TIP. From that humble beginning, my wife Sandra and I, along with some of our closest leaders, have walked through every season of Steve's journey, which began in the Philippines, time back in the US to care for family members, then Malaysia, Thailand, and finally, Africa. Steve went from a minister and teacher in our Bible schools and others, to a director of our schools and other ministry schools, to a seasoned leader in a nation of his own.

It is more than fulfilling to see where God has taken him and his willingness at every stage to say "Yes, Lord." This is a story of faith. Unreasonable faith. This is a story of trust. Unwavering Trust. We worked with Steve through the deep healing of his early life, the loss of family members, and the trials of new nations, cultures, changing ministry leaders, and models. Steve encountered all these things as a single young man.

This a story of challenges and personal sacrifice, but more than that, a story of unrelenting tenacity and a willingness to trust and obey, to hold fast and stay the course no matter what the circumstance. This is a story of the spiritual process, the journey it takes to go from "anointing" to "appointing." Scripture tells us, "many are called, but few are chosen." Calling is a gift from God, but being chosen is based on the fruit of our lives. Steve's story shows us why so many never move from being called to being chosen.

Steve had plenty of opportunities to quit along the way. ALL for good reasons. If he had, he would not be where he is today. He would never have reached that set-in place of appointment that comes as the fruit (not a gift) of a life of persistent faith, trust, pruning, and proving. All promises, destinies included, follow a path that leads through the wilderness, cave, pit, and/or prison for seasons of time.

In many ways, Steve's story may not be unlike the stories of many others. With the exception being Steve's unwillingness to give up and settle. All along the way, God's supernatural influence pulls Steve from season after season, all in preparation for Divine Setup. With God, it is always about the process which leads to fulfillment. The difference between the "calling of God" and the "choosing of God" rests entirely upon our willingness, commitment, and obedience every step of the way. By laying out his journey for us here and bringing us into his story, Steve challenges each of us in our journeys. Or we could say God, the Holy Spirit, through Steve's life, experiences, choices, and example, is challenging every one of us.

When missions were being considered by my generation, we read the stories of those who had gone before us. Men and women who spent decades in unfathomable circumstances and opposition for the least amount of fruit. All to prepare the way for us to go and continue where they had left off. Missions in this generation are so much easier, effective, and empowered than it was one hundred years ago. But many challenges remain the same—personal, cultural, and spiritual challenges. Missions is a lifetime venture and take fully invested lives to see His kingdom come in STILL unreached cultures, societies, and nations of this world.

Every believer with a call from God, no matter how simple or how great, should read this book because Steve highlights the principles that take us from ordinary to extraordinary. What is the difference between an ordinary life and an extraordinary life? EXTRA! As you take this journey with Steve, you have a front-row seat to the EXTRA it takes to move from "called" to "chosen," "ministry" to "leader," a "child of God" to a "son of God," and "using your gift," to "growing your fruit." These are some EXTRAS it takes to truly see God's plans and purposes worked in you, to you, and then out through you. God uses the foolish things of this world to confound the wise. My story, Steve's story, and others like us are living examples of that. Jesus calls "whosoever will" to come follow Him. This is a "whosoever will" story with eternal results.

One of my favorite verses is from a poem by Robert Frost, "The Road Not Taken." The verse states, "Two roads diverged in a wood, and I, I took the one less traveled by, And that has made all the difference." Steve has taken the Road Less Traveled. That has made a difference not only in his life but in the lives of countless others along the way, at home, and in nation after nation. Is this not the road the Lord would mark out for us all if we were willing?

Craig Kuehn
Executive VP of Global Ministries,
Go To Nations, United States headquarters

PREFACE

It has been my privilege and honor to serve the Lord for over twenty-five years as a full-time missionary in southeast Asia, east Africa, and short-term missions ministry when I lived in the United States.

The seed for writing this book was planted in my heart when the Go To Nations leaders, my ministry family for those twenty-five years, asked me to share some of my experiences for a book being written to celebrate our fortieth anniversary as a ministry.

In writing this book, my desire was to leave a written legacy of the life I have been blessed to live. When I surrendered my life to the Lord in 1987 as a twenty-four-year-old man, I had no idea the plan the Lord had for my life, nor did I know how adventuresome it would become.

Within these pages are stories of the incredible ways God used my life, the challenges I faced, and the obstacles I overcame in pursuing the Lord's will for my life. God's grace has surely been evident in my life, and He has kept me safe in the palm of His Hands.

Steve Wheeler

ACKNOWLEDGEMENTS

I am extremely grateful to Janet Meyers, who assisted me in so many ways throughout the process of writing my life story. Her work on this project has been more than editing. Being an author herself, Janet reviewed the chapters as I wrote them and made recommendations for improvement. She understood my goal of sharing my adventures and experiences for the benefit of others. She has provided valuable insights into such areas as using more descriptive wording, sentence structure, and giving advice for chronology. Janet has been a source of wisdom in each part of the writing process, from the beginning ideas for the book to exploring different avenues for publishing.

Janet has been a longtime friend, mentor, advocate, and now, Grandma to our daughters, Grace and Sarah. She has been a constant source of encouragement, especially when writing about some of the more difficult and challenging seasons of my life. I am grateful for her friendship, her loving moral support, and her inspiration.

I am grateful for my Go To Nations family. Much thanks to my leaders, Dr. Jerry Williamson, Craig Kuehn, and Tim and Nancy Lovelace, among others, who have stood with me, encouraged me, and corrected me when they needed to over these past twenty-five years.

Thank you to those who have taken time out of their busy schedules to read this book and give their endorsements. Each of you have encouraged me in this endeavor.

I'm thankful for the Holy Spirit's leading and work in my life. It was amazing that as I wrote this book how the Holy Spirit brought back events I had completely forgotten about.

PROLOGUE

A relative who was a Mormon prophet came to the home to pray over the child who needed a life-saving operation. "Briggie," as he was known, picked up the child and held him in his arms. He anointed him with oil, laid his hand on him, and prayed. After praying for some minutes, he looked at the anxious mother and said, "This child shall live and not die, and he will preach the gospel one day." In the earliest moments of life, the Lord's destiny and purpose for that child had been declared and proclaimed.

I was that child. I was born on July 11, 1963, at St. Jude's Hospital, in Fullerton California. I was born without a soft spot, and my skull bones had grown together, causing pressure on my brain and stunting its growth. I needed an experimental operation to correct that problem. The doctors were unsure if I would survive the risky procedure. The surgery involved removing the parts of my skull bones that had grown together and replacing them with a titanium plate, securing it with metal screws on the sides.

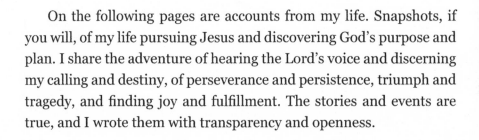

On the following pages are accounts from my life. Snapshots, if you will, of my life pursuing Jesus and discovering God's purpose and plan. I share the adventure of hearing the Lord's voice and discerning my calling and destiny, of perseverance and persistence, triumph and tragedy, and finding joy and fulfillment. The stories and events are true, and I wrote them with transparency and openness.

PART I

The Early Years

1

For I Know the Plans
I Have for You, Jeremiah 29:11

I was living in Bullhead City, Arizona, on the banks of the Colorado River in the tri-state area of California, Nevada, and Arizona. I had been a part of the drug culture, and I left California to get away from it. I had four arrest warrants out for me, and I was afraid of being caught and going to jail.

My offenses were not serious. I mostly got tickets for not having car insurance or an up-to-date drivers' license. Each of those four tickets turned into warrants because I did not appear at my court date. The last time I got pulled over, I was arrested and spent the night in jail, so I needed to appear in court and stand in front of a judge. I was told at the hearing, "Mr. Wheeler, if these go to warrants again, you will go to jail for one year." Well, I did not take care of those warrants, and I just got out of California.

I was soon doing drugs again and realized I couldn't control my addiction. I had gone to Laughlin, Nevada, which is on the Nevada side of the Colorado River, at the urging of a drug buddy. He told me, "You can get a job easily here in Laughlin, and the pay is much higher." When I arrived, I found the casinos did a background check. I had those four warrants, so I did not apply for any jobs lest someone would find out about my past, and I would go to jail.

My drug buddy kicked me out of the house, and I found work at a restaurant across the river in Bullhead City. I would go to work and shower in the bathroom, and after my shift, I would sleep on the grass at a casino. I was homeless, although not for long.

I was twenty-four when I accepted Jesus as my personal Savior in September 1987. I was filled with the Holy Spirit in October and called into ministry in November. Those first three months of my new life in Christ were incredible. For the first time in my life, I had a purpose for living and something to do for the Lord, but I had no idea what.

I met a couple who had a homeless ministry. They took me into their home, which ironically was right across the street from the police department and courthouse. In that house, I prayed and asked Jesus to come into my heart and accepted Him as my personal Lord and Savior. I remember praying for Jesus to break my drug addiction. That was one of the hardest prayers I ever prayed!

My bedroom faced the street, and every night during the shift change in the police department, the police cars would test their spotlights and sirens. The spotlight and red and blue spinning lights shined into my window. It's funny now, but I would wake up terrified because it looked and sounded like the police were at the door looking for me. I began attending Neighborhood Foursquare Church right around the corner from where I was staying. It was a small church with friendly people.

Early Experiences

I lived in the church parking lot in an Airstream travel trailer for a season. It didn't have running water or plumbing, but it was connected to electricity. That season was wonderful, although uncomfortable. I didn't have anything, but I felt rich because I had Jesus. I used the bathrooms in the church and for showers, I had a little portable water container I filled with water and set out in the sun. Then, in the afternoons, I would shower on the church's porch.

During that time, I bought my Fender guitar from the pastor. I wanted to worship the Lord in my way, but I only had a small cassette player. My heart longed to play music, so I was excited to have an instrument! I had been playing for a few months and learning the songs we sang in church. I got excited when my pastor asked me to play on the worship team. That first Sunday morning service, I had not tuned my guitar with the pastor's, so we were not in tune with each other when we played. I was so embarrassed; I played "air guitar" for the remainder of the service.

I was determined we would be tuned properly for the evening service, so I arrived early, and we tuned our guitars together. It was sweet! When we began the worship service, my guitar strap fell off, and I dropped my guitar on the ground. I put the strap back on and played again, and it fell off again! That was my first "ministry" experience, and I was mortified. I was so proud of myself for being invited to play on the worship team, but the Lord used that embarrassing experience to bring humility into my life.

As I entered God's presence in private worship times, the Lord taught me the principle that what you are in private will be what you are in public. I had some incredible intimate times with my Father in that little Airstream trailer in those early days of walking in faith with the Lord.

Learning to Listen to the Holy Spirit

From the beginning of my walk with the Lord, the devil has tried to kill me. Over the years, I had several near-death experiences where I could have died but didn't. I want to share a few experiences in my early days of learning to be led by the Holy Spirit.

One day I was out for a walk. I don't remember where I was going, but I remember vividly what happened. I was waiting for the light to change to cross the street. When the light turned green, I started to walk, and I heard an inward voice telling me to stop. I looked to my left. I was standing in front of an eighteen-wheeler truck, blocking my view of the traffic. I couldn't see past the truck, and I assumed the oncoming traffic had stopped, so I walked. I heard the voice again loudly telling me to stop, so I stopped and again looked both ways. Nothing seemed out of the ordinary, so I walked again, and I heard that voice a third time. It seemed like it was yelling, "STOP! STOP WALKING." I stopped, and when I did, a pick-up truck ran the red light and sped through the intersection. If I had not listened to the Holy Spirit prompting me to stop, I would have walked directly into the path of the truck that ran the red light. Undoubtedly, I would have died instantly. The Word of God says the children of God are led by the Spirit of God (see Romans 8:14), and I learned a valuable lesson about walking in step with the Holy Spirit.

During that time, I worked across the river in Laughlin, Nevada, for a janitorial services company with a contract at an electric power plant. I had been working there for a few months. One night my project was to strip the wax off the floor of an administration building, put new wax down, and buff everything to a nice shine. The process was to first cover the floor with about an inch or so of water and then mix the wax remover and let it sit for a few minutes. Then I was to use a huge buffer machine with mesh pads to remove the wax.

4

The floor was ready, and I was standing in about two inches of water and chemicals when I began. I held the power cord in one hand as I moved the buffer in wide angles from left to right. I suddenly felt a holy presence, an angel of the Lord, come up behind me. I felt a hand cover the hand I had the power cord in. Then in a flash, the cord I was holding shorted out, burst into flames and engulfed my hand with fire.

I could have been electrocuted, but the angel of the Lord protected me. The only evidence of the incident was my finger had a black burn mark where I held the power cord when it burst into flames. The rest of the night I showed everyone at the power plant my finger and told them how the angel of the Lord delivered me from certain death.

I often meditated on John 10:28: "I give to them the gift of eternal life and they will never be lost and no one has the power to snatch them out of my hands" (TPT). The devil continually tried to stop God's plan for my life from coming to fruition, but God's hand of protection was upon me. I was a drug addict before the Lord intervened and saved me, and I wondered what it could be that the Lord had for me to do.

2

Bread of Life Rescue Mission

One church member had a homeless ministry in our area called Bread of Life. Homelessness was and still is a huge problem in the tri-state area along the Colorado River. In those days, it was estimated up to thirty-thousand people in that area were homeless. Our friends had a heart for helping those on the streets. Bread of Life had a small building where they held services and served hot meals on Mondays, Wednesdays, and Fridays. Clothes and food items were given away. While volunteering there once a week to help serve food, I also shared the Word of God from time to time. I am so grateful they mentored me in those early years.

Miracles

I learned so many things and experienced miracles when I was volunteering at Bread of Life, but I want to share two. On a hot summer day in Bullhead, the truck transporting the homeless men to

Bread of Life for the service had just arrived. About fifteen people got out of the truck and entered the building, but one man stuck out to me. He was blind and wearing thick glasses. The Holy Spirit spoke to me that He wanted to heal him that day! It was my day to preach the Word of God, and I don't remember the message I shared, but what happened afterward is still fresh in my memory.

As I ended my message, I gave an altar call for those who wanted to accept Jesus as their personal Lord and Savior. I watched for a response from the blind man. He was squirming in his seat but did not raise his hand. I just knew he would be healed that day, so I sat down and talked with him after the service.

He said he had been blind for several years. I told him God wanted to heal him and asked if he would allow me to pray for him. He agreed, and I laid my hands on his eyes and commanded the blindness to go in the name of Jesus. After praying, I asked him to tell me what had happened. He took off his glasses and said, "I can see light!" I prayed for him again, opened my Bible, put it in his hands, and asked him to read it. He read John 3:16, "For God so loved the world that He gave His only begotten Son, that whoever believes in Him should not perish but have everlasting life" (NKJV). God had healed him! I was so excited, and the man was thrilled God healed him too!

Then he did something I didn't understand. He put his glasses back on. I wanted so much to throw those glasses away since he didn't need them anymore, but I remember the pastor telling me, "You can't do that. He has to learn to walk out his own healing." I never saw the man again. Like most of the homeless population, he just disappeared. About a year later, he showed up at Bread of Life again and gave this testimony. "I was healed last year here at the mission. When I left that day, I continued to wear my glasses, but I soon discovered I couldn't see while I was wearing the glasses. The Lord spoke to me one day and said I didn't need the glasses anymore, and when I stopped wearing them, I could see perfectly."

Brother Boyd

Brother Boyd was homeless and regularly came to Bread of Life Rescue Mission. He had received the Lord and volunteered at the mission, helping serve, and the pastors discipled him. Several years before, Boyd had been in a terrible accident, resulting in him having one foot four inches shorter than the other and sticking out at a weird angle. The accident also caused him to need a partial lobotomy, where part of his skull had been crushed. Because of the head injury, he was slow to speak, and it took him time to form words and answer questions. Boyd was highly intelligent, but to have a conversation with him required a lot of time.

Brother Maurice Martin and his wife were elderly evangelists with the Foursquare denomination who came and held a series of meetings at the church on the believer's authority. I soaked in everything they preached like a sponge. We witnessed several miracles and healings as he taught the Word on our authority over sickness and disease. It was an amazing week of ministry, with miracles and healings every night.

Ironically, Brother Maurice had one ear plugged up, and he was deaf in that ear. His wife had suffered a stroke, and she was still in recovery. When he prayed and laid hands on people, he stood his wife up and leaned her against the wall, and she would pray.

I just knew God would heal Brother Boyd, but he didn't come to any meetings, and I kept wondering where he was. I remember what happened the last Sunday of the meetings like it was yesterday. I had such faith God wanted to heal Brother Boyd, but we didn't see him in the service again.

After it was over and most of the congregation left, Brother Boyd arrived, and Brother Maurice talked with him for a few minutes and offered to pray for him. Someone brought a chair for Boyd, and Brother Maurice kneeled before him and grabbed his feet. I was right next to them, watching with my eyes wide open. I didn't want to miss what was about to happen. I remember some of Brother Maurice's prayer, "Lord, we are asking for a creative miracle. We command this foot to grow in Jesus' name!" What happened next was incredible! His foot moved! I was stooped over and just inches away from Boyd's foot, so I had a clear view. Boyd's foot grew out two inches but was still crooked and at an angle. Brother Maurice then took off Boyd's boots. We could see his foot had grown but was still about two inches shorter than the other foot. He prayed again, and I watched as his foot grew out the other two inches and straightened as well!

We had witnessed a creative miracle! God grew four inches of bone and straightened Boyd's foot. At the evening service, Brother Maurice encouraged us that everyone could see miracles if we just stepped out in faith and exercised our authority. He asked for a show of hands of those who would lay hands on the sick. I was sitting on the front row, and I shot my hand up. I would have an opportunity to put into practice what I had learned that week the next day.

I was working at Walmart, and on Monday morning, I went to work as usual. There was nothing special about that day. I was a department manager and had a couple of people who worked in my department. When I arrived, I saw Linda's eye was swollen and black and blue. She was in terrible pain, and I asked her what happened. She said, "I was lifting a box to put on the shelf. I dropped it, and the corner hit me in the eye." Before I knew what was happening, I heard these words coming out of my mouth, "Can I pray for you?" She agreed, so I told her after my shift, I would pray for her. I had never laid hands on anyone before and didn't know what to do.

I avoided her the rest of the day, and I was hoping to sneak out without her seeing me so I wouldn't have to pray for her. As I walked out of the store, I thought, *I made it without seeing Linda.* I took a few steps, and there she was on her break, sitting outside with about fifteen other employees, smoking a cigarette. She saw me and came to have me pray over her. I was committed now, and I was so scared! She stood there looking at me, waiting for me to pray. I looked at her and past her to see the other employees watching me.

Thoughts of what I would do flooded my mind. Brother Maurice didn't show us how to lay hands on the sick; he just said do it. I thought, *this is terrible, and I am going to make a fool out of myself.* I would just touch her eye and pray. As I fearfully reached out to touch her eye, my hand and fingers were shaking. What happened next was like watching a movie in slow motion.

Before I even touched her eye, she fell under the Holy Spirit's power. She hit the ground with a loud "thud." There weren't any ushers to "catch" her, as you would see in church. I looked at the other employees. They heard the thud, and when they turned to look, they dropped their cigarettes, and their mouths were open. I looked to the sky and said, "This is Your fault, Lord. I have killed her." She wasn't moving. *Oh, why did I raise my hand at church last night?* Then Linda stood up, and her eye was completely healed. The swelling disappeared and was no longer black and blue. I tried to look like I did this all the time, but inwardly I was thinking, *Praise the Lord, I didn't kill her.* I was so excited and relieved that I forgot to lead her to the Lord!

3

I Will Make Even Your Enemies Be at Peace with You

I worked for a company that specialized in cleaning homes after fires or floods. One morning my boss called me and said, "We have a house across the river in California that I need you to go look at. Four people were murdered there, and I want you to pray over the place before we start repairs."

Fear immediately gripped my heart. When I left California, I vowed I would never return. I explained I had four arrest warrants for me. He was sympathetic but still wanted me to go. I was terrified I would be arrested as I crossed the river into California. The next day my boss encouraged me, "You need to take care of those warrants. You don't want to have that hanging over you." I pondered my options and prayed. *One year in jail is a long time. If I could just do my time, then I would be free.* I asked the Lord what He wanted me to do. As I was praying and crying to God, I felt led to open my Bible to Proverbs 16:7 and read these words: "When a man's way please the Lord, He makes even his enemies to be at peace with him" (NKJV). My heart leaped for joy!

God had just spoken two powerful things to me. My life was pleasing to Him, and He would make my enemies be at peace with me. I had the assurance everything would be okay, so I appeared at the Bullhead courthouse. I remember that day vividly. It was 4:30 in the afternoon, and I decided to talk to the judge hearing court cases. I walked into the courthouse, sat, and waited until the judge heard the last case. As the judge stood to walk out, I stood and approached the bench. A deputy immediately stepped in front of me, but I called out to the judge and asked if I could ask a question. "What can I help you with?" the woman asked. I then gave her the unvarnished truth.

I was excited to share with the judge what had happened, just like a little child who had no guile. I said, "I have four arrest warrants and was told the last time I appeared in court that if these tickets went to a warrant again, I would be put in jail for a year. I gave my life to Jesus and have gotten cleaned up. I was praying the other day, and the Lord said my life was pleasing to Him, and He was making my enemies be at peace with me. I want to take care of the situation, but I do not know what to do. I came to ask for help." The judge replied, "Are those warrants in this jurisdiction?" "No, they are from California," I said. We talked for a few minutes, and she suggested I call the court in California and see if I could take care of the warrants and set up a payment plan without having to appear before a judge. I thanked her and left the building. I thought, *What just happened? I just walked into the judge's court, approached the bench, and talked to her like she was my friend. Who does that and gets away with it?* I made the call to California, and true to His word, my enemy was made to be at peace with me.

I was given a fine of one thousand dollars. I set up payments of fifty dollars a month, and I didn't have to go to California and appear before a judge. I took care of everything over the phone.

God set me free and removed one major obstacle from my past that haunted me. I could now serve the Lord and go forward without fear. I was faithful to make my payments and eventually paid my fines off. I was free!

4

Ministry Experiences: Sharing My Faith

We were in between pastors at Neighborhood Foursquare Church when I had my first opportunity to minister. I hadn't been born again for too long and was still pretty rough around the edges. The Lord spoke to me about sharing my testimony with those outside my church, and I looked for opportunities. The first church I contacted was a Baptist church around the corner and down the block. I made an appointment to visit the pastor, Bob Rose, and said I wanted to share my testimony with the church.

The time came for my appointment with Pastor Rose, and I wasn't sure what I would say. We were from two different streams of Christianity. I wondered if I heard the Lord correctly that I was supposed to share my testimony at that church. Pastor Rose greeted me warmly and welcomed me to sit in his office. After a minute or so of small talk, the pastor said, "We don't usually allow someone we are not familiar with to share in our services, but thank you for coming by." With that, he stood, signaling our meeting was over. "Since I am here, can I just go ahead and share my testimony with you?" I replied as I shook his hand. He motioned for me to sit back down, and I shared my life story. When I finished, he wiped a tear from his eye and said, "I can see you love the Lord, and you are genuine. God has touched your life in a mighty way. Can you come and share your story with our congregation on Wednesday night?" I gladly accepted the invitation and visited the church the following Wednesday night.

I had one suit, one dress shirt, and one tie. I put on my best and arrived at the church a few minutes before services started. Pastor Rose greeted me and ushered me into his office and talked about the order of the service. After the worship service, he introduced me to the congregation. "I met this young man on Monday. I was moved by his testimony and have asked him to come share it with us tonight. Would you please welcome Steve Wheeler?"

Many people were in attendance, and they were polite and listened intently to my story. As I was sharing, I saw people wiping tears from their eyes. When I finished speaking, I sat in the front row while the pastor closed the service. The pastor gave the announcements, and then he called me to the platform and said, "Maybe you have been touched by Steve's story. I don't usually do this, but if you would like him to pray for you, I invite you to come to the altar." I was shocked! I had no idea I would be praying for anyone.

I prayed for six people at the altar that night. One woman I prayed for fell under the power of the Holy Spirit. The ushers had no policies or procedures for that type of thing, so they left her on the floor while I prayed for the others. I left the service with the deep abiding peace that comes from having been obedient to the Lord. That was the only time I shared at that church, but Pastor Rose had a warm spot in my heart, and I never forgot him. We saw each other from time to time, usually at a restaurant after mid-week services. I always said hello, and he always greeted me warmly.

The second church I approached was Calvary Chapel, which Chuck Kelly pastored. Pastor Chuck and I frequently ministered together at Bread of Life Rescue Mission. I talked with him one day about sharing my testimony, and he invited me to come on a Sunday night, which was their "family night" service. Back in those days, I knew nothing about protocol as I do now, so I didn't have a follow-up call with Pastor Chuck, confirming my visit.

I showed up on Sunday evening, and Pastor Chuck wasn't there. I found someone who looked like a leader and let him know I was scheduled to share that night. The person in charge did not know that and wasn't expecting me. Neither of us knew what we were supposed to do. It was decided I would share briefly before the message. I shared for about ten minutes, then sat down and listened to the message. Later, I found out some members thought what I shared was not appropriate for a family night. Many had young children, and I did not know enough to soften my testimony.

On another occasion, my mom and many relatives met in Laughlin at the Ramada Hotel and Casino for the weekend to gamble. I was bold back then and told my mom I wanted to have a family meeting while everyone was together. I wanted to share my testimony of drug addiction and the deliverance and freedom I had found in Christ. Sharing my testimony to strangers in a church setting was one thing but sharing with my family was another. I was not sure what I would say or how they would receive it. The meeting time arrived, and everyone met in my mom's room. Cigarette smoke filled the small room, so someone opened the window for fresh air.

Everyone was respectful and listened quietly to what I said. I spent about twenty minutes sharing my testimony. I didn't give the "sanitized" version but went into great detail about my drug addiction and how Jesus saved and delivered me. At the end, I asked everyone to bow their heads and close their eyes, and I gave an altar call. I said

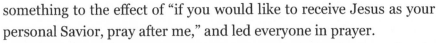

something to the effect of "if you would like to receive Jesus as your personal Savior, pray after me," and led everyone in prayer.

I don't remember many comments after I finished. Some family members got up and left quickly while others mingled, talking about what to do next. My Aunt Gaye came up to me, gave me a big hug, and whispered, "I am so proud of you. I am a Christian too, and I pray every day for your dad." I don't know what the heavenly results of that meeting were, and I had completely forgotten about it until writing this book. As I shared this story with my wife, we both laughed as I said, "I probably wouldn't have the audacity to do that now!"

Therefore, if the Son Makes You Free, You Shall be Free Indeed

I attended Neighborhood Foursquare church and served on the worship team. For some time, the church was without a pastor, and different ministers came weekly to preach while the denomination looked for someone to pastor the church. Many people left during this challenging time, but a small core group of about fifteen to twenty stayed, which I was part of.

One Sunday no one was scheduled to preach, so we gathered together for worship and prayer. I was on the platform playing my guitar with the worship team leading the small congregation in praise and worship when a woman came in and sat in the back row. We were a small church, so I knew everyone, but I didn't recognize her. As we worshiped, I heard the Holy Spirit whisper, "I have brought her here to set her free." After a few minutes, she got up and walked out of the building. I saw my friend John Turpin follow her outside, and after a few minutes, he came back in by himself. After worship was over, I asked John, "Is she still here?" "Yea, she is outside and doesn't want to come in," he replied. "God told me He wants to set her free. I'm going out to talk to her," I said. He replied, "Be careful; she is whacked out."

I walked outside and struck up a conversation with her. She lit a cigarette, so I lit one as well. Even though I was a Christian and on fire for the Lord, I still smoked. It's funny now, but back then, I didn't think anything about ministering the love of Jesus to her while smoking a cigarette. I told her God loved her. She replied angrily, "What do you know about love?" She turned to walk away. Then I did something I had never done. "In the name of Jesus, you come back here!" I shouted. When I said those words, she turned around violently and started contorting. I thought, *wow, the name of Jesus works.* Every time she turned around to walk away, I said, "In the name of Jesus, turn around," or "the blood of Jesus," and each time I said those words, she turned around, and the demons in her would manifest.

The Holy Spirit brought things to my mind when I talked with her. When I spoke out what I heard, she admitted they were things that had happened in her life. I said, "Jesus brought you here to set you free. If you come into the church with me, we can pray for you." When she got to the church's door, she put her hand on the handle and began to open the door. Then the door slammed shut. She tried the second time to open the door, and again the door slammed shut. Finally, on the third time, she opened the door, and we went into the church.

The congregation was gathered in a circle holding hands and praying. I walked to the group and said, "I don't know what else to do, but I got her in the church." While others prayed quietly, I sat next to her while we talked with her. I don't remember her name, but I will call her Debbie. The demons kept manifesting, and she clenched her fists so hard her knuckles turned white. She did this several times while we were ministering to her. When we asked her if she was ready to receive the Lord, she turned to me and said, "Steve, I think you better take this." I stuck my hand beneath hers and wondered what she had. *Is it a bomb?* I was a little scared over what she would deposit into my hand. She tried to open her hand a couple of times but couldn't.

When she finally released her hand, a double-edged razor blade fell into my palm. That she did not slice her hand to pieces was a miracle. Someone prayed for her to receive Jesus, and she was set free from the demons. When we opened our eyes, we saw her countenance had completely changed. She now had a glow about her and a big smile on her face. Someone asked if she was around here, and she said, "No, I don't live here. I was just passing through town and somehow ended up here at the church. I don't even know how I got here." As we were about to leave, we prayed for her to receive the Holy Spirit, and she wonderfully received the infilling of the Holy Spirit. One church member gave her money to get home to her family, and we never saw Debbie again.

When we talked later, we discovered when the church members were inside praying, someone would pray for a specific thing, and I would talk about that specific thing outside when I was ministering to Debbie. It was awesome to see Jesus completely save and set free Debbie. I learned a great deal about the power in the name of and the blood of Jesus available to us as believers today.

PART II
Preparing for Ministry

5

Do Not Lean on Your Own Understanding

I don't remember the specific date, somewhere around 1991 or 1992, but I remember that night before I left Bullhead City, Arizona, very well. I was sleeping on the floor of a friend's house. I had loaded my Mazda B2000 pick-up with all my belongings. I was to depart in the morning for Tulsa, Oklahoma, and I couldn't sleep.

As morning dawned, I felt the Lord speak to me to give my most prized possession away. The first guitar I bought when I became a Christian was a Fender, and it was the most valued thing I owned. As I gave it to the person, he was shocked. He told me the Lord spoke to him in the night to begin playing worship, and he would be given a guitar.

As I drove to Tulsa, I was alone with my thoughts. I applied to attend Victory Bible Institute a few months earlier and hadn't received notice I had been accepted. I was sure that was the next step, so I left in faith, believing the school accepted me. I could transfer with the company I was working for and had a job waiting in Tulsa, but everything else was unknown.

It was difficult to leave my church family for the unknown, and as I drove, I struggled with my emotions. *Am I doing the right thing? Had I heard clearly from God? What would happen to me?* I drove to Tucumcari, New Mexico, where I stopped at a hotel to rest for the night. After I settled in my room, I went to the restaurant and ordered food. My emotions got the best of me, and I broke down and cried uncontrollably. It seemed the tears just wouldn't stop. My poor waitress asked if I was okay, and I mumbled I was.

When I got back to the room, I cried out to God, "God, I need to know what I am doing is what You asked me to do! If I am making a mistake, tell me, and I will turn around and go back to Bullhead." As I cried before the Lord, I saw a Bible in the drawer from the Gideons. I picked it up and cried to the Lord for a Word as I opened to Proverbs chapter 3, verses 5 and 6. The words jumped off the page at me as if I had never read them before. "Trust in the Lord with all your heart and lean not on your own understanding; In all your ways acknowledge Him, and He shall direct your paths." My heart jumped with joy! Then I read the passage in Proverbs 4 verse 7. "Wisdom is the principle thing; therefore, get wisdom. And in all your getting, get understanding." My soul overflowed with joy, and I praised the Lord with all that was in me! Those two Scriptures, given to me in a hotel room on the way to the destiny the Lord had for me, assured me I needed to take the leap of faith and have led me on this adventure. Even now, almost thirty years later, I still vividly recall exactly where I was when I heard from the Lord.

Victory Bible Institute: 1993-1994

A year or two before I moved, I attended a conference in Tulsa and toured a local Bible college. The tour guide was Mary Gervase, and as we went through the campus, I felt the Lord speak to me to support her while she went to school. After the tour was over, I told her what the Lord spoke to me and got her name. When I returned to Arizona, I sent money to the school on her behalf, and I supported her for some time.

During the school year, she was hit head-on in a car crash. She lived, but it took a long time to recover. The accident took her out of school, and we eventually lost touch. Every time I sent a check to the school, I prayed, "Lord, when it is time for me to go to school, I ask that I can go debt-free and pay for my schooling upfront and not have to go into debt." Sowing finances into Mary's life was one of the most fruitful things the Lord led me to do. Those seeds have continued to produce a harvest in my life, as you will see throughout this book.

After I had been in Tulsa for a few months, I went to the VBI office to inquire about being accepted into the school. I was told the letters hadn't been mailed out yet, and they couldn't give me any information. "You don't understand," I said. "I moved here in faith believing I was supposed to go to Bible school, and I don't live at that address in Arizona anymore." The woman smiled and said to wait. She came back and handed me an acceptance letter! I was going to Bible school!

When I enrolled in VBI, I paid for my first year in cash. It cost $1,370, and in those days, that was a lot of money. I got all my textbooks for free because I paid in full. Anyone who knows me well knows reading is one of my passions, so I was excited to have so many new books to read.

I remember the first days of the Bible school like it was yesterday. I came out of a pretty rough lifestyle and needed help. I knew I couldn't change in my power, and I desperately needed the Word of God. I had a calling for ministry, and for the first time in my life, I knew I had a purpose. I was serious and didn't have time to fool around, and I let everyone who sat around me know not to disturb me because I needed the Word of God to fix me. I sat in the second row and listened intently to every teacher that came, wanting to squeeze everything I could from them and get my money's worth.

Monday was the first day of school, and I went home into my prayer closet and prayed, "My first day of Bible school was amazing, Lord, but my life hasn't changed yet. I am still the same as I was yesterday." The second day was the same. It was amazing to sit under the Word, and I soaked in everything that was said, but my life was still the same. I went home again and prayed, "Lord, my life hasn't changed a bit. What is going on? Please change my life." The third day was the same as the rest, and I went home mad. When I got into my prayer closet, I blamed God that I had been in Bible school for three days, and my life hadn't changed a bit. I sputtered, "If You're not going to change my life, then give me my money back and send me back to Bullhead."

That evening when I went to church, there was a pause during worship, and a holy hush fell in the auditorium. After some time, someone prophesied, "You said to Me today, 'if You are not going to change my life, then give me my money back and send me home.' But I say if you will just trust Me, the change I do in your life will be astounding. You will not recognize yourself when I am finished with what I am doing in you." I slunk down into my chair, embarrassed my prayer was broadcast to the entire congregation. At the same time, I was excited God knew who and where I was. I didn't know what was in store for me as the year went on.

One day during chapel, Pastor Sharon Daugherty came and led worship. As she played the piano and worshiped, God got a hold of my heart. God was digging deep and doing a powerful work in me. I got out of my chair, knelt before the Lord, and wept uncontrollably. I had never wept like that, and it went on for thirty minutes. I couldn't pray or talk; I could only sob and wail from deep within my soul and spirit. When the burden lifted and I got up off the floor, I had soaked the carpet with my tears about twelve inches around the place where I was lying.

After that, Pastor Billy Joe Daugherty came in and talked about having a heart for the world. I wept again uncontrollably, so much so that he looked at me as if I was disturbing him. But God was grabbing my heart again and breaking it for the world's peoples and solidifying my call to the nations. All I could do was say through my tears, "I will go, Lord." I am sure those sitting around me wondered what was happening, but all I can say is it was one of those times where the Lord came in and did a deep work in my heart, and I walked away changed. That was a day of consecration for me, setting myself apart for the work the Lord was calling me to. From that day forward, I lived life looking through a different set of lenses. I lived determined to go and do wherever and whatever the Lord wanted me to.

Bible school was a great experience. It was great to sit under the Word every day, but the *life* experiences I gained served me well even today. By the time I graduated, the Lord truly had done a great work in my life, and I was a different man. I graduated with a sense of purpose, destiny, and vision for my life and ministry. I discovered what I was born to do while I was in VBI.

6

Will You Go for Me?

It was November, and I had been in school for a couple of months. A short-term mission trip to Mexico was planned for over the Thanksgiving holiday, but I didn't put my name on the sign-up sheet. I had the money to go, and I felt the Lord speak I was to go, but I didn't sign up because I knew I couldn't take time off from work.

I remember one chapel service that changed my entire life. The church's missions' director led the chapel service. He rebuked the class, "You are Bible school students, many of whom are preparing for ministry. We made this mission trip affordable for everyone to go on." As he spoke these next words, it seemed he was pointing his fingers right at me, "and only one student has signed up to go on this trip." He said other things, but all I heard in my heart was, "And only one person signed up for this trip." I knew I was supposed to go, and I was being disobedient. After chapel, I told him I would go.

I went to my supervisor and asked for time off. She listened politely and then said she couldn't give me the time off during the holiday. The company I worked for had an open-door policy, meaning you could appeal to higher management if you wanted to. I said to my supervisor, "I am sorry, but I want to go to your manager and ask approval to take this trip." I went to the manager and got the same reply. I spoke with four different management levels and got the same reply. Then the Lord spoke to me, "Are you going to trust in your ability to take care of yourself, or are you going to trust Me with your life?" So, I gave my two-week notice and quit my job to go on a mission trip.

Quitting my job was one of the hardest things I ever did up to that point. God gave me that job, and it was the only thing that brought stability to my life other than my relationship with the Lord. I don't remember much of the specific ministry we did during that two-week trip because the Holy Spirit was breaking my heart every day for the nations, and every day I cried. The other team members left me alone because I would just cry if anyone said anything to me. The Holy Spirit had my heart in His hands. One day He asked, "If I called you to come here, would you?" Another day, He asked, "If I asked you to come and live here in a dirt floor house, would you?" Every day He would ask, "If I asked you, would you go for me?"

I still vividly remember the exact day I said "Yes" to the Lord. We were driving back from a ministry event. It was raining, and I looked out the window, watching the people as we drove by. My heart was breaking, I was crying, and I heard the Holy Spirit whisper, "Will you go for Me?" I broke down and said, "Yes, Lord, I will go for You. Wherever You want me to go, whatever You want me to do, I am Yours. There is no price I could pay that would ever compare to the price You paid for me."

For We Walk by Faith and Not by Sight

There was so much to process after that first mission trip. I came back a different person, knowing the Lord's calling for me and having a new direction and purpose for my life. When I returned, I felt the Holy Spirit speak to me, "The places I will send you to will require you to walk in faith and believe Me for meeting your needs. For the next season, I do not want you to work but to trust Me and ask Me to provide for your needs.

That was a real challenge for me! I was excited and a little nervous; would the Lord meet my needs? What if I failed? Some school leaders did not think I was hearing from God and told me I needed to get a job, often telling me, "If you won't work, you won't eat..." I learned from that experience it is not always best to tell people what you have heard from the Lord.

My first need arrived quickly. My $48.23 electric bill arrived. I went into my prayer closet, set the bill on the floor, and prayed, "Lord, You said You wanted me to believe You to meet my every need. I have an electric bill due now, and I need $48.23." While I was thanking the Lord, I heard the phone ring in the other room. After praying, I played the message. The caller said, "While I was praying, I felt the Lord speak to me to give you money. I have one hundred dollars I want to give you." I was shocked and astounded! God answered my prayer quickly!

Next, my rent was due. I needed $485, and I didn't have two nickels to rub together. I prayed and presented my need to the Lord, and again, I got a phone call while praying. "Steve, I feel led to give you five hundred dollars. Can I come by later? That season lasted maybe two or three months, and eventually, I got a job waiting tables. That was when I learned to believe and trust God for my future ministry finances I would need, and this is where I learned how to trust God to provide for all my needs.

During that time, I began a ministry called "Bread for the Nations." I felt the Lord say if I couldn't meet the needs of people in my community, how could I expect to go meet the needs of the people in the world? Shortly after that, I received my first monthly financial partner. A good friend in Bullhead called me one night and said, "I am going to send you twenty dollars a month for you to use for your feeding program." She remained a faithful twenty-dollar a month partner for the next twenty-five years.

Our church did monthly crusades in the city's lower-income housing areas, and I bought food to hand out to people. During that season, I held two evangelistic crusade meetings in those housing complexes. The first crusade was exhausting. I did all the work myself, setting up the venue, preparing the food baskets, preaching, giving the altar call, etc. When it was finished, I swore I would never do another crusade again. After that, the Holy Spirit "debriefed" me about the crusade, and I realized I had done many things wrong.

The Lord stirred in my heart to have another crusade, and I determined to implement the things the Holy Spirit had taught me. During the Thanksgiving holiday, I led a team to do a crusade in one of those projects. I had a Thanksgiving dinner along with a gospel presentation. That time, everything was done differently. First, I prayed every day for the crusade. One day I was praying, "Lord, it would be nice to have turkey we could have as a meal. Thank You for providing that need. Oh, and dinner rolls would be great too." I got up and got ready to go to church, and when I opened the door, someone had put a few bags of food on my doorstep while I was praying. Inside was a turkey and dinner rolls. I got other people involved, and I didn't do anything at the event. The night of the service was special, and the results were gratifying. I introduced the ministry team, and they handled everything. I don't remember how many people gave their hearts to Christ that night, but I remember it was far more than the previous crusade I did by myself.

During that time, I sent out my first newsletter, "Bread for the Nations." I sent them to my dad in Hesperia, California. I never preached to him; I just, matter-of-fact, sent him information about what I was doing. I didn't realize it then, but God used my newsletters to reach some of my family, but more on that later.

7

Mexico Missions

I spent the next two years traveling and ministering in Mexico. The language barrier affected me during my first mission trip. It was frustrating to not communicate in Spanish.

My pastor had written a book called, *This New Life* that had been translated into Spanish. I determined on my next trip, I would present the gospel in Spanish. I memorized the book and learned how to present the gospel and lead someone to the Lord in Spanish.

On my second trip to Mexico, I would go up to a crowd and say, "I want to practice my Spanish with you." They were always excited and eager to hear me practice. I would begin by saying, "I talk; you listen." Then I would present the gospel without stopping. It usually took about twenty minutes or more. Afterward, I would give an altar call and lead those who wanted to receive the Lord in prayer, asking Jesus to come into their hearts. That was a powerful tool the Lord had given me, and I led hundreds of people to the Lord during that time.

On one trip, we had evening outdoor crusades in an open lot across from our hotel. During the worship service, which usually lasted between one and a half to two hours, a friend and I walked up and down the street evangelizing. It was so easy to preach the gospel and pray for people to receive the Lord. Every person we talked to invited Jesus to come into their hearts. After one crusade, I asked our team leader if we could go back out and evangelize. We were given permission, and we headed out the door. I was confident we would reap a harvest of many souls just like we did earlier during the crusade.

We spent the next four hours walking up and down the same streets, and not one person received the Lord. We walked into a bar and sat down with someone. I spent two hours trying to convince that man to give his heart to Jesus, but he wouldn't budge. My friend translating got upset with me for my persistence in trying to convince this person, who I felt was so close to giving his heart to the Lord. That caused a split in our friendship, and we were never close after that trip. My friend just couldn't understand the passion for lost souls driving me.

I learned a valuable lesson about the power of worship, though. While worship was happening, it seemed the heavens opened, and everyone's eyes and hearts were opened to receive the gospel message. When worship was finished, the atmosphere was different. I felt the Holy Spirit speak to me that worship pushes back the darkness and creates an atmosphere for miracles to happen.

Miracles in Mexico

I frequently traveled to Nuevo Laredo, Monterrey, and Mexico City. I usually went with a team from the church or other Bible school students. After graduating from VBI, another graduate and I traveled to Nuevo Laredo and spent a month volunteering with a ministry. I was praying about moving to Mexico, which would be an opportunity to get to know the ministry better. Many things happened during that season of traveling, but I remember two events vividly.

On one trip, I felt the Lord say He wanted me to teach on the Holy Spirit and divine healing. On the Saturday before I was to preach, the team was having a meal near our hotel. It was raining that night, and after I finished eating, I left to go to the hotel to prepare for the next day. I had only one pair of dress shoes, and the bottoms were slick, so my feet often slid from under me when I wore them. I started to cross the street, and out of the corner of my eye, I saw a truck barreling toward me. I ran across the street, and when I reached the curb, my feet slipped on the wet pavement. I fell and twisted my ankle, landing half on the curb and half on the sidewalk. I was in excruciating pain and couldn't get up. I was crying out for someone to help, but people kept walking past me.

Some of our team exited the restaurant and saw me across the street and came and picked me up. My ankle wasn't broken, but it was swollen twice the normal size, and I was supposed to preach on healing the next day! I thought, *God, how can I preach on healing when I need healing myself? What will people think when I hobble up to the platform to preach?* The Lord spoke to my heart, "My provision for healing isn't based on you but on My Word." I decided to preach the next day as planned.

After the long worship service, I was introduced to come to the platform. I explained what happened the night before and preached on the will of God to heal. The pain in my ankle left as I was preaching! When I gave the altar call to pray for the sick, many people received healing. One woman had a large tumor in her stomach that was instantly healed.

We were in Monterrey on another trip with a large youth group from a Florida church. We had to use three vans to transport all of us. The schedule was packed with three ministry events planned for each day. I remember the motto that served me well on that trip, "Eat when you can, sleep when you can, and go to the bathroom when you can because you don't know when you can again."

We finished the first ministry event and were driving to the second when the lead van's engine completely stopped running. We pulled off to the side of the road and tried to determine the problem, but the van would not start. The ministry leader said, "We are next to a university, so let me inquire if we can do our evangelistic outreach on the campus." He left and came back a few minutes later, saying we were permitted to do our outreach. So we rushed onto the campus and set up our equipment, and a large crowd gathered.

The program consisted of dramas, testimonies, and a short gospel presentation. Several people responded to the altar call, and as we packed up our equipment, we noticed a young woman crying. Someone went over and talked to her. "I have been praying for years for God to send someone to our campus." She was so happy the Lord had heard her prayers. The funniest thing was when we got into our vans, the one with the problem started right up. It seemed the Lord wanted us to be at that campus that day. Later in the evening, we heard we were the first Christian group allowed to do a program on the campus, which was where many of the nation's leaders went for training.

8

Roommates and
Ministry Beginnings

Dan Skerbitz was one of my closest friends while I lived in Tulsa. We went to VBI together, and we shared an apartment. Dan had been doing a cell group for singles at the church, and when I moved in, we ministered together. One week I would lead worship, and he would teach the lesson, and the next week, we would reverse that.

We made a great ministry team, and our gifts complemented each other, so we flowed together well. Dan was strong teaching in the Word of God, and my strength was in leading worship and flowing with the Holy Spirit. One of my best times was after the cell group was over. We would debrief and talk about the meeting, what went well, how the Holy Spirit moved, etc.

During that time, I got invitations to minister in church services. I didn't have much experience preaching and was just learning how to present the Word of God. Dan often accompanied me when I had the opportunity to preach, and we led worship together. We both played guitar, so we would play and lead the congregation in praise and wor-

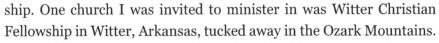

ship. One church I was invited to minister in was Witter Christian Fellowship in Witter, Arkansas, tucked away in the Ozark Mountains.

When I talked to the leader who invited me, he said there wasn't a pastor in the church, and different speakers came every week. He told me, "People are a little different here, and many members are elderly. Most don't think drinking is a sin. Many chew tobacco and make whiskey, so it would be best to not preach about sin." I hung up the phone and thought, *well, this should be fun!*

Dan traveled with me to Witter. I still remember the small white one-room church with a steeple on top and a graveyard on the property. We got there a bit early, and they were in the middle of Sunday school. We walked in and sat in the back. I looked around the small room, which had a wood-burning stove in the middle of the sanctuary. Six people were there, mostly elderly. I remember the leader's question, "When is it okay to ask God for help?" An elderly woman next to me raised her hand and answered, "First, you must do all you can for yourself. After you have cut your firewood, canned all your fruits and vegetables, then you can ask God for help." Another younger woman raised her hand and said, "We can go to God for anything, anytime we want. He loves us and wants to provide for all our needs."

I thought *I have to preach after this!* This will be unique. Dan and I led worship, and then I shared a short message. I was nervous and spoke quickly and didn't preach long. I don't remember the message, but I remember Dan and I had a debriefing on the way home. He told me something I never forgot, "Good preaching is like getting ready to sit down and watch a movie. You are relaxed, you have your popcorn next to you, and you are ready to enjoy the movie. When you are preaching, people are supposed to be relaxed and ready to hear what you say. You seemed nervous, and because you were nervous, the congregation felt that and became nervous too." That was the gist of what Dan said, and I have kept that in my heart ever since.

Because so few people attended the service, I thought the offering would be small. Maybe enough to grab a cup of coffee or give Dan money for fuel. I was pleasantly surprised to receive an offering of over six hundred dollars. That church became a partner, and they supported me during the entirety of my first stint on the mission field. The church leader told me a couple of years later, "We have never had a missionary come to our church, and you are the first missionary we ever supported."

9

Victory World Missions Training Center

After graduating from VBI in 1994, I planned to attend Victory World Missions Training Center in February 1995. After graduation, I would move to Mexico, but the Lord had something else planned. As is always the case with me, I had made my plans, but the Lord was directing my steps.

Several months before school started, I went to Bullhead City for a few weeks. I had been praying I could pay my tuition in cash and have my rent and utilities paid for the duration of the school so I wouldn't have to work. The school schedule was Monday through Friday from 8:00 a.m. to 4:00 p.m., so it was important I not work. The school lasted three months and ended with a two-week mission trip to Guatemala and El Salvador.

I had the finances saved to pay for the tuition. However, when I returned to Tulsa, I was informed the next year's tuition would increase by five hundred dollars. That was a huge amount in those days, and I was discouraged to hear this news. On January 30, 1995, I received an unexpected letter. As I opened it, I read these words, "Brother Steve,

I had some junk and scrap metal to sell. I said to the Lord, 'If it sells, I will send it to Steve.' It sold within three weeks for the full amount. Jesus is alive. Signed, Brother Joel." Inside the letter was a check for one thousand dollars more than the amount I needed! He also put his business card in the letter. On the back of the card was a tiny mustard seed and the Scripture, "If you have faith as a mustard seed, you can say to this mountain, 'move from here to there and it will move' and nothing will be impossible for you."

I had no idea who Brother Joel was, but with that check, I could pay my tuition and not work the entire time I was at Victory World Missions Training Center. After I received that letter, I met Joel. He reminded me of the time we were evangelism partners during one of our church's crusades in the low-income housing areas. He said I had shared with him about going to school. I still have that letter and look at it from time to time to encourage myself that God can speak to anyone. Joel and his wife and I became great friends, and they were faithful partners when I first went to the mission field in the Philippines in 1996.

Leading Worship

I gave my guitar away when I moved to Tulsa and had been without one for a couple of years. I had been asking the Lord for an Ovation guitar. When I lived in student housing, the couple who were the house parents had become my friends. One night I was at their house for dinner, and a guitar case was placed before me. I was told, "We want to give this to you. We feel the Lord said you are going to need it." As I opened the case, I cried. Inside was a beautiful Ovation guitar. God had answered my prayers! I spent the next several months having a great time worshiping the Lord and learning how to flow with the Spirit in worship. God would use me in that area in the future.

During the first week of the Victory World Missions Training Center, the school's director, Hal Boehm, wanted someone to lead a time of worship every day before class. Two people could play instruments in the class, I and a fellow student. Hal met with both of us one afternoon after classes. He talked to us about worship and said, "I want to give you each a week to lead the class in worship. Then I will choose one of you to lead worship for the duration of the school."

After we both took our week leading worship, Hal came to me and said, "Steve, I want you to lead worship for this class." That is where I learned to lead worship and discovered the anointing and gift God gave me. I learned many valuable leadership lessons from Hal during that time that still resonate in my heart today. He gave me general direction about how he wanted worship to go and then released me to develop my gift and learn to lead worship. He met with me once or twice during the school year to give me encouragement and direction. That is one of the best examples of leadership I experienced in my early days of walking with the Lord, and I have never forgotten Pastor Hal's example.

Guatemala and El Salvador Missions Trip

The class spent the last two weeks of training on a mission trip to Central America. I don't recall much of the ministry in Guatemala or El Salvador. I remember we did several evangelistic outreaches in parks where we did dramas and preaching.

I have always been a person with many questions. Mostly the questions went in this order:

1. Where are we going?
2. How are we getting there?
3. What will we do once we get there?
4. How long will we be there?
5. What time are we coming back?

I asked Hal those questions frequently during the trip, and one day when I again asked the question, "Where are we going?" He replied, "I am going to put you on a three-question-a-day diet. From now on, I am going to answer only three questions a day from you." "Are you kidding me?" I asked incredulously, to which Hal replied, "No, I am not kidding, and that is question one. I will only answer two more questions for you for the rest of today, so think carefully before you ask any more questions." It was a humorous but gentle way for Hal to remind me to relax and enjoy the trip.

Appearing on Trinity Broadcasting Network

We spent six days in Guatemala doing ministry on the streets and in church services. Then we rode a bus for six hours to El Salvador and spent another six days doing ministry. We rented a school bus for our transportation during the ministry trip. We had just finished a full day of ministry and were heading back to the hotel. It was sweltering. Everyone was sweaty, stinky and tired because we had been in the park all day.

Hal was sitting in the front of the bus when his cell phone rang. He talked for a few minutes, and when he got off the phone, he had exciting news. He said, "We've been given an incredible opportunity. I just got off the phone with TBN, and they want us to come appear on their show tonight, which will be broadcast live. This is the first time we have been invited to be on the show. When we get to the hotel, we will have only about ten minutes before we leave for the studio."

When we got to the hotel, the Holy Spirit said to me, "Wear your suit tonight. I am going to put you on television to share your testimony." I put on the best one I had—a dark blue pinstriped suit Dan had given me. We didn't have enough time to shower, so I washed my face and put cologne on to help hide the smell from the day. We boarded the bus and started on our journey to the TBN studios. Pastor Hal was communicating by phone with the TBN contact, and after he got off the phone, he told us two people would go on the show with him to be interviewed. When he announced who would be interviewed, my name wasn't mentioned, so I lowered my head on the seat in front of me and prayed and rested my eyes. After some time, Hal came to the back of the bus and sat next to me. He said, "Steve, I feel you are supposed to be on the television program with me tonight, so be prepared to join me on the stage."

Even though the Lord had already told me He was putting me on TV, I was excited and a little scared at the same time. The questions rolled off my tongue, one right after another! What questions am I going to be asked? What am I supposed to say? Can I have the questions in advance so I will have time to formulate my answers? I remember Hal putting his hand on my shoulder, looking me in the eye, and saying, "Steve, don't worry about the questions. Most people do not have a difficult time talking about themselves. You will be fine."

That TBN station had the largest viewing audience outside of the United States, with millions of viewers watching from various parts of Central America. When we arrived, my classmate Diane and I and Pastor Hal were ushered backstage, where we were introduced to the show's host. I remember his greeting was warm and inviting as he thanked us for coming onto the show.

One episode that evening would be taped and aired later, and the other episode would air live that night. It was decided I would be interviewed first, and Diane would be interviewed in the live show. The worship band played, but I couldn't concentrate. I was so nervous. I was standing on the TBN stage! My mouth was dry, I couldn't focus, and I wondered what the host would talk to me about. A thousand questions ran through my mind!

When the worship service was over, the host introduced Hal, who then introduced me to the viewing audience. Hal and the host talked for a few minutes, and then the host turned to me and asked, "Brother Steve, tell me, how did you come to know the Lord?" These thoughts raced through my mind, *"Did he just ask me to share how I met Christ? Is this really happening?"* I shared my story of redemption and how Jesus came into my life and delivered me from drug addiction. I shared the good news of the gospel for about thirty minutes. When I finished, the host looked at me and said, "Brother Steve, what would you like to say to those watching tonight? Would you please pray with those who would like to receive Jesus as their personal Lord and Savior?" I looked straight into the camera, sharing from my heart, and then led people in the "sinner's prayer."

As we went to a commercial, the host, Hal, and I exchanged pleasantries. As I sat in the audience with my classmates, I was stunned at what just happened. Quietly, I thanked the Lord for the opportunity. I prayed my story would inspire others and bring hope to the hopeless, and God would use it for His glory.

The next episode would be aired live, and Diane and Hal would be the guests. Diane had been raised in a Catholic home and had come to know Jesus as her personal Lord and Savior. Someone came out during a commercial break and said the phone lines were ringing off the hook with people calling in. I remember one caller we were told about, who said, "I am a Catholic, and I was asking the Lord what I must do to be saved, and He said, 'turn on TBN tonight. There will be a woman named Diane who will tell you what to do.'" There were many testimonies that night of people who called in response to Diane's interview. I never learned what the response was when the episode with my testimony was aired, but it has been a highlight of my walk with the Lord. We were each given a videotape of the program as a keepsake, and I still have that tape packed away in a box somewhere.

10

Connecting with Calvary International

Victory World Missions Training Center invited many ministries from around the nation to come pour their lives into the students. I first encountered Calvary International (now Go To Nations) when Dr. Jerry Williamson, the International Field Director, spent two weeks with our class, teaching on culture shock and fundraising.

I was struck by his passion and zeal for the Lord. I spent most of my breaks in between sessions peppering him with questions about Calvary International. After he finished teaching in the school, he set up a booth at the Oral Roberts University campus, where a conference was taking place. I stopped and talked with him several more times. He was patient in answering my questions and gave me his business card.

He encouraged me to attend the Field Candidate Preparation and Orientation training in July of 1995 at the Calvary International World Headquarters in Jacksonville, Florida. FPCO was a fourteen-day course for potential missionaries who wanted to learn more about becoming a missionary with Calvary International. I prayed and felt I was to attend, so I filled out my application and prepared to travel to Jacksonville. When I arrived at the offices, Dr. Jerry met me with these words, "I had you pegged wrong. After I left Tulsa, I said to myself, 'I'll never see that guy again.'"

The training during those two weeks was invaluable. We learned everything from dealing with culture shock, raising your ministry budget, and solidifying your calling. We also learned Calvary International's standards and procedures of being a missionary with them. I officially joined Calvary International as a missionary after I completed the FCPO program. That was the beginning of a relationship that has spanned twenty-five years thus far.

Originally, I planned to move to Mexico to begin my mission's "career," but during my exit interview on the last day of FCPO, I was recruited to join the team in Manila, Philippines. The team of three missionary couples had recently gone through a leadership change and was in a time of transition and rebuilding. Craig and Sandra Kuehn were the Regional Directors for Southeast Asia. The other missionaries in Manila were Bruce and Emma Behnken and Eric and Therese Nehrt. It would be a great opportunity to be on the ground floor of the new thing the Lord was doing within that team and region of the world.

I developed my financial support base and ministry plans right away. There was no time to lose, and I wanted to get on the field as soon as possible. After about eight months of fundraising, I raised about 70 percent of my ministry budget. I had a few "pledges" from people who said their financial partnership would begin once I moved to Manila. When I was released for field departure on March 4, 1996, I was vastly under budget. I started my mission's career in a financial deficit. I am happy to report that today's missionaries with Calvary International (Go To Nations) are not released for field departure until they are 100 percent fully funded.

PART III
First Missions Assignment: The Philippines

CHAPTER

11

Field Departure

In February of 1996, I was cleared for departure to the field! The last few weeks were filled with giving away possessions I couldn't take. I was excited and scared. So many thoughts raced through my mind during those days leading up to my departure. I was leaving the safety and security I knew to go to a country where everything was unknown. I didn't know what the future held, and I felt the "finality" of my life in the States as I prepared.

I was leaving my home country and giving my life away so that God could use me in the nations, and I never planned to return. It was a huge leap of faith, as I didn't know anyone in Manila. I had only met Craig Kuehn, the Regional Director for Southeast Asia, once during the Field Candidate Preparation Orientation class. I didn't have a clear vision of the ministry the Lord was calling me to do; I just knew I was to go, and as I was obedient, He would direct my steps.

Airlines then allowed two seventy-pound luggage pieces at no charge. Although I didn't have many possessions, it was difficult de-

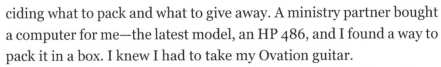

ciding what to pack and what to give away. A ministry partner bought a computer for me—the latest model, an HP 486, and I found a way to pack it in a box. I knew I had to take my Ovation guitar.

By March 3, 1996, I had finally finished packing my boxes. I cannot tell you how many times I packed, unpacked, and repacked those boxes during those last weeks in the United States. Do I need to take these books? Is it necessary to take this appliance? Even though I was provided a checklist of things to bring and things to leave behind, I still changed my mind about certain items. My roommate Dan watched me and gave me advice from time to time.

The cell group Dan and I led had a goodbye party for me. It was the night before I was to leave my country, and the silence hung heavy as Dan and I were lost in our thoughts. Dan looked at me and said, "Steve, you are really doing this. It's hard to believe tomorrow you will get on a plane and leave." We talked about the process I had been through and how hard it was for me to leave. After some time, Dan said, "How do you want to spend your last night in the States?" I wanted to get out of the house and get my mind off leaving, so I said, "Let's go to a movie." I don't remember what we saw, but it was a great way to spend my last night in the States.

Early the next morning, Dan and I loaded my luggage in the car, and he drove me to the Tulsa International Airport for my flight to Manila, Philippines. I was stepping into the destiny the Lord created me for. After I got checked in for my flight, I grabbed a cup of coffee and found a chair to relax in. Everything seemed so surreal to me. I was getting on a plane and moving to the other side of the world!

I somehow got the idea I should write on paper the past experiences I was leaving and throw that list away as a declaration of putting the past behind me. I had written a few things and was quietly praying over each item on the list. After I finished praying, I crumpled up the paper, put it into the wastebasket, and boarded my flight.

Welcome to Manila!

After a long flight, the plane touched down in Manila, Philippines, and taxied for quite some time before we arrived at gate B29. As I exited the plane and walked through the airport terminal toward Immigration, I heard these words on the intercom, "Welcome to Manila." *I am here!* It was so euphoric!

However, that euphoria was short-lived and replaced with a healthy dose of culture shock once I arrived at Immigration. Thousands of people were crammed into a room that only had the capacity of about five hundred. It was chaos! I didn't know where to go or which line to get in, and no one stood in any clear line. Everyone jumbled together, jockeying to get to the front. People coming in from behind thought nothing of cutting in front of you. It took several hours to clear Immigration and Customs. I was relieved to see someone patiently waiting for me outside the terminal. We loaded my bags into the van and started our journey to Pasig, Manila, where the team was based.

Those first few days and weeks were a blur as I tried to navigate my new surroundings. I was the only single missionary among a team of three married couples. I remember it was extremely hot all the time. While Filipinos, in general, are friendly toward Americans, it was hard to adjust. Everywhere I went, I heard people calling out to me, "Hey Joe!" Americans were called "Joe," which was short for G.I. Joe and originated in the early 1900s when the United States had governorship over the Islands and had given the Philippines their independence as a nation. I tried to ignore them, but they just called out louder and louder until I acknowledged them. I stood out everywhere I went for two main reasons. For one, my skin was pale white. I also had facial hair and hairy arms, which intrigued every Filipino, as most Filipinos are brown-skinned, without facial or arm hair. Anytime I talked with a Filipino, they would stare at my arms, and they worked up the courage to touch my arm hair. "Ooh, very hairy. You're hairy. Hairy like a monkey," they would say while petting and stroking my arm. Then the grand finale would come as they tried to pull my arm hair out!

My personal space was invaded every time I stepped out of the house. As an American, I was accustomed to having about two to three feet of space between the person I talked to and me. However, Filipinos did not have that custom, so I would step backward whenever someone invaded my space. Then the person I was talking with stepped forward. It took me a while to get used to this.

I remember my first attempt at riding public transportation. I was given instructions during my orientation about getting on and off the bus, the price, and how to pay. I remember the day I ventured out. The trip into town went okay, but as I was coming back, I needed to signal I wanted the bus to stop, and I forgot what to do. I remember two or three ways to signal the driver to stop, but I couldn't remember what they were. I remember being told to say, Alto, to say stop, or was it, Para? I didn't know, so I tried saying both, which the driver ignored. My stop was approaching quickly, and I thought, *okay, so that wasn't it. What do I do now?* Then I remembered someone saying I was to hit a coin on a metal bar. Or was it to hit the roof with the back of my hand? I wish I had paid more attention during that meeting. Oh, Lord, help me get off this bus, I said to myself as I saw my stop passing by. I walked toward the front of the bus, shouting, "Alto! Para!" over and over while hitting the back of my hand against the roof. That got the driver's attention, and he stopped several blocks away from my destination, and I walked the rest of the way home.

Culture Shock

Culture shock is a real phenomenon that hits missionaries in different ways. It hit me with a vengeance as soon as I got off the plane.

I constantly struggled with culture shock during most of my time in the Philippines. For the first several months in Manila, my new Filipino friends would come up to me and start a conversation. As we talked, they would look me in the eye, then would reach out and rub my stomach and say, "Oh, you are fat. So very, very fat!" and I got so offended. Who are you to tell me I am fat? I may have gained weight since I have been here, but I am NOT fat! Which would then lead to a time of introspection...maybe I could try to lose some weight, maybe I should exercise.

During one team meeting, we had some Filipino associates with us. One of them came up to me and rubbed my stomach and said those words I dreaded to hear, "Oh my, Steve, you are so very fat!" Anger rose on the inside of me, and I exclaimed to my friend, "Why do you people keep calling me fat? It's so incredibly rude!" Then I learned something I'd never forget. My friend replied, "When we call you fat, we are saying you are prosperous, that you are blessed by the Lord." Oh, so all this time, I was being told God had prospered me. *Why couldn't you just say that instead of making me feel like I was overweight,* I thought, embarrassed by the scene I caused.

During the 1990s, the population of Metro Manila was over eight million people. Most of them went to and from work at the same time every day. It was a twenty-minute walk from my house to the main road where I could catch public transportation, and as I walked to the street, I had a clear view of traffic. The police managed traffic by opening all the lanes so commuters could drive in one direction for twenty minutes, while people driving in the opposite direction stopped and waited for their turn. This gave drivers going in each direction about twenty minutes to drive. Many times, you waited up to sixty minutes before your turn to arrive. Often when I walked to the street and saw traffic at a standstill, I would think, *nope, not going to do this today,* and would turn around and go home and stay in the house for the rest of the day.

63

I went to the post office almost every day. Even though the post office was about three miles away, it often took two to three hours to travel that distance and the same amount of time for the trip back home. If you happened to be in the city around rush hour, which started at about 3:00 p.m., it would often take four to five hours to travel home. The Lord was so gracious to me during that time. It seemed I somehow just knew when mail was waiting for me in the mailbox. I would arrive with great expectancy and anticipation to find a piece of mail with my name on it.

I remember one day I just knew I had mail. As I journeyed to the street to get a bus into town, I saw the traffic at a standstill. I didn't let that deter me, as I wanted to; no, I *needed* to get my mail. It took four hours that day to travel the three miles to the post office. When I got to the mailbox, I had great anticipation of retrieving that piece of mail that surely was waiting for me. I opened my mailbox with great expectations and peeked inside. It was empty! I was dismayed and disappointed. With tears in my eyes, I went to the counter to ask if the mail had been delivered yet, and the woman said, "No, not yet, come back later." In desperation, I replied, "I see a bag of mail behind you. I know there is a letter inside there for me."

The postal employee and I went back and forth about me coming back later to check the mail, and before I knew it, I was walking into the room where the mailbag was. "I just know there is mail for me in that bag, and if you just let me look inside, I know I can retrieve it." I wasn't listening to the employee protests as I walked past the counter. I opened the bag and rummaged through the mail, and it only took a few minutes to pull out a letter addressed to me. "Aha!" I exclaimed. "I told you I had mail, and here it is!" I left the post office triumphant. I had a letter from home! I had no inclination my actions were revealing culture shock.

I quickly realized the pace of life was different in the Philippines. I was used to accomplishing several things in a day while I lived in the United States, but in Manila, it was vastly different. At most, if you were extremely blessed by the Lord's favor, you could accomplish one task on your To-Do list whenever you went into town. If your task on any given day was to buy groceries, pay bills, go to the post office, then have lunch, you would have to choose which one was the most important to accomplish. Because it normally took six hours to travel into town and back on public transportation, that meant you would have about an hour or so before rush hour traffic began. You never wanted to be stuck in the city during rush hour.

Culture shock seemed to hit me in waves and differed in intensity. Sometimes I would handle it well, and it would last for a day or two. Other times, it was difficult and seemed to last for weeks. During one extreme season of culture shock, everything seemed to bother me, and I couldn't get a breakthrough.

I went to church with our team members one Sunday afternoon, thinking listening to God's Word and spending time in worship would relieve the cultural pressures I was experiencing. I don't remember what the pastor preached about, but it was probably about having patience or loving people. Anyway, the preaching made me mad, and I left the service to go home. By the time I got to the bus station, it was the middle of rush hour traffic, but I didn't care. I just wanted to get home, close the curtains, and "lick my wounds."

It was chaos trying to get on a bus. People didn't stand in line. About fifty people crowded the bus entrance, trying to get on a bus while passengers were trying to get off. I tried to get on three busses but was pushed aside each time. When the next bus arrived, I grabbed both sides of the door, and when the door opened, I shoved my way onto the bus and sat near the front behind the driver. The seat was just big enough for one person, and I was comfortable.

As passengers got on the bus, I looked up and saw a large woman looking at my seat. I realized she wanted to sit next to me. I quickly surveyed the situation and thought, if she sits on the outside of the seat, I will be crushed against the window. If I sit on the outside, I will only have about three inches to sit on, but I won't be crushed. I moved and let her sit next to the window.

I will never forget what happened next. Since I had just come from church, I was dressed in black slacks, a nice dress shirt, and nice dress shoes. A man and his child, who I imagine was about seven got on the bus, and as the boy passed by, he looked straight at me... and threw up on me! Not just a little, but a big gushing throw-up! It hit my neck, ran down my shoulder and my pant leg, and collected in a huge puddle on the floor. The man patted his child on the back as if to say, "Congratulations, son, you just puked on an American" and kept walking. Well, that was the last straw, and I yelled at the father, "Are you kidding me? Your kid pukes on me, and you're going to just walk past me and not clean it up?" He replied, "So sorry," and handed me a small handkerchief to clean myself up with. I was infuriated, to say the least. I cleaned myself off the best I could and threw the handkerchief on the floor.

To keep from falling out of the seat, I had to brace myself by placing my feet at different angles for the rest of the ride home. The only place to put my right foot was in the middle of the vomit puddle, so my shoes kept sliding out from under me, spreading it around the bus. I finally got home and was disgusted with myself and the Philippines. Of course, the devil used this to his advantage. These thoughts raced through my mind. *You are a Christian, and you acted terribly on the bus. What a wonderful witness you are. You are a terrible missionary, and you should go home.*

Housing Challenges

One contributing factor to the cultural stresses I experienced in Manila was finding adequate housing. I bounced around from place to place for the first several months of living on the mission field. In the first few weeks, I stayed with Bruce and Emma Behnken in their home. After that, I moved to Davao in the southern Philippines to work with one of our missionaries. I stayed in their home but quickly discovered it was not a good fit for me, and after about a month, I went back to Manila. For the next couple of months, I stayed in Eric and Therese Nehrt's home while they went to the United States to itinerate. When they returned, I realized I did not have the necessary funds to rent my own place.

The team was preparing for a set of new missionaries coming for the first Timothy Internship Program. Part of this was to set up housing the interns could move into, and a two-bedroom house was rented in the same village where most of the team lived. I was invited to stay in that home until the new interns arrived, and I believe I stayed there for a few weeks. As the date for the interns' arrival drew closer, I wasn't sure if I could afford to secure my own place. I found a potential place to look at—a two-bedroom house quite some distance away. An add-on was under construction where the owner was adding bedrooms. The owner was a young woman planning to move out. She seemed pleasant enough, so I signed the contract and moved in.

I noticed things out of place in the home and heard noises at night. One morning I inspected the add-on and found women's clothes and discovered the owner was sneaking in and living in the construction area at night! When we confronted her about it, she said she wouldn't move out, so I had to leave. I stayed in that house for about a week. I gathered my few belongings and didn't know what to do. One of our missionaries knew of someone who had rented a house and was renovating it and said I could stay there. I was told construction crews would come every day to work, and I needed to take care of their two Doberman Pinchers and make sure they didn't get out of the house. It was incredibly stressful, but I was relieved I had a place to stay, even if temporarily.

Because it was hot at night, it was my custom to sleep naked. The first morning a construction worker startled me when he walked into the bedroom to get something while I was sleeping. It was as if they didn't care someone was sleeping in the room; they just came in and started working. The next night, I stopped sleeping naked, and I also locked the bedroom door. Obviously, the workers had keys, so they just unlocked the door and came in and started working.

One afternoon after the construction workers finished for the day, I opened the bedroom door and was ready to go out and look for a house to rent. I evidently scared the two Doberman Pinchers, who must have thought I was an intruder, and they charged at me and chased me back into the bedroom. I was terrified. Every time I tried to open the door and leave, they would charge at me. I was trapped and afraid. I didn't know what to do, so I called Bruce, one of our missionaries who lived near me. "Bruce, you got to come and help me. I am trapped in my bedroom. Every time I open the door, I am attacked by the dogs, and I can't escape," I cried into the phone. I'm sure Bruce thought I was crazy, but he came and rescued me from those terrible dogs. Soon after that, I rented one side of the duplex and finally had a home I could afford. It was a new two-story, two-bedroom duplex, and I was the first tenant. I lived in this home for the remainder of my time in Manila. I had moved seven times in seven months, and I was glad to finally have my own place before the Timothy Internship Program started.

12

The Timothy Internship Program

The Timothy Internship Program is a practical, hands-on mission-ary training internship developed by missionaries for missionaries. The first internship program for Calvary International was launched in October of 1996 in Manila. I was privileged to be one of the first students to participate in this valuable training.

My classmates were Anthony and Laura Morris, Tami Hammond, and Becky Herro. Classes were about three to four hours each day, and we met in different homes, depending on what was being taught that particular day. We learned about the Filipino culture, culture shock, language learning, and many other things vital for a new mis-sionary to succeed on the mission field.

During our internship, we were introduced to Pastor Noel Alber-to, who was involved in prison ministry in the Metro Manila prison. He had been incarcerated there once and had received Jesus as his personal Lord and Savior. Upon his release, the Lord spoke to him to return to the prison and minister to the inmates. He invited us to minister in the prison with him every week.

We met at 5:00 a.m. on Tuesdays to journey into the city where the prison was. We began our trip on either a public bus or a private taxi, which would take us to downtown Manila. That portion of the drive usually took two hours or more, depending on traffic. It was common for rush hour traffic to begin at 5:00 a.m. and last until about 10:00 a.m. Sometimes we found a bus right away, and other times we had to wait. The trip's final leg included a ride on the LRT (Light Rail Train), which dropped us off near the prison.

Taking the LRT was quite an experience. By the time we got downtown, it was the middle of rush hour traffic. Hundreds, if not thousands, of people would be waiting for the LRT to arrive, and many times we would wait for up to an hour just to board. When we got on, we would be so stuffed between passengers that it was often hard to breathe. We often were "up close and personal" with other passengers on this portion of the trip. When we arrived at the stop near the prison, we would wait for Pastor Noel to meet us at Jollibee's—a famous fast-food restaurant in the Philippines.

Our scheduled time to minister in the prison was from 9:00 a.m. and usually lasted about an hour or two. The trip usually took about three hours, so we arrived at Jollibee's by 8:00 a.m. and waited for about an hour for Pastor Noel to arrive. When we arrived at the prison, we went through security, did our ministry program, and usually finished by 11:00 a.m. Then we started our journey back home. By the time we got off the LRT and back into the heart of Manila, it was usually the beginning of rush hour traffic. All the people we met on their way to work were now going home. We often had to wait for an hour or so for a bus or taxi to arrive. We usually got to our village between 3:00 and 5:00 p.m. Most Tuesdays, we spent up to ten hours in traffic to minister for about an hour or two. By the time we got home, everyone would be exhausted, dirty, sweaty, dehydrated, and hungry.

Prison Ministry Experiences

The Metro Manila City prison was unique in that those incarcerated were allowed to have their families with them. Areas were set aside for inmates who had their wives and children living with them. The prison was overcrowded, and the prisoners' conditions were deplorable, especially for the wives and children.

We did children's ministry because many children were being raised in the prison. I didn't like children and was not happy about doing children's ministry. I often thought about when I was in Bible school, and one subject was children's ministry. I didn't pay attention during the classes, and my mind wandered constantly. I thought children's ministry training was a waste of time because I had no desire to minister to children. I remember the teacher saying, "You may think ministry to children is a waste of time, but I tell you that you better get ready because I guarantee you will do children's ministry at some point."

When we began doing ministry to children, I thought, *why, oh why, didn't I pay more attention in that class?* I was a target for every child wherever we went. I had pale white skin, but mostly the hairy arms drew the children's attention. First, they would look at me, and I could tell what they were thinking, wow, the American is hairy. Then they would work up the courage to walk up to me while looking at my arm hair. Then with excitement in their eyes, they would reach out and touch my arm and stroke it like they were petting a dog. Then they would grab a tuft of my arm hair, pull it out, and run off squealing with delight. This was the extent of my children's ministry experience.

One morning as we were going through security to begin our program, there was an undeniable tension in the air. We didn't know what was going on, and we could hear distant shouting. I usually followed

Pastor Noel's facial expression. That day he looked concerned as we walked to the family area and began our children's program. We had just gathered the kids and were doing songs and skits when Pastor Noel leaned over to me and whispered, "We must quickly finish what we are doing and leave right now." When I asked him what was happening, he replied, "The inmates are going to start a riot today. Out of respect for us, they are waiting until we leave. It is dangerous, and we need to get out now." We gathered our things, and a few minutes after we cleared security, we heard the riot begin.

On other morning, we arrived at Jollibee's and heard loud shouting and distant clanging. We didn't think much about it, but the noise steadily grew in intensity as we waited for Pastor Noel. When he arrived, he told us, "I just came from the prison, and we can't go today. There is a riot happening now, and the prison is locked down." We talked about what we should do. We traveled four hours that day to get to the prison, and we didn't want to waste our day in the heart of the city. As we were talking over breakfast, Pastor Noel got a gleam in his eye and said, "I know what we will do. Gather your things, and let's go."

We had no idea what we were about to get ourselves into, but we knew Pastor Noel well enough to know that whenever we saw that gleam in his eyes, we were about to have an adventure! He stopped along the way and got a big white piece of cardboard and a black marker from an art supply store. Then, he just stopped, stooped down, grabbed the marker and cardboard, and wrote in big letters, "Jesus Saves," and then said to us, "Okay, now stand on this car and share the gospel to the people passing by."

None of us had ever done anything like that, and no one wanted to be the first to begin. I mean, it was a complete stranger's car. What if the owner came and saw us standing on the roof of his car? We were stalling, and Pastor Noel grabbed the sign, climbed onto the car's roof, and preached. After a few minutes, he climbed down and handed the sign to one of us and said, "Now it's your turn." Each of us took a turn standing on the roof of this car and preaching. It was an incredible experience, even though we were extremely embarrassed. Americans just didn't do that type of thing!

13

Learning Experiences

I Am the Lord That Heals

It was always extremely hot in the Philippines. In my early days there, I didn't have an air conditioner. In the hottest part of the summer months, I slept on average about three hours a night. During the hot season, I would sleep downstairs on the cool marble floor. I dunked a sheet in water and covered myself with it. Then, to make things complete, I turned on my floor fan and set it by my head. Even with all that, it still wouldn't get cool enough to sleep until about one o'clock in the morning, and by four o'clock, it was already too hot to sleep.

One night about 2:00 a.m., I was trying to drift off to sleep, and suddenly, I felt like someone had thrown a blanket over me, and I got chills. I got every blanket and sleeping bag I owned and covered myself, but nothing helped. I was shaking so hard that I was moving along the floor. I thought *I need to call for help, but I can't get to the phone.* All I could do was say the name of Jesus over and over again. "Jesus, heal me, Jesus, heal me," I prayed. After some time, the chills

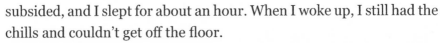

subsided, and I slept for about an hour. When I woke up, I still had the chills and couldn't get off the floor.

I was pondering what to do when the Holy Spirit had a conversation with me. "Did you ask Me to heal you?" He whispered to me. "Yes, I did," I replied. "Do you believe I have healed you?" He questioned. "I do believe You healed me," I said. The Holy Spirit said, "Then what do people who are healed do?" I thought, *well, I suppose you would get up and get dressed and start your day.* "Then, if I have healed you, what should you do?" He pressed, trying to teach me something. "Well, I guess I should get up and get dressed and act like I am healed," I said. Even though I still felt sick, I got up, got dressed, and started my day. It was a Thursday, which was the day of our weekly team meeting, and by the time I got to Craig and Sandra's house, I was completely healed.

Steve Is Single and Available

While I was in Bible school, most of my classmates were getting married and going into ministry. Those in leadership encouraged us to find a spouse. However, I had decided I would never marry. I had purposed in my heart to serve the Lord as a single man for as long as I lived. When I moved to the Philippines, I was a curiosity to Filipinos wherever I went. In their culture, most people got married young and started a family, so it was unusual for them to meet someone my age who wasn't married. People constantly tried to set me up with a sister, mother, or aunt who would be "just perfect" for me.

One of the most embarrassing experiences I had was when I was invited to preach in a Sunday service. I had never been to the church and met the pastor for the first time a few minutes before service began. He asked general information about me so he could properly introduce me to the congregation. "Do you have a family, Brother Steve?" he asked. I replied I was single and didn't think anything of it.

After the worship service was finished, the pastor called me up to the platform. While the pastor introduced me, I was mentally going over my notes. I really wasn't paying too much attention to what he was saying until I heard, "This is Steve, and he is single and available." All the single ladies in the congregation let out a delighted squeal, and I thought, *oh, here we go again.* I heard this all the time wherever I went to preach, "This is Steve, and he is single and available," and usually, that was the end of it. This time, the pastor went further when he said from the platform, "And Brother Steve, this is Sister Agnes sitting in the front row. She is also single and available. We can arrange for you to meet privately after the service is over." With that, he gave me the microphone and turned the service over to me. I was so embarrassed and upset the pastor would do this to me in public that I had difficulty ministering the Word.

Team Ministry Experiences

First Peter 4:10 encourages believers to use whatever gifts they have received to minister to one another. One of my responsibilities within the Calvary International team was leading worship at our weekly team meetings. The many years of practicing in God's presence during my personal worship time allowed me to cultivate an anointing for leading worship. I continued to develop my skills as a worship leader in those meetings. The weekly team meetings were a lifeline for us, as it was a consecrated time to connect with God and each other in worship and prayer. I looked forward to each meeting and always left encouraged and edified. In those early days, God would often take over our meetings and release His prophetic voice as we turned our ears and hearts toward heaven. It surely was a unique thing that happened in our midst, and I've never seen it replicated anywhere else.

One Thursday in particular, I remember well. It was a normal day for me. I arrived at Craig and Sandra's house a few minutes early for our weekly team meeting. I was leading the worship time during those days, so I got there early to prepare. When I arrived, I set my guitar case down by the foyer door, opened it, got my guitar out, and tuned it. After tuning it, I set my guitar back in the case and left the case open. Soon other team missionaries arrived, and while I was talking to someone, I heard a loud thump and then a crack of breaking wood. I turned to see the commotion and saw a child had tripped while coming into the house, fell on my guitar case, and broke my guitar.

My beautiful Ovation guitar had a crack in the wood that ran along the guitar's top side. I could still play the instrument, and the sound quality was the same, but it was completely ruined as far as the value. Ovation guitars are normally expensive, and this one was worth about one thousand dollars. This guitar had a special place in my heart. I had asked the Lord for an Ovation guitar when I gave my first Fender guitar away many years before when I left Bullhead to go to Bible school.

I went into the bathroom to gather my thoughts and stayed in there for quite a few minutes. "Lord, I know this was an accident, and I forgive from my heart. I'm sorry for leaving my guitar case open and leaving it in an unsafe place. You know this has been my favorite guitar. Would You replace it for me?" I prayed silently. When I came out of the bathroom, it seemed everyone was staring at the door waiting for me to come out. The child came up to me, hugged me, and said, "I'm sorry for breaking your guitar." I hugged her back and told her it was okay, and it was an accident. Now I was to lead worship. When I played, my arm hair would get caught in the guitar's broken crack and would be pulled out. After I finished leading worship, I picked several strands of stuck arm hair from the crack.

Supernatural Season of Fasting

During that first year in Manila, a lot of transition was happening. Not only was there a leadership change, but also the team grew. Several new missionaries came to Manila to go through the Timothy Internship Program. As a team, we experienced a time of supernatural fasting. In our weekly meetings, the Holy Spirit was supernaturally directing people to fast and pray. There was overlap, where one person would say, "I stopped my fast yesterday," and another would say, "I started fasting yesterday." For an entire year, someone was always fasting and praying. It was incredibly unusual.

Eric and I both were led to do a forty-day fast, and we did it together. It was the first time I fasted for forty days. Up to that time, I had never fasted for more than a few days, and I was thankful the Lord had spoken to Eric at the same time. Eric had experience in fasting for long periods. Before we started our fast, we talked about what type of fast we would do. We agreed we would only drink water for the first ten days—no coffee, soft drinks, or fruit juice—just water. After those ten days, we would continue with just water only if we could. But if it became difficult, we would drink a little fresh-squeezed fruit juice in the evenings. Then about ten days before we were to stop our fast, we would add a little broth in the evening to get our stomach prepared for eating again. It was such a wonderful time of fasting, and I experienced the Holy Spirit in powerful ways!

As we ended our fast, I told Eric, "When I can eat, I am going to have a cheeseburger with French fries." Eric just laughed. The day came when I could eat again, and I was so excited. I went to a restaurant and ordered a cheeseburger, French fries, a coke, and ice cream to finish the meal. I had that plate of food sitting in front of me, and I was expecting to eat everything. However, I could only eat one cheeseburger bite and one French fry, and I was completely full.

During that season of supernatural fasting, the Holy Spirit led me to do several long fasts. It was an incredible experience. I learned many things about fasting. Those long fasts were so easy because the Holy Spirit was leading me. I didn't struggle with hunger as much as I had previously when I fasted. I learned there is a fast when you put the flesh under and do your fast in your strength, and other times, the Holy Spirit leads you to fast for specific reasons you may not understand. I have found both types are valuable. There is less struggle physically when the Holy Spirit is leading the fast.

Give Us Thailand!

During that fasting and prayer season, the Holy Spirit worked within our team on many different levels. It was only after several years had passed that we could look back and see why the Holy Spirit had led our team to fast and pray.

One weekly team meeting I specifically remember was significant in Calvary International's Southeast Asia history. I woke up with such an expectancy in my spirit as I got ready to go to our meeting. I had spent time worshiping the Lord and preparing to lead worship like I normally did for our gathering. As I was on the bus on the way to Craig and Sandra's house, I felt it would be a powerful time, and God would move in our midst that day. I was learning God works through authority, and our worship creates an atmosphere for the Lord's voice to be released. As the team's worship leader, I would often catch glimpses beforehand of what the worship would be like, and that day I knew in my spirit God would move in a mighty way.

During our worship, a holy silence filled the room. The Holy Spirit's presence was so tangible we just basked in His presence. Many members were sitting in their chairs; others were kneeling with their faces to the ground. I was standing in the middle of the living room and had stopped playing. We were quiet before the Lord for several minutes.

One missionary, Derek Cardwell, prophesied, saying in effect, "I feel like the Lord is saying if we ask Him for a nation, He will give it to us." After several minutes, Craig said, "Lord, give us Thailand!" When he said that, we all wept and wailed uncontrollably, crying out to God to give us Thailand. I put my guitar down and cried out to God. It was an intercession that came from deep within my spirit I couldn't control or contain. That weeping and wailing went on for about thirty minutes before subsiding. We knew God had given us Thailand that day in 1997, but it would be another eight years before Calvary International planted a team in Thailand.

Furlough to the United States

I led worship with my broken guitar for quite some time and continued to pull my arm hair from the cracks. About six months later, I went to the United States on furlough. One of my partnering churches in Jacksonville, Florida, was hosting a missions' conference, and I planned to attend. That church financially supported many Calvary International missionaries, so I expected to see several of my co-workers during this conference.

I arrived a week before the conference and traveled to Largo, Florida, to visit another partnering church. I had been invited to give a ministry report and share with the congregation a message about missions. We had a wonderful time, and after the service, the pastor and I went to his office to visit before lunch. We were talking about the service when the pastor said, "I felt the Holy Spirit speak to me during the worship service to give you something." He pulled out his guitar case and set it in front of me. "I felt the Lord say I was supposed to give you my guitar," he continued. I was dumbfounded and didn't know what to say. I looked at the case and saw the word Ovation written across it. When I opened the case, I saw a beautiful red Ovation guitar. It was the exact model of my guitar that had been broken in Manila. God not only replaced my guitar, but He replaced it with exactly the same model! I was so excited God heard and answered my prayer.

Several weeks later, I was itinerating on the West Coast, visiting family and ministry partners. I was in Bullhead City, Arizona, where I lived for several years when I first received the Lord. I still had many friends and ministry partners in that area. I stayed the weekend in a friend's home, who also happened to a financial partner, and I was scheduled to share in their church.

My longtime friend was teaching Sunday school, and she had asked me to come share with her class that Sunday. I wasn't excited about that because I wasn't good around children and had no idea how to relate to little people. She said her class had adopted me as their missionary and had been praying every Sunday for me. The children had never met a real missionary, so they were excited to meet me.

After worship, I followed Sandy back to the Sunday school room. In the middle of the room was a single chair, and I was asked to sit in it. One child presented me with a gift, and when I opened it, it was a big box of Jelly Belly jellybeans, which was my favorite candy. My friend said, "Every Sunday for the past year, the children brought an offering for you," and one kid handed me an envelope with money. Then all the kids gathered around, laid their hands on me, and prayed fervently. I was so blessed that Sunday being with that church and Sunday school class.

On Monday morning, I was preparing to leave Bullhead for my next destination. My friend and I were talking over breakfast when he got up from the table and went into the other room. He came out and said the Lord had told him to give me one of his guitars. He handed me a guitar case, and when I opened it, I saw a beautiful Fender guitar. God sure gave me double for my trouble during that time of visiting the United States. I was blessed to return to Manila with two guitars! In the Philippines, I learned Becky, one of my classmates in the Timothy Internship Program, desired to learn to play guitar. I wanted to bless her and gave her the Fender guitar I had been given in Bullhead.

14

Ministry Trips

Calvary Bible Institute, Metro Manila, Philippines

One result from Calvary Bible Institute leadership training during those days was a rapid multiplication of schools starting. Many students were pastors. Once they graduated from Calvary Bible Institute, they would take the material and start their own leadership training within their churches. Several Calvary Bible Institutes were running in different parts of Metro Manila during that time.

I was scheduled to teach The Power of Praise and Worship in one school. The church's pastors where I was scheduled to teach attended one of our weekly Thursday team meetings and wanted to talk with me. They wanted to promote Calvary Bible Institute and make posters to invite pastors from their area to attend the classes at no charge. They wanted to get information about the class I would be teaching. The pastor asked me, "Pastor Steve, what will be the theme of the teaching?" Immediately, the Holy Spirit inspired me to respond, "First, we will teach on the foundational aspects of worship. We will

85

deal with why we worship and the importance of worship, then on the practical aspects of worship, developing a worship team and musicians and singers. Finally, we will teach on the spiritual aspect of worship, how to flow with the Holy Spirit and release the prophetic in worship." I was stunned as the words poured out of my mouth. The Holy Spirit was definitely speaking through me.

As we continued talking about the logistics, the pastors suggested we turn this into a worship conference and open it to the public. It would be a great way to train worship leaders from different churches and promote the training course. Calvary Bible Institute was taught on Friday and Saturday evenings because most pastors being trained worked secular jobs during the day to supplement their incomes. I had never done a conference before, so I was both excited and nervous.

We spent the first weekend teaching on worship foundations and the second week on practical aspects of worship. In the final week, we taught on the spiritual aspects of worship. After each night of teaching, we spent time praising and worshiping and practicing what was taught. The final night was the most powerful. After teaching how to flow with the Holy Spirit in worship and release the prophetic ministry, the host church's worship team led worship. It was an incredible experience as the prophetic ministry was released.

The Dead Live

Craig received an invitation to travel to Bulacan and visit Pastors Ariel and Paz Acuna, who were Calvary Bible School graduates. It was about a four-hour drive from where we lived in Pasig City, and it would be the first time for Craig to preach in their church. We arrived Saturday afternoon and spent the night. Craig ministered in Sunday morning service and returned to Pasig Sunday late afternoon.

We met Ariel and Paz at McDonald's and had a time of fellowship before going to their house. While we were eating, Ariel told us this incredible story that had happened the night before. After Friday night prayers, many church members got into a Jeepney to go home. The Jeepney rolled off the side of the road several times before it finally landed upside down in a ditch, throwing many people from the vehicle. People rushed to the scene to help, and they discovered a church member was crushed under the vehicle. When they pushed the Jeepney over and pulled the man out from underneath the vehicle, they found he was already dead.

The church members loaded the man into a vehicle and drove him to the hospital. They leaned the dead man in the backseat of the car, and it was told to us that while they were driving, this man's head kept falling over because his neck was broken. The first hospital they went to would not receive the man because he was already dead, so they traveled to another hospital.

Meanwhile, the church was praying. As they drove to yet another hospital, the dead man suddenly came back to life! He raised his head up, took a deep breath, and prayed in tongues! This man was in church the next day, completely healed! He just had a couple of bruises, but other than that, he was fine. I had read the Bible stories where Jesus raised the dead and had heard testimonies of people being brought back to life, but I had never seen it or met anyone who had been raised from the dead.

It was a lot to take in that weekend, and on the way home, Craig and I talked about the events that had transpired. I felt the Holy Spirit speak to me, and I told Craig, "I feel like the Holy Spirit said I would work together with Pastor Ariel and Paz someday." That was sometime in 1997, and it would be another ten years before I would move to Khon Kaen, Thailand, to work with them.

Catanduanes, Virac, Philippines

I met Pastor Rene through Pastor Noel while doing prison ministry during the Timothy Internship Program. Pastor Rene and I had become friends and had done ministry together. We met for lunch one day, and he told me about a leadership conference he and five other pastors were hosting, and he invited me to be a speaker. Up until then, the only ongoing ministry I participated in was our weekly prison ministry, so I was excited to have the opportunity to travel and preach.

Before accepting the invitation, I talked with my leaders about the trip. I would be the only American among the six Filipino pastors leading the conference. I was used to doing ministry with Tami, Becky, Anthony, and Laura, who were in the Timothy Internship program with me. This would be the first time I would do ministry without my classmates, and I was apprehensive. I would be gone for about ten days, but we all agreed it was a great opportunity, and I was given permission to accept the invitation.

On the day of our departure, I was on my way to meet Pastor Rene and the other pastors. I wasn't settled in my spirit, and I had a strong urge to call my family in the United States. I didn't know what was going on, but I didn't have peace. I felt I needed to call home. When I arrived at the church, I pulled Pastor Rene aside and said, "I feel like I need to call home and make sure everything is okay before we leave. Do I have time to go back to our office and make a phone call?" In those days, cell phones were not readily available, so calling the United States was difficult and expensive. It would take about a day to travel to Catanduanes, and Pastor Rene didn't think the group had time to wait for me to call home.

I struggled with what I should do. In my spirit, I knew something was wrong at home, and I needed to find out what was going on. On the other hand, people were depending on me to keep my word and go on this trip. Pastor Rene left me alone for a few minutes while I wrestled with what I should do. Suddenly, I had lost my peace about taking this trip, and I knew the Holy Spirit was telling me I shouldn't go. Pastor Rene and the other pastors were in the Jeepney waiting for my decision. At that moment, I did something I would later regret. I ignored and disobeyed the Holy Spirit's prompting and got into the Jeepney. As we started our journey, I felt terribly anxious.

We departed for what would be a fourteen-hour drive through the mountains, driving on dangerous, winding roads. We had a good time of fellowship and singing songs, but I still did not have peace. One by one, we fell asleep. The winding roads caused us to brace ourselves so we wouldn't fall over while we slept. The Jeepney stopped along the side of the road for a snack late in the evening. A favorite snack in the Philippines is Balut. The Filipinos love them, but I could never bring myself to eat one. Who wants to eat a fully developed baby duck embryo? Pastor Rene put one in my hand and said, "You want to try?" I cracked it open and bravely ate the whole thing, including the bones.

We arrived at the boat dock at dawn. The final part of our journey was a two-and-a-half-hour ferry ride to Virac Island. The Philippines is notorious for overloading passengers on ferries, and this trip was no different. As we loaded the ferry, I felt someone behind me put their hand into my pocket. I grabbed the hand and held onto it, but the person disappeared into the crowds. Luckily, I didn't have anything of value in that pocket.

As we neared the island, the ferry listed as it turned. We were standing at the rail staring down at the water, and we were frightened. Pastor Rene instructed us, "If this boat capsizes, jump out as far as you can in the water and swim as fast as you can, as the water will suck you in, and you will drown as the boat sinks." It was pretty scary, but after about twenty minutes, we were docked and on dry land.

Catanduanes is known as the typhoon capital of the Philippines and experiences typhoons almost year-round. On Thursday, it was announced a category-five typhoon was heading straight for the heart of the island and was expected to make landfall the following day. During the conference, one pastor from the island came to the podium and shared the following story. He said the island had a history of being hit by devastating typhoons that would destroy much of the island. A pastor of a small church used to stand on the beach and stretch his hands out and rebuke the typhoons as they formed. It was said during the time he was alive, the island was spared from many devastating storms because he stood and prayed. However, after the pastor died, no one took up the mantle to pray, and the island had experienced several devastating typhoons.

The pastor encouraged the other ministers who lived on the island that it was time for them to take up that mantle of prayer. We all went to the beach, and it was quite a sight to see all the regional pastors stand at the water with their hands outstretched toward the sea and rebuke the storm and command it to dissipate. I was frightened, and although I was praying, I must admit I wasn't praying in faith. I was wondering if we would die in this devastating storm. Friday was the last day of the conference. After the worship service, the pastor who rallied the ministers came to the podium and said, "I am here to announce today the typhoon heading straight to the island has disappeared! The storm has dissipated as we commanded it to do, and we are no longer in danger." Praise erupted as we gave thanks to the Lord for such a powerful display of His power.

On our one day to relax, we visited a well-known beach in that area and enjoyed a time of refreshing and relaxation. I tried to enjoy it, but I just wanted to get home. I had lost my peace the day we left and had not gotten it back. The week had been good but also traumatic, and I was anxious to get home.

Sunday came, and we planned to preach a short message in the host church and then get to the boat dock after the service. The last boat for the day left at 3:30 p.m., so time was of the essence. One pastor from our team was preaching, and he just went on and on, with no signs of stopping. I have never been good with people who drone on and on, and I rolled my eyes and breathed with heavy sighs. Pastor Rene leaned over to me and whispered, "What is wrong with you?" I replied in an angry tone, "We have got to get out of here. Can't you make him stop peaching? We are going to miss the last ferry, and I don't want to be stuck here for another night." The pastor preached for another forty-five minutes, and I grew more anxious with each passing minute. I was desperate to get off this island and get home.

We reached the last ferry with just minutes to spare. By the time we got to the mainland, it was getting dark. We started our journey and stopped in the middle of the night at someone's house who had prepared a meal for us. We were tired and hungry, and we all agreed we wouldn't stay long, and we would eat quickly and leave.

The host was pleased to serve us a meal she was obviously excited for us to eat. She set a bowl down in front of each of us. The bowl contained what looked like liquid and a bone. I looked at the other Filipino pastors and saw the look of horror on their faces and knew we were in trouble. When a Filipino doesn't want to eat what is placed before them, you know you are in for a shock. We blessed the food, and I quietly confessed it would not harm me if I ate any deadly thing. I took the spoon, brought some liquid to my lips, and immediately gagged. It was slick and absolutely horrible! It was like taking lip balm or cooking oil and rubbing it all over your face. I could only take a couple of sips, and the other pastors could not choke it down either. While we were eating, the host looked at us with a big smile, and we tried to look like we were enjoying it, but it was so hard. My lips continued to feel the effects of that liquid the rest of the trip home.

The mountain road was a series of dangerous twists and turns. At about 1:00 a.m., when everyone was sleeping, I felt a jolt and then another jolt as the Jeepney stopped abruptly. "What's going on? What's going on?" I shouted to everyone and no one as we were all startled awake. We discovered the driver had fallen asleep and crashed the vehicle into the mountain. We were fortunate the accident happened while he was taking a corner and turned into the mountain instead of going over the cliff. Needless to say, I did not sleep for the rest of the journey.

We got to Manila at 6:00 a.m., and I said my goodbyes to everyone and found a bus home. It was the middle of rush hour, so it took several hours to reach home. I immediately stopped at Craig and Sandra's to check in and let them know I made it home. Sandra met me at the door and said, "You need to call home. Right after you left, your brother called, looking for you. Your mom had a stroke. She seems to be okay now, but we had no way to contact you. We didn't have any phone numbers and didn't know how to reach you." My heart sank. That was why the Holy Spirit was telling me I needed to call home. Looking back, my brother called at the exact time I felt the Holy Spirit telling me to call home and not to go on this trip. I often wondered what would have been different if I had listened and not taken the trip. I struggled with guilt for a long time that I was not there when my family needed me.

After I got home and repented to the Lord, I called my brother, who filled me in on what happened. I talked with my mom, and she cried, "I had a stroke. Are you coming home?" She was partially paralyzed on her left side and in rehab, making slow progress. I planned to take a trip home to see Mom and see how everything was going. It took me a few days to get a flight to the United States. I went first to my brother's in California, then we traveled to Arizona to where my mom was.

As I walked into her room, she cried. I hugged her, and she pathetically asked, "Are you moving home now to take care of me?" It was heartbreaking as I gently replied, "I will be going back to Manila in a few days, but I wanted to visit and see how you are recovering." I don't remember how long I stayed in the States, but my heart was heavy as I headed back to Manila.

Ho Chi Minh City, Vietnam

Calvary Bible School began training leaders in Vietnam in 1995. We worked with pastors of the underground church in Ho Chi Minh City, Vietnam's capital. In those days, it was dangerous to travel and minister in Vietnam. The communist government persecuted the underground church. We often heard stories of pastors who had been tortured and killed. If a foreigner was caught ministering in the country, they would be deported. The punishment was much worse for national pastors if the government caught them. Many times, pastors would simply vanish, never to be seen again. Despite the persecution, the underground church was thriving and growing at a rapid pace.

Sometime in 1997, I was hanging out with Eric and Therese like I did most days. Eric looked at me and said, "Have you read through the Holy Spirit curriculum yet?" Craig, Sandra, Eric, and Therese were writing and developing the courses that would form Calvary Bible School's curriculum during that time. Eric had just completed writing that course. I gave him a puzzled look and replied I hadn't seen the material. He gave me a copy of the outlines and asked me to look it over and let him know my thoughts. I thought it unusual that Eric would ask for my opinion, but I took the outline home and studied it.

A couple of weeks later, Eric asked me if I had looked over the course. I replied I had been studying the material, and I really liked how they wrote the course. Eric asked, "Do you think you would feel comfortable teaching the course?" I still had no idea why he had asked me to look over the material and was puzzled by this question. "Yeah, I probably could teach this subject," I said. Eric grinned and replied, "That's good to hear because Therese and I want to send you to Vietnam to teach this next month." He told me he was scheduled to teach the Holy Spirit syllabus in Vietnam, but something had come up that prevented him from traveling. Instead of canceling the training, Eric and Therese decided to send me in his place. They agreed to pay for my airfare and visa, while I would be responsible for covering my lodging and food.

I was so excited to have this opportunity to travel and teach. This would be the first time I would teach in the Calvary Bible School and the first time to travel to Vietnam. It would have been impossible for me to take this trip without Eric and Therese's financial help, as I continued to struggle with low finances. It was extremely dangerous to travel in Vietnam in those days, so Eric and Therese prepped me on precautions to protect myself and the pastors we were training.

One day we had a meeting to talk about the trip details. Eric began, "You will need to make sure you don't stick out in the crowd. Cover all the white skin you can. When you are in public, you need to wear a long-sleeved shirt, a floppy hat, a pair of sunglasses, gloves, and a face mask of some kind." I listened intently. "Oh, and you should shave off your arm hair before you go." With that, our meeting was finished, and I went home and obediently shaved off my arm hair.

The next day I walked into Eric and Therese's house for another meeting. When Therese saw my naked, shriveled arms, she immediately burst out laughing uncontrollably. She said, "I can't believe you took Eric seriously and shaved off your arm hair!" Eric was and still is a prankster and loves pulling a practical joke, and this was my first time being on the receiving end of one of his pranks. Eric saw my expression and tried not to laugh as he encouraged me that I did the right thing.

The day of my departure to Ho Chi Minh arrived, and I was apprehensive. I was traveling by myself and had no idea who would pick me up or what hotel I would stay at. I got to the hotel in mid-afternoon and noticed a barber across the street. I thought it would be a good idea to get a haircut, so I went to check it out. I stepped into the shop and saw a man sitting in a chair getting his hair cut. I watched as the barber pulled out a straight-edged razor and shaved around the man's forehead. I thought that was unusual. Then the barber took the razor and shaved the outside of the man's ears, and I thought, *nope, not going to happen,* and went back to the hotel.

I was advised I needed to be transported to the school in the early morning when it was still dark. This would help alleviate some risk to the pastors who attended the class. The first day I was picked up at 4:00 a.m. I had on my floppy hat, a pair of sunglasses, a bandana covering my face, and wore a long-sleeved shirt and a pair of gloves. I have a photo, and I looked like a bank robber.

We arrived at the house church and were whisked in the back door and up three flights of stairs. I was taken to a room where I would have breakfast and be allowed to sleep until classes started at 8:00 a.m. The breakfast was a bowl of soup and a piece of bread, along with coffee. I was famished, so without thinking, I took a big spoonful of the soup. My tongue was on fire! I had never tasted anything so spicy hot in all my life. I tried the best I could to eat everything, but I couldn't. It felt like I had burned off three layers of my tongue, and my lips burned the entire day.

Someone came to get me at 8:00 a.m. and took me to the class. The men sat on the floor on one side of the room and the women on the other. They closed the windows and praised and worshiped the Lord. It was incredible to experience their exuberance in praise! The leaders constantly looked for the secret police and were ready to whisk me away to safety if needed. The students hung on every word I said and listened intently to the teaching on the Holy Spirit. We completed the first class successfully without being raided. I was taken back to the hotel to rest for the evening.

The next morning, I was downstairs in the hotel lobby at 4:00 a.m. waiting for my ride, but to my frustration, no one came until 8:00 a.m. I got on the back of the scooter, and we took off. We rode for what seemed like an hour. I started seeing the same buildings over and over again, and I realized we were going in circles. After some time, we finally got off the main road and went down a single-lane dirt road. We stopped at a building, and the driver got off the scooter and said, "Wait here and don't stand out, and try to blend in." Well, I was dressed like a bank robber, with my floppy hat, sunglasses, and bandana. I felt terribly out of place, and people passing by looked at me suspiciously. The driver appeared a few minutes later with a look of terror on his face and said, "We must hurry; the police are coming!" We got on the scooter and drove away. I was terrified! I laid my head against the back of my driver and sang quietly in the Spirit.

What happened next was like a movie scene. As we drove, a scooter would pull up alongside us. Without looking at us directly, the driver would say words of instruction and then pull away and go in another direction. We turned left. After a few minutes, a different scooter pulled up alongside us, gave other instructions, and pulled away again. Then we made another turn. We drove like that for two hours, with different scooters pulling up beside us, giving instructions, and then pulling away.

We finally arrived at the house church and began our classes at 10:00 a.m. We were told the police raided early that morning where we were the previous day, and the students had to scatter. We finished the week of teaching without any further incidents. I arrived back in Manila with incredible memories of my first experience in Vietnam!

Taipei City, Taiwan

During the first few months of living in Manila, I moved several times, and I was extremely frustrated with my living conditions and lack of finances. I was having challenges with culture shock and finding my place within the team. One of my financial partners happened to be visiting Taipei City, Taiwan. They worked with a team of doctors from the United States, conducting disaster relief training for police and medical officials from around the city. They wanted to see me and invited me to come and visit. They offered to pay for the trip expenses, and I was happy for a chance to get out of the Philippines. They purchased my airline tickets, gave me the flight details, and I put it out of my mind since the trip was still a few weeks in the future.

I was visiting one of our missionaries in the village where I lived one day, and he asked me about the trip. "Aren't you supposed to leave today?" I replied, "No, I leave tomorrow on the fifteenth." "Today is the fifteenth!" They replied. I looked at my calendar, and he was right! It was 1:00 p.m., and my flight would depart that afternoon at 3:00 p.m., and I was frantic. I hadn't packed or prepared in any way, and the airport was at least three hours away on a good traffic day. "What do I do?" I exclaimed. I contacted my friends in Taipei City and didn't even know if I could get to the airport in time to catch my flight.

I rushed home, threw a few things in my suitcase, grabbed my flight itinerary, and ran to the main road to get a taxi to the airport. I didn't know whether I would make my flight, nor did I know if my friends knew I would be coming. Miraculously, I made it to the airport and boarded my flight with a few minutes to spare. I had no idea what I would do when I arrived in Taipei City if my friends were not there to pick me up. I didn't know where they were staying, and I didn't have their phone number. I arrived in the early evening. As I exited the terminal, I was greatly relieved to see my friend standing among the crowd waiting for me.

The disaster relief training was at a military base outside Taipei City, where the government trained the national police force. For the first time since I had left for Manila, there was hot water and a bathtub! It was nice to take a hot shower or even a hot bath!

One afternoon my friends decided we would go into the city and have a nice dinner at a seafood buffet. We hailed a taxi and started on our journey into the heart of the city. I was sitting in the front seat, and my friends sat in the back. A song by The Captain and Tennille was playing on the radio with catchy lyrics, and my friend hummed along in the back seat. This upset the taxi driver. He turned around and shook his fingers at him and said sternly, "My song. You no sing." I chuckled quietly. Well, the tune is catchy, so he soon hummed along to the song again. At that point, the taxi driver took both hands off the steering wheel, turned around in his seat so he could look him straight in the eye, and shouted, "My song. You no sing. My song!" I could see brake lights ahead. The driver was going fast, and he was not looking at the road while scolding him for singing. I tapped the driver on the shoulder and exclaimed, "Brake lights. I see brake lights. Please stop!"

Thankfully, we made it safely to the restaurant. We paid our fare and said goodbye to the taxi driver, who was still upset my friend sang his song. We were famished and looking forward to a good meal. We walked into the restaurant and asked for a table and were told the restaurant had just closed. When we asked why the waiter replied, "Typhoon coming." We hadn't heard of a typhoon in the area. We took a bus back to the military base and fortunately got back in time to be served a meal.

Despite the taxi drama, it was a relaxing trip, and I enjoyed being with my friends and sitting in on the training. When I returned to Manila, I felt refreshed. That trip came at just the right time, and I was so thankful I had the opportunity to visit my friends in Taiwan.

15

Dad Is Proud of Me

I was fortunate to have the opportunity to travel to the United States and be with my family for Christmas, and I was happy to be home. I still struggled with a lack of finances, so my plan was to itinerate and raise funds while visiting family. I was staying with my brother and his family, who lived in Victorville, California.

I visited my dad, who lived at 17581 Sultana #45 in Old Towne, Hesperia, which was not too far from my brother's house. Dad lived in a hotel room for his last eighteen years. When my dad first rented that place, he, my older brother Phil and his dog and puppies, and I and my cat and kittens lived in that hotel room. It had one double bed my dad slept in, a single bed my brother and I took turns sleeping in, and a small foam mattress we kept on the floor. It was cramped, to say the least. I left Hesperia when I was twenty-three and had not lived in that area since then.

Dad was sixty-eight. He was a lifelong smoker, and his health was declining. He could only walk a few steps without stopping to rest and catch his breath. He would carry a small folding chair when he went outside and walk until he got out of breath and then sit in his chair until he was rested. There was a restaurant around the block from his room where he would eat occasionally. When I was twenty-one, I worked at that restaurant as a manager. Dad told me it took him thirty minutes or longer to walk there because of his breathing issues.

One of my partnering churches invited me to preach on a Wednesday evening, and I asked my dad if he would come with me, and to my surprise, he said yes. When I picked him up, I was both excited and nervous. I do not remember the message, but I remember inviting people to receive Jesus. From the platform, I led people in a prayer to receive the Lord. As I prayed, I watched my dad to see if he was following the prayer and thought I saw him praying. I wasn't sure if he accepted the Lord that night, but he had the opportunity.

We hardly spoke on the way back to Dad's house, as we were each lost in our thoughts. When I pulled up to dad's hotel room, he looked at me and said, "I know you will do what you are supposed to be doing. You want to know how I can tell?" "How's that, Dad?" I replied. His voice trembled with emotion as he said, "Because I can feel it when you talk," and with that, he got out of the car and left. I was stunned. Blinking back the tears flowing down my face, I sat there for a minute. Dad wasn't good at expressing what he felt. Although he regularly received my newsletters, I had never heard him tell me anything about the ministry work I was doing.

A few days later, we were all having dinner with my brother Glen and his wife, Carolyn. Dad's favorite meal was hamburger pizza. When Carolyn told him she was making pizza, he got excited. During the meal, we made small talk, and I could tell Dad was having trouble breathing. Dad looked at me and said, "I don't think I will be here the next time you come for a visit." It took me a minute to realize what he was trying to tell me. Dad somehow knew he wouldn't live too much longer, and he was trying to tell me goodbye. I brushed the conversation off because I wasn't ready to accept that reality. I said, "Oh, Dad, you're going to be here for a long time." I remember Dad looking at me with sorrowful eyes as he said, "No, I don't think so." That was the last time I saw him, and it was the last conversation I had with him before he died.

The Letter

I returned to Manila with a heavy heart, and life seemed to carry on, but I was just going through the motions. One day in early March of 1998, Tami, Becky, Anthony, Laura, and I were coming back from the prison ministry outreach. We couldn't go into the prison that day because the prisoners were rioting, so we had lunch in the city before heading back to our village in Pasig City.

After lunch, we stopped by the post office and got the mail. In the mailbox was a letter from my dad. It was postmarked on January 20, 1998, but the letter took just under two months to arrive in Manila. I was thirty-five, and this was the first letter my dad had ever written me. As we got on the bus for the ride home, I held Dad's letter in my hand and cried softly. Suddenly, I missed home and regretted being in Manila.

When I got home, I opened the letter. It was a short, one-page letter. Dad mentioned Christmas was not the same without me there. I had spent the previous Christmas with my dad and Glen and Carolyn in California, but that year I was back in Manila. He commented on the change in my life and told me how happy he was I found what I wanted to do in life. As I read through the letter, I cried. He closed the letter with: "I think of you often and love you very much. Love, Dad." I burst into tears, sobbing uncontrollably. Dad never told us "I love you" when we were growing up, and he wasn't good at sharing emotions. This was Dad's goodbye letter to me, and he made sure I knew

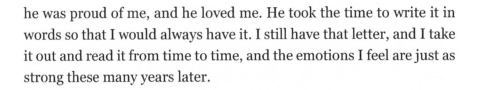

he was proud of me, and he loved me. He took the time to write it in words so that I would always have it. I still have that letter, and I take it out and read it from time to time, and the emotions I feel are just as strong these many years later.

The Phone Call

On the evening of March 28, 1998, in Manila, I got a call from Glen letting me know Dad passed away on March 26, two days after his sixty-ninth birthday. I received my dad's letter less than two weeks before he died. Glen told me Dad had died in his sleep, and my older brother, Phil, found him. He said it looked like Dad was playing a game of solitaire and fell asleep and died.

News spread among our team in Manila, and I got a call from my best friends, Eric and Therese. "Steve, we don't want you to be alone, so come to the house and spend the night with us." I was thankful to not be alone with my thoughts and went to Eric and Therese's and arranged my flights to the United States. I got my flight booked, called my brother, and gave him my arrival details. I tried to sleep, but sleep wouldn't come. I tossed and turned most of the night until finally, morning came. As I lay in bed, suddenly, a wave of grief came over me, and I let out a deep wail and cried, mourning the loss of my dad.

As I worked out my flight details, I was overcome with many emotions. The thoughts rolled around in my head, *I have given up everything to serve You, God.* In my grief, I looked to the heavens and blurted out to God, "I live in a country not of my choosing, among a people I am not familiar with because You said so." I wondered if the sacrifices I made to answer God's call on my life were worth it. The two years I had been on the mission field had been extremely difficult. I was misunderstood, my motives and character were questioned constantly, and my finances were a continuing struggle. On top of all those stresses, my mom suffered a debilitating stroke, and now, the death of my dad. As I left the Philippines, I was heartbroken and dejected.

When I arrived in the United States, Glen had taken care of most details concerning Dad's funeral. Dad had served in the Korean War, so he would receive a twenty-one-gun salute, and my brother would receive the folded flag that covered the coffin. I was asked to give the eulogy. The ceremony was small, with just our immediate family. My brothers Phil, Glen, and I were all together for the first time in a long time. My uncle Jerry, my dad's half-brother, was there, and a stranger showed up. I had never seen him, so I walked up to him, said hello, and asked how he knew my dad. He introduced himself as my dad's brother, Donald. I didn't know Dad had another half-brother, and I must admit I didn't treat him respectfully. I said to him in a sarcastic tone, "Wow, it is so good to meet you after my dad has died," and walked away.

Dad's Important Drawer

We had many details to take care of after the funeral. One main thing was to go to Dad's hotel room and clean it out. I was staying with Glen, and we put it off for several days. We decided Phil should meet us at the room so the three of us could go through Dad's stuff and clean everything out.

Glen and I arrived at the hotel first, and when we walked into my Dad's room, memories came flooding back, and I stepped back in time. Everything looked exactly the same as it did when I left in 1986. I silently glanced around the room, and it seemed as if I could hear conversations that took place many years previously. Scenes played back in my mind like a movie reel. My brother and I stood there without speaking, each lost in our thoughts. I was brought back to reality when Glen said, "Well, I guess we should get started."

I stood in front of the nightstand in between the beds. That was Dad's drawer where he put anything and everything important and had value to him. We had taken the beds out to the trash dumpster, and I investigated what was in that nightstand. As I pulled the drawer open, I was stunned at what I saw inside. I stood there for what seemed like an eternity staring in unbelief. Inside Dad's *important* drawer were my newsletters. Every newsletter I ever sent was stuffed into his important drawer, from the oldest to the newest, so tightly that the newsletters didn't fall out when I turned the drawer over. I could hardly believe what my eyes were seeing.

I put Dad on my mailing list and sent him newsletters in 1993 when I was in Bible school and giving food to the needy. I never preached to my dad or anyone else in my family, for that matter. I just simply sent him updates so he could read about what was happening. Now, it was 1998, and there I was, looking at about one hundred of my newsletters, a written history of God's working in my life. I was lost in my thoughts, reliving past ministry in my mind, when I heard Glen say, "Uh, what are you doing?" bringing me back to reality. "Looking in the drawer. I can't believe Dad kept all my newsletters." Tipping the drawer upside down and shaking it, I said, "Look, there are so many they won't fall out." Glen replied matter-of-factly, "Yea, he kept them and read them over and over again. He talked about you all the time. He was proud of you." I couldn't believe it. I had no idea Dad kept them, or he was proud of me. Nor did I know how God used those newsletters.

Transition

After returning to Manila, I realized I couldn't live and sustain ministry with the financial partnership level I had. I needed to do something but didn't know what, so I prayed and sought the Lord. I sensed a change was coming and talked with my leaders about increasing my financial partnership.

I was checking my emails one morning when I received a note from a partnering church in Arizona. The pastor said they had exciting news to share with me in confidence. An exchange of emails would be the catalyst for the change I had been sensing. The pastor shared they had been praying about planting another church in Henderson, Nevada. They had been making plans for several months, and they asked me if I would pray about moving to the United States to help plant the church. This seemed like an incredible opportunity and an answer to prayer.

We continued discussing back and forth until we agreed on what seemed to be a perfect fit. I would move to Nevada for a year to help plant the church and be the Missions Pastor. I would focus on raising my financial support for missionary service while assisting in the church plant and would return to the Philippines the following year in a better position financially. It seemed to be a win-win situation for everyone involved. I had never planted a church, so it would be an incredible learning experience. Craig and Sandra, my leaders in Manila, agreed it was a good move and the Lord's timing.

The last couple of months in the Philippines went by in a blur. I was excited and apprehensive about the change taking place. I came to Manila in 1996 with two seventy-pound boxes and a guitar. It was now September of 1998, and I was leaving with four seventy-pound boxes and my guitar, filled with hope and expectation. I stayed at Craig and Sandra's house the night before I left the Philippines. I couldn't sleep well, tossing and turning most of the night. Finally, 3:00 a.m. came, the time for Craig to drop me off at the airport with my life's belongings.

Looking back twenty-two years later, with the benefit of hindsight, I can see God's hand and how He had a bigger plan for my life than I could see then. He had a purpose for moving me to the States that was much more important than I could grasp. I planned to be in the States for one year, but it ended up being nine. I did not know I would be heading into some of the most difficult times of my life.

PART IV
Interregnum

16

Life in the United States

I faced a difficult transition. I had been a missionary for some time, and now that season was coming to a close, and I would find myself living in the United States, feeling dejected, rejected, and alone. I didn't think what missiologists call "reverse culture shock" would be a problem for me, but it was. Reverse culture shock is the emotional and psychological distress some people suffer when they return home after a number of years overseas. It can result in unexpected difficulty readjusting to the culture and values of the home country, now that the previously familiar has become unfamiliar.

Viva Las Vegas

It was October 1998. My dad had passed away in March, and I was moving to Las Vegas, of all places. My first home in Las Vegas was the Tropicana Royale Apartments, on Tropicana Avenue and Eastern

Street. It wasn't the best part of town, but it was centrally located and affordable. It seemed those first few months went by in a blur.

Most of my friends in the States had moved on and didn't seem interested in my missionary exploits. When I lived in the Philippines, I was treated with respect and honor. Because the Filipinos looked at me as a pastor, I carried a certain amount of authority and what I said carried weight with those I knew and ministered with. When I returned to the States, I was just like everyone else. I no longer had the prestige the title "pastor" carried, and I found no one really cared what I had to say. Almost no one cared I was a missionary or had ministry experience. It was a rude awakening.

I had heard it said the majority of missionaries leave the mission field within the first two years of service. I came to believe I was part of that majority, thinking I had only been on the mission field for about one-and-a-half years. When I talked about my first stint on the mission field, I hung my head in shame when I told people I was only on the field a short time. It was only when I researched for this book I realized I believed a lie all these years, and, in fact, I lived in Manila for almost three years.

When I returned to the United States, my plan was to spend a year raising my financial support to return to the mission field. It was now 2000, and I was stuck in the United States with no clear plan for returning to the Philippines. At that time, Calvary International gave a two-year grace period for missionaries to return to the field once they returned stateside. Since I had no immediate plans to return to the mission field, I resigned from Calvary International. It was hard to do, and I felt the door was permanently closed to missions for me once I did. I was assured that if and when I had plans to return to the field, I could rejoin my Calvary International family.

I was depressed and felt like a failure. I knew I was called to be a missionary, and that was what I was supposed to with my life. I knew my purpose, but now I was off the field and felt like life was over. None of my church community friends knew I had been a missionary. I never talked about my time in the Philippines. That was a different person, and I felt shame whenever I thought or talked about my time as a missionary. For the next year, I was in a funk and settled into a routine of going to work and church. I had no hope of returning to missions.

2001: The Year of Destiny

I don't have the exact date I heard God's voice about returning to the mission field written down in my Bible, but it was in early 2001. This day was like most every other day—nothing out of the ordinary. I certainly wasn't expecting to hear from the Lord, nor did I have faith that life would ever be anything different than what it was.

As I was resting, God spoke into my heart, "Return to the place where you failed, and this time, you will be successful." Suddenly, the memories of being a missionary came flooding back. The life I was meant to live that I had tried my best to push aside and thought was over forever, experienced a resurrection. Light and life flooded into my being. The calling on my life, the purpose for my existence, my God-given destiny, which was ordained from the world's foundations, was spoken back into existence—risen from the dead, with just one Word from the Word. My life changed forever that day. I would never be the same.

I turned to my Bible and read from Romans 11:29 AMP: *"For the gifts and calling of God are irrevocable [for He does not withdraw what he has given, nor does he change His mind about those to whom He gives His grace or to whom He sends his call]."* There it was, in black and white, written and inspired by the Holy Spirit eons ago so that I could read it at just the right time. God's message to me: *I Have Not Changed My Mind.* I sat there, stunned and shocked out of my depression. God wasn't disappointed in me. He hasn't changed His mind about me. It was time to rise up out of the ashes of failure and try again, this time with the promise of success.

A few months passed since God spoke to me about returning to the mission field, and I was no closer to fulfilling that dream. I still had no clear, concrete plan about the timing, and I questioned God. I remember praying, God, have You forgotten me? Do You even know where I am? I was frustrated.

I planned to attend a conference in Phoenix one weekend. The time for the conference had come, and I was preparing to leave. It was Friday, and I had packed my car. I started my drive to Phoenix. But I felt in my spirit I was to go to California instead and attend Full Gospel Church (now called The Church for Whosoever) on Sunday. The church had been a faithful financial partner to me when I was in the Philippines. I attended services there from time to time when I visited my brother. I made my reservations for the Phoenix conference months ago, but the feeling was so strong that I was to go to California; I couldn't ignore it. I put my car in drive and headed south to Victorville, California.

Sunday morning came, and I hadn't planned on being in California. I followed the prompting of the Holy Spirit, and now there I was, sitting in the congregation, wondering why I was there. During the worship service, I became lost in the Lord's presence, lifting my hands and heart when a holy hush descended upon the congregation. For several minutes, no one moved. Then someone prophesied. *I have led you to the place where you are, and I will also lead you out in My time. I have brought you to the place where you are, and I have not forgotten about you, and I know how to lead you out. Where you are is good for you, and what I am doing in you now is good for you.* I cried softly, thanking Jesus, over and over again, as His peace flooded my soul. From then on, I knew I was walking in His plan, and no matter how long it took, I would return to the field. I also realized it wouldn't happen right away, but I was okay with that. I knew God was doing something good in me. I felt free, and God was faithful to continue His work in my life.

God's Confirmations

My circumstances didn't change immediately, but I was growing spiritually. I still worked at the bank and served at the church. But inwardly, God was doing a work deep inside me, molding me and preparing me. He was faithful to confirm His Word to me from time to time. The following *"mile markers"* are written in the margins of my Bible.

September 30, 2001

My closest friends, Eric and Therese Nehrt, had come off the field and were now living in Dillsburg, Pennsylvania, where they were missions' pastors at Christ Community Church. It was soon after the 9/11 attacks on the World Trade Center, and I had flown out for a visit. On Sunday morning, we all went to church together. During worship, someone came and laid their hands on me and prophesied, *"Go back to where you failed and try again, and this time you will not fail."* This was an exact confirmation of the word the Lord gave me. God repeated word-for-word what He told me several months before when He spoke to me about returning to the field.

November 1, 2001

During a season of uncertainty, I questioned God about going to the field. Thoughts raced through my head. *Did I hear God correctly? Is this really God's will or my own?* I was involved in the cell group ministry, and one particular Thursday, there was a moment of silence after worship. After several minutes, the group leader said, "I feel like I have a word for someone." He opened the Scriptures to Proverbs 16:33 and read: *"The lot is cast into the lap, but the decision is wholly of the Lord (even the events that seem accidental are really ordered by Him)"* (AMPC). I stared at the group leader in disbelief. He had no way of knowing I had just asked the Lord if I was walking in His will. But. God. Spoke. It was God's decision I return to the mission field and not mine. My moving to the States and all that had happened was not an accident. I was encouraged God knew where I was and was directing my steps.

I made plans to return to the Philippines, but there was a process. I needed to rejoin Calvary International as a missionary. I telephoned Janet Meyers, a leader at our world headquarters, to discuss how to renew my missionary status. When we talked, Janet said, "No one who has resigned from Calvary International after coming off the field has ever rejoined. We usually never hear from them again. You will be the first missionary to resign and rejoin Calvary. I am sure there is a process, but I don't know what it is." Janet then referred me to Cheryl Bessinger, who said the same thing. She would research the policies and procedures for that situation. After a couple of days, I got a call from Cheryl. "You will need to come through the Missionary Preparation Orientation here in Jacksonville, and after that, we can renew your status as a missionary."

Divine Delay

I felt like I was given a new lease on life, and I enthusiastically raised my ministry budget. I scheduled meetings with my former financial partners, and I was pleased that, without exception, they indicated their intention to partner with me again. I worked hard throughout the end of 2001 and most of 2002, building my ministry budget. I had met my financial goals and was ready to go. The last thing I needed to accomplish was to go through the Missionary Preparation and Orientation at our Calvary International World Headquarters in Jacksonville, Florida. I submitted my application to attend the next class in July 2002. My plan was to depart for the Philippines as soon as I completed the training. The only thing left to do was to pack my bags and purchase my airline ticket. Then everything changed.

June 3, 2002: The Call

My stepdad had been ill for some time with bone cancer in his jaw, and his health had been steadily declining. I got a call from mom on the morning of June 3, and in between her sobs, she told me he had passed away during the night. The next few days went by in a blur as my brothers, and I gathered in Parker, Arizona, where they had lived for several years. As we planned the memorial service, my brothers and I talked about the best living solution for Mom. As a family, we decided it would be best for Mom to come and live with me in Henderson, Nevada. I had never cared for another person before, and I wasn't sure if I could give Mom the care she needed.

Over the next few days, we packed Mom's belongings. We did everything in such a hurry in those days, and we left behind many family heirlooms. Looking back now, I wished we would have taken more thought and consideration when we moved Mom. We loaded my brother's truck, mom's car, and my car with her things and drove to her new home in Henderson. We drove mostly in silence. I think Mom and I were lost in our thoughts. I broke through the quiet when I turned to her and said lightheartedly, "It's just you and me, kid."

It was June, and I had already made plans to attend the upcoming MPO in Jacksonville in July. I had already bought my airline tickets and paid for the class, so we all agreed I would go ahead and attend the class.

The Associate Missionary

I lived in a tiny one-bedroom apartment when Mom moved in with me. We put her hospital bed in the living room and tried to find space for her and her things. It was an adjustment for both of us as we settled into our new living conditions.

I quickly realized Mom required a lot of help. She just couldn't do much for herself. She was partially paralyzed on her left side, and the stroke left her unable to walk more than a few steps, dress herself, etc. Although her mind was still sharp, she needed much care. I had never been responsible for anyone but myself, and it was challenging to take care of another person. I have the type of personality that thrives on a routine, and we quickly established one for our lives. I would wake up in the morning and get ready for work. Then Mom would wake up, and before I left for work, I would give her a shower, get her dressed, and make her breakfast. At lunchtime, I would leave work, go home, make her lunch, and then go back to work. After work, I would cook dinner, and after dinner, I would get her into her nightgown and watch TV for a little bit. Then I would shower and go to bed.

I was single, so I didn't cook much, and when I did, it was usually something I could microwave. However, Mom came from a generation where meals were cooked from scratch. When I got home from work, I cooked a complete meal from scratch that included meat, potatoes, veggies, salad, and dessert. Cooking a meal like that took a lot of time and some getting used to. I worked a full-time job, and I quickly discovered taking care of Mom was a full-time job too, and soon I was exhausted. Because Mom was on Medicare, she was eligible for in-home health care, but it took about nine months before receiving health care services. After the first few weeks, I got used to going without sleep, and we both settled into our new lives together.

Soon the time came for me to travel to Jacksonville to attend Missionary Preparation Orientation. By this time, I had communicated with Nancy Lovelace about my change of plans in returning to the mission field. Everyone at the Calvary International World Headquarters was so supportive, and I felt so loved and appreciated.

At the end of the training, each person has an exit interview, and mine was with Tim and Nancy. During the interview, Nancy turned to me and said, "We are developing a program for people who, for whatever reason, can't go to the mission field full-time. We are still working out the Associate Missionary status details. We won't be launching the program officially until next year. However, the leadership has talked about it, and we have agreed we will start with you as our first Associate Missionary." I was stunned. God surely answered my prayer to continue to be involved with missions while caring for Mom.

I was an Associate Missionary from 2002 through 2007. Being an Associate Missionary gave me the ability to raise funds for short-term trips. It was an incredible blessing to be the first missionary for this pilot program. God worked miraculously in many ways on my behalf during this season. By that time, my job with Wells Fargo gave me thirty-five vacation days yearly. I took two short-term mission trips a year for the next five years and used my vacation days, so in effect, Wells Fargo paid me to be involved in missions. When Mom could begin receiving home health care services, she received a voucher every year that she could use to pay family members or friends to come stay in the house and care for her while I was gone.

17

Short-term Mission Trips

Amazon River Missions Trip: Columbia, Brazil, and Peru

I took my first short-term mission trip since becoming an Associate Missionary in April 2003. My colleagues with Calvary International had invited another pastor and me to go to Columbia, Brazil, and Peru. The purpose was to minister at a scheduled conference. The pastor would teach on inner healing, and I would teach on the Holy Spirit. I was excited to be getting out of the country and was especially excited to be going to South America. It would be one of the most defining and chaotic trips I had taken.

We arranged to meet in Leticia City, Columbia. Leticia City was on the Amazon River and bordered Columbia, Brazil, and Peru and would be our operations base. We stayed at a compound called the Casa Blanca. It was the mansion of a drug lord who had been put in prison. The missionary community somehow took the mansion over, and several ministries used the home for their short-term mission trips. The main transportation was by boat on the Amazon River. We had to obtain visas for Brazil and Peru to travel up and down the river. It seemed from the beginning of the trip the enemy threw everything he could to stop the conference. The pastor we were with commented to me one day that he had done several conferences on the subject of inner healing, and every conference faced obstacles.

Plans had been made to travel about twelve hours up the Amazon River to visit remote villages in the region my colleagues were doing ministry in. We would spend the night and then visit other villages as we came back down the river to Leticia City. The day came for us to depart, and we discovered the pastor missed the memo we needed to have a yellow fever shot to travel up the river. There was a lot of back and forth about him getting a shot, and finally, the pastor consented. We went to the clinic, but the doctor had not arrived, and we needed to wait. It was now noon. We were supposed to leave at 7:00 a.m. and were behind schedule. We sat at a table and ordered coffee and waited hours for the doctor.

While we were talking, I gazed out at the mighty Amazon River and saw its strong current carrying trees, logs, and other things past us. I looked up at one point and saw a large island slowly being swept past us by the surging current. On this island, an indigenous woman was washing clothes. I couldn't believe what I saw and watched the scene unfold as the island was carried past us.

The doctor arrived and gave the shot at 4:00 p.m. We had wasted the entire day waiting at the clinic. My colleague was networking with another missionary couple, and there were heated discussions about what we should do. I thought it best to stay where we were and start our journey fresh in the morning. The missionaries we were working with wanted to leave that afternoon. We were behind schedule and were supposed to be at the conference. But nothing had gone according to our plan. Only two hours of sunlight were left, and it was dangerous to be on the Amazon River at night.

It was decided we would start our trip to a village located two hours up the river and spend the night at a church, then continue early the next day. Five of us were in this little boat as we began our journey. The sun had set, and the missionary couple argued about where the church we were supposed to stay at was. It was now completely dark, and we were still on the river. One missionary stood at the front of the boat, waving a spotlight across the waters to help the driver see ahead. We constantly hit logs and trees, causing the boat to sway from side to side. I thought the boat would capsize, and I wondered if I would live through this trip. Finally, we heard the voices of the pastors we were to meet in the distance, and we made it ashore. We slept in the church that night, and even though I was exhausted, I didn't sleep well.

Up the Creek without a Paddle

We left as soon as the sun came up the next morning. We had about a ten-hour trip up the Amazon River ahead of us. The Leticia conference was supposed to be in its second day of teaching, and yet we were in the middle of nowhere. After two hours on the river, we stopped seeing any sign of human life. No boats, no villages, no people, no smoke, nothing but water and jungle as far as the eye could see. This was the most desolate and isolated place I had ever been in, and I felt the river closing in on me.

About eight hours into our trip, the boat's engine stopped. There was a lot of commotion as the missionaries worked frantically to find the problem. We drifted downriver. The spark plug blew out, and no one found a spare on the boat. The missionaries argued about not having an extra sparkplug, and the boat continued drifting downriver.

The jungle closed in on me, and I didn't know what to do, so I leaned forward, put my head on my folded arms, and prayed. Inwardly, I panicked and struggled to control myself. I heard other missionaries talking about what to do, but their voices seemed far away as I was lost in my thoughts. Someone said it would take three days to float back down to civilization. Someone else said there was not enough food or water.

The pastor's words brought me back to reality briefly. "I've got to do something; I just can't sit here," he said. "Do you have a paddle?" The missionaries looked around and found one paddle. We were five people in a little boat, up the Amazon River, with just one paddle between us. The pastor grabbed the paddle and paddled the boat.

I battled fear; the tangible feeling of the desolation and isolation of where we were hit me in waves, pushed aside by prayer, only to come rushing back again and again. The jungle seemed to whisper, you are not going to get out of this one. No one knows where you are. Then in the midst of all this, God spoke clearly, "I have brought you to this place of isolation and desolation physically to show you how isolated you are spiritually. You need to be in a place where you are known and where you can know people." In a flash, the Lord peeled back the veil over my heart and allowed me to see where I was spiritually from His perspective. I knew I was in a dangerous place, and the enemy would devour my life if I continued on this path. I repented to the Lord, oblivious to what was happening around me.

We drifted down the Amazon for what seemed like hours. We saw distant smoke rising into the air. Human life! Civilization! A woman was on the riverbank cooking a meal, and the pastor paddled the little boat toward her. The local missionary got out of the boat, spoke with the woman for a few minutes, and came back with four paddles. Oh, we were ecstatic! Now, we all had a paddle to use.

As we each paddled our way back into the river, I turned behind me. I saw two canoes filled with who I imagined were the warrior men of that clan, paddling frantically toward the woman. They were quite focused as they paddled. I suppose they saw us in the distance and thought we were attacking the woman, and they were coming to the rescue. I paddled a little faster and with more purpose.

Then, we heard a distant sound. As it got closer and louder, we heard an engine. We saw a boat. Our second sign of life on the river! It was unusual to see a boat that far up the river. The local missionary stood and frantically waved a shirt and screamed, and the boat turned toward us. It turned out to be a boat taxi ferrying passengers. The only reason they stopped is they recognized the missionary. They asked what the problem was, and we told them about our predicament. Someone looked around and found an extra spark plug, and it just happened to fit our engine! I don't know much about mechanics, but we counted it as a miracle. Our little boat started right up.

We got back out into the river. The local missionaries turned the boat around to continue our trip up the river. I don't know what came over me, but I stood and said, "No! I want to get back to civilization!" Everyone but the missionaries agreed with me, and we headed back to Leticia City.

I learned a powerful lesson that day. Sometimes we settle for "good," and we miss God's best. We were ecstatic we each had a paddle. It would now only take a day and a half to float and paddle back to civilization. That was good, but God's best was for us to have the sparkplug. How many times had I settled for good and not pressed into God to receive His best? When we got to dry land, I knew I had an encounter with God, and He had powerfully spoken to me. He went to extraordinary lengths to get me into a place and position where I could hear Him. That place happened to be ten hours up the Amazon

River in total isolation. That is how much He loves me! I was happy to set foot on dry land.

We came to the end of the mission trip, and we still had not done the conference. What was originally planned to be a five-day conference turned into a three-hour conference. The pastor from the United States spoke to a group of indigenous pastors for about an hour and a half about inner healing. I spoke for about an hour and a half on the Holy Spirit's baptism. The translation was into three languages, which was unusual.

We said our goodbyes and went our separate ways. The trip was organized especially by God to get me to a place where I could hear His voice. I knew I had to find a church family to be a part of where I could be known and have meaningful relationships. I needed to let people back into my life and heart.

The Church at South Las Vegas

When I returned to the United States, I knew things were going to change. I knew things *needed* to change, but I didn't know how the change would come. I was still processing what had happened to me on the Amazon River and how clearly God spoke to me. I wanted to meet with a financial partner. When I spoke with her on the phone, she mentioned a church that had just started having services in a movie theater. She and her family were going to attend the next day. We planned to meet in the lobby before services, and I hung up the phone intrigued.

The church officially started the weekend before, which was Easter Sunday, April 20, 2003. The church conducted a free, city-wide Easter egg hunt at a local high school's football field. I was so impressed hearing testimonies of the thousands of kids and families touched by the church through that event.

During the pastor's message, he looked up, pointed his finger in my direction, and said, "There is someone here who God is saying that you need to be in a place where you can be known and where you can know people." Those words penetrated into my spirit. Those were the exact words the Lord spoke to me on the Amazon River. I don't know why, but I was shocked to hear those words coming from the mouth of Pastor Benny. After the service, I knew that was where I was supposed to be. My pain and wounds ran deep, and it would take a long time to recover, but the healing process had begun. For the next six months, I faithfully attended services and purposely did not get involved in serving in any capacity. I needed to sit under the Word, let the Word wash over me, and bring healing to my soul.

After that, I began serving, and it was exciting to be a part of a growing church. The church continued to do Easter egg hunts for the next several years, and the congregation continued to expand. The church moved from the movie theater into a high school auditorium. Eventually, they bought a piece of property and built a building. I stayed planted in the church and faithfully served until I left for the mission field in 2007, and I am still a member.

Lahore, Pakistan

In 2003, I received a call from the International Victory Bible Institute director. I graduated from Victory Bible Institute in 1994 and became an International Victory Bible Institute teacher. A Bible school had just opened in Lahore, Pakistan, and I was asked about my availability to go there and teach.

Pakistan was an extremely dangerous country and traveling to the city of Lahore was particularly risky. It was just a couple of years past the 911 attacks. While the government was officially a partner with the United States in the war on terrorism, the general population of

Pakistan did not like Americans. I remember the director telling me he had difficulty finding teachers to go to Pakistan. One reason was a few months before our proposed trip, there had been a bombing at the hotel where we would be staying. Several Americans and other foreigners had perished in that attack, and terrorist groups operating within the country were specifically targeting Americans. I prayed about it and felt at peace, so I accepted the invitation. I would be the first person to arrive in Pakistan and the last to leave. It would be the most dangerous trip I ever took.

I was sitting in McCarren airport in Las Vegas waiting to board my flight for Lahore when I felt an urge to call my mom. I didn't pay too much attention to it because I had just said goodbye to her. There was the pre-boarding announcement, and the first-class passengers were boarding the plane, and the prompting to call Mom became stronger, and I thought, *this is weird*. Then came general boarding, and inside, the urge became a shout, call Mom now! I found a payphone and called her. No one answered, and I checked a new message on my phone. When I played the message, I heard, "This is 911; what is the nature of your emergency." I didn't know what to do. The plane was boarding, and something had happened to Mom.

Boarding continued while I made phone calls. I called the apartment complex manager. They told me Mom fell out of her wheelchair and tumbled down the embankment and had been taken to the hospital. Boarding was almost completed, and the airline agents wanted to know if I would be boarding. I contacted the emergency room and talked with my aunt. Mom had taken a pretty bad fall and had cuts and bruises but seemed okay. I asked Mom if she wanted me to come home, but she encouraged me to get on the plane, and she would be okay. I hung up the phone, raced to the plane, and was the last passenger to board.

As I exited the Lahore airport, I found someone holding a sign with my name on it. It was extremely hot, and I sweated profusely. We walked to the vehicle that would transport me to the hotel, and it was surrounded by guards holding AK-47s. The other two teachers soon arrived, and we began our week of training. The church bishop who had started the Bible school hired a private security firm to protect us as we traveled back and forth from the hotel to the school. Every time we walked out of a building, we were surrounded by ten guards holding AK-47s with their fingers on the trigger, ready to shoot. Every day was incredibly intense, and we continuously felt a tremendous added stress level. When we drove down the street, people looked at our caravan and saw we were Americans. They looked at us with such hatred in their eyes. It was a terrifying experience to be the object of such hatred.

I taught the Power of Praise and Worship. My teaching sessions happened in the evenings, and every time I got up to teach, the electricity went out. I taught every night in the dark, with the only light being a little rechargeable lantern by my notes. I still have videos somewhere of the entire class I taught. The only thing you can see is the lantern.

While the training continued during the week, the bishop heard one of his pastors who had recently been kidnapped had been found alive. He had been tortured and had miraculously escaped, and I had the opportunity to interview him. During our conversation, the pastor lifted his shirt and showed me where he was shocked by electric prods. His body still had the torture marks he endured. He told me details of his escape. His captors were stopped at a border crossing in the late night and examined by the border guards. He realized if he didn't escape, he would be killed. Even with bound hands, he managed to open the door and roll out of the vehicle and down a hill. I had heard and read stories of people who had been tortured for their faith, but this was my first and only opportunity to speak with someone who lived through that experience. I have this interview on a videotape stored somewhere.

After I finished teaching my class one evening, I prayed and thanked God for sending me to Pakistan. Who was I? I was awed I had this opportunity. I was just a regular guy who loved the Lord. I remember the Holy Spirit spoke to me, "You were not My first choice. The first two pastors I asked to go to Pakistan told Me *no*. You were the third person I spoke to about going, and you were the only one who said *yes*." I have never forgotten that conversation with the Holy Spirit. I have strived in my Christian walk to always be obedient to the Holy Spirit's leading.

India

I had the opportunity to travel to India several times between 2004 and 2006. I taught in two Calvary Bible schools that were train- ing leaders. One school was in the city of Hyderabad, which had a population of six million people. The other school was tucked in the Himalayan foothills in the northern region of India. The two regions were vastly diverse. The people and cultures were totally different, so much so that it was like being in two different nations. I was seriously praying about moving to Hyderabad and had several conversations with Craig Kuehn about relocating to India in the future.

Gangtok

It was extremely difficult to reach Gangtok and took two days to reach the Sikkim region. I needed three different transportation modes to reach the area where the Bible school was. First, I flew into Bodogra City. Then I took either a motorbike or a taxi to reach the bus stand at the edge of the Himalayan Foothills. The last part of the journey was a minivan someone from the host church drove.

I had an adventure the first time I traveled to Gangtok by myself. I was told someone would be at the bus stand to pick me up when I arrived. I was advised several vans took passengers into the Himalayan Foothills, and I would be approached by several wanting to take me, but I should wait for the pastor's minivan. "They will know who you are because you will be the only white person, so just wait until they come," was the sentence I usually heard when I traveled by myself.

When I arrived at the crowded bus stand, several van companies approached me and offered to take me to Gangtok. I kindly refused and said someone was coming to get me. As I waited and the crowd thinned, the vans departed one by one. I was now completely alone at the bus station. It was getting late, and my ride still had not arrived. I didn't know what to do. I didn't have any cash on me, and the last van for the day would be leaving soon. If I didn't take that van and my ride didn't show up, I would be stuck at the bus station for the night. I was negotiating with the van company, explaining my predicament, when I heard someone in the distance call out to me in broken English, "You, Steve?" My ride had come, and I was relieved!

The road to Gangtok was a little wider than a single-lane dirt road, with just enough room for oncoming traffic to pass at certain spots. On one side of the road was the mountain; the other had a straight down drop with no guardrails. It was frightening, but also picturesque. As we drove into the foothills, the driver stopped at a specific spot, and everyone got out and put on their parkas. I followed and put on my jacket. When we got back into the vehicle, we turned a corner on the road, and immediately, the temperature dropped considerably, and it got cold. The scenery was beautiful, and as we came around one corner, I was surprised to see a Coca-Cola plant in the middle of nowhere.

The Gangtok hotel was filthy, perhaps the dirtiest I had ever stayed in. It was also extremely cold. There was no heating or hot water in the room, so it was constantly cold throughout my stay. The hotel provided five heavy blankets for the bed that looked and smelled like they hadn't been changed and washed in several years. When I got under the blankets for the night, I could not move, but at least it kept the cold off. Once I stepped outside, I either walked uphill or downhill. No level roads or walkways were anywhere, but it was so beautiful. Sometimes the clouds would part, and I could see Mt. Everest in the distance. The Calvary Bible school was a short distance from the hotel, making it a convenient place to stay. I always had a great time when I traveled to Gangtok, and the students were attentive and asked questions after each class.

It was discovered many years later that some graduates started a Calvary Bible school in Bhutan. It was believed Calvary Bible School was the only school in the nation training pastors and leaders then. At this writing, I believe there is still leadership training in that nation.

Hyderabad

I taught two subjects at the Calvary Bible school in Hyderabad, Divine Healing and the Power of Prayer. When I traveled to India, I had no idea how life-defining it would be. It was a powerful week of ministry. With the benefit of hindsight, I see how that trip set the direction for my life and ministry, continuing to this day.

During the teaching of the Divine Healing course, I felt the Holy Spirit speak to me that some students had issues with their backs. Over the years, I witnessed several people who had been healed instantly of back problems as I laid hands and prayed for them. I was confident the Lord was present to heal that day. At the end of one session, I gave an altar call for those who needed healing, and specifically those who needed healing in their backs. Amazingly, six students with back problems came forward. I laid hands on each one and prayed for them, and they were all instantly healed!

As I taught on the Power of Prayer, we experienced God's move in the classroom. After one of the sessions, I stopped the class and invited everyone to pray. In India, when you announce it is time for prayer, people pray immediately and forcefully! It was no different on that day. A holy roar ascended as we all lifted our voices.

I was praying in one corner when the Holy Spirit spoke to me. I had been asking the Lord questions over the past several months. I had flowed in some gifts of the Spirit previously that seemed to be waning and were not as prevalent, and I asked the Lord the reason. The Holy Spirit said He was leading me into a teaching ministry. I would operate in the office of a teacher, and those previous giftings would not be as prevalent as they once were. I was stunned, as I wasn't expecting the Lord to speak to me in such a powerful way.

We prayed for quite some time. Afterward, I allowed the students to share what they felt the Holy Spirit was speaking. It was exceptional that every student who testified shared similar things. The common theme from all who shared was a change of direction or ministry happening. It seemed the Holy Spirit was birthing new ministries, new visions, and new giftings in that prayer time.

18

Foundations for the Future

Life was not the same when I returned to the United States. I pondered the things the Lord had spoken to my heart about becoming a teacher in the body of Christ. I took stock of my life and experiences. When the Lord spoke to my heart about ministry in 1987, there was a preparation season which included going to Bible school. When the Holy Spirit spoke to me about becoming a missionary in 1993/94, I went for training at Victory World Missions Training School and joined Calvary International.

In each step of my journey as a Christ-follower, whenever there was a calling and ministry birthing, there was a period where the Holy Spirit worked to build the foundation for what He wanted to accomplish in and through me. It took years, and I knew the importance of working with the Holy Spirit to build a strong, firm foundation.

I thought about the foundation the Lord had built in my life up to that point. I knew the Holy Spirit wanted to birth a new teaching ministry in me. What tools did I currently have that would help me? What did I lack? What did I need to incorporate into my life that would push me forward? I realized I only had one year of Bible school and three months of missions training, so there were gaps in my foundation. I lacked important tools and skills. I needed more training, and I needed to go to seminary.

I approached Dr. George and Janet Meyers for help. It was natural to seek them out as they had been incredible mentors to me over the years. Dr. George had been instrumental in helping me see the value of planning for the future. With his guidance and encouragement, I saw the wisdom of investing in a 403-b Calvary International made available to missionaries. Dr. George and Janet have impacted my life in countless ways, and they both mentored me in that planning process.

I was visiting our home office in Jacksonville and staying with Dr. George and Janet. I talked with them about looking for a seminary to attend, and the first question Dr. George asked me was, "What are you going to do with your education in the future? What are your long-term goals for attending seminary?" I hadn't thought about my long-term goals. Dr. George gently asked me two questions to think about the big picture: "Do you intend to use your education to help you teach in Calvary Bible School only? Do you wish to be a professor in a Christian university in the United States in the future?" He said, "If you wish to be a professor in a Christian university, you will need to attend a seminary with regional accreditation, which can be an expensive investment in your future. If your desire is to teach in Calvary Bible schools, you can choose a seminary with national or local accreditation, which would be less expensive." I was at a fork in the road, and determining the answer to these questions would help me choose which road I would take.

I spent the next year discovering the answer to Dr. George's two important questions. It was something I took seriously, and I spent much time in prayer about what the Holy Spirit was leading me to do. I learned as much as I could about the different accreditation types.

I researched various seminaries and sent out applications to a few schools. During that season of introspection, prayer, and counting the cost, I discovered my desire was to focus mainly on teaching in the Calvary Bible schools. I had spent a year doing due diligence and research. Standing at that fork in the road, I understood the Holy Spirit's leading. I had discovered the answer to the questions Dr. George had asked, and I knew which road to take.

Logos Christian College

I heard about Logos Christian College through Calvary International. I had visited their website several times during the previous year to learn about their degree programs. I was pleasantly surprised to learn Logos and Calvary International had formed a partnership that gave missionaries tuition discounts. I enrolled with the school and worked on obtaining a bachelor's degree in New Testament theology.

Many years ago, I had financially supported someone attending Bible school. Every time I sent a check to the school on behalf of that student, I prayed that when it was time for me to go to school, I could pay for tuition upfront and not incur debt. After I enrolled in Logos' degree program, I learned I was awarded a 50 percent discount on my tuition, and I completed that degree without going into debt!

I started working on my degree soon after my mom came to live with me. My life was already full, and I wondered how to add one more thing to my busy schedule. I heard a teaching about the power of ten, and I incorporated that principle into my studies. I did not have large time blocks to dedicate to studying, but I had ten minutes here and there to dedicate to reading and writing throughout the day. I carried my textbook with me everywhere I went. Whenever I had a few minutes free, I read a few sentences or a paragraph and made notations in the book.

That degree took well over a year to complete as I did my work in ten-minute blocks. Each subject consisted of a textbook to read and a series of cassette tapes to listen to. Then there were tests to take and papers to write. The work I did at the bank gave me a great amount of privacy as I worked in a cubicle by myself. I would take my cassette tapes to work and listen to them with my headphones over and over again. Once I had the material digested, I would write my papers at home, usually a paragraph or two each day.

The Timothy Internship
The Peten, Guatemala

Mom had been living with me for three years, and we had settled into a routine. Her health was precarious, but despite that, she did well for most of that time. However, in 2005, she began falling, and as time went on, she fell more often. She had a lifeline necklace, so she would press the button, and the fire department would come pick her up when she fell. It got to where she was falling two or three times a day, and we concluded she could no longer stay at home. It was a challenging time which we both realized would happen at some point, but neither of us was prepared for the reality she needed full-time skilled nursing care.

After research about appropriate facilities, we moved her into a nursing home. It was hard on both of us, and it took time to adjust to our new living situation. It was challenging as Mom had previously been waiting by the door when I came home from work, and now I came home to an empty house.

My long-term goal was to go back to the mission field. I needed to go through the Timothy Internship, which is a ten-week practical mission training program on the field with mentoring from veteran

138

missionaries. I had been part of the first internship program in 1996, but it had been a few years since I had been on the mission field full-time. By 2005, attending the internship was a requirement for all candidates intending to go to the field. I talked with Mom about my going out of the country, and she agreed it would be okay knowing she would be well taken care of while I was gone. I promised I would call at least once a week to check on her.

It was January of 2006 when I applied to the Timothy Internship Program. I would spend ten weeks in Peten, Guatemala. The class was small and consisted of Patrick Courtney, Scott and Susan Oldaker and their children—Joy, Arial, and Faith—and me. By the time the internship started, I had completed my studies with Logos Christian School. I was ready to graduate and receive my degree. The graduation ceremonies were scheduled, I had made my final payment, and I was ready to "walk." The graduation would occur in January, which unfortunately coincided with the first week of the Timothy Internship in Guatemala. I was given grace to miss that first week to graduate and receive my degree. I was the first missionary to take advantage of the partnership agreement with Calvary International and Logos Christian College and graduate from that institution. I had dropped out of school in the eighth grade, so it was quite an accomplishment to receive that degree.

In the internship, we were scheduled to visit La Nueva Sesaltul, a village out in the bush where Calvary International had been working. A previous team had built indoor stoves in each grass hut of the village, and our purpose was to repair the stoves. We were scheduled to spend the night in the jungle, and I was not looking forward to it. I was a city boy and not handy with tools, and definitely was not into *roughing it* outdoors. We bought hammocks and hung them between posts for sleeping. I tried my best to sleep, but I was extremely uncomfortable and became frustrated. I remember getting up and storming out

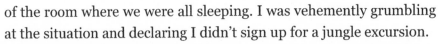

of the room where we were all sleeping. I was vehemently grumbling at the situation and declaring I didn't sign up for a jungle excursion.

I found a small building that had been used as a school. I took my flashlight and looked around inside to see if I could find anything to sleep on. In one part of the room was a mattress with no stuffing, and all that was left was the coils and springs. I threw my sleeping bag on it and laid down. It was worse than the hammock. I then spotted what looked like a picnic table just long enough to stretch out on, so I threw my sleeping bag on top of it, climbed in, tucked my flashlight next to my side, and zipped the sleeping bag up. I was so exhausted that I fell into a deep, deep sleep.

Evidently, I turned over in my sleep, and when I did, I felt something move next to me! It felt like a snake had crawled into my sleeping bag. So I instinctively beat the snake with my fist while trying to unzip my bag and escape the horrible death that surely awaited me from the snake bite. I remember screaming while I was beating the snake on the head. Once I got out of the sleeping bag and regained my composure, I discovered the snake I was hitting was actually my flashlight. When I rolled over and felt the flashlight next to me, I imagined it to be a snake!

Morning finally came, and we were having breakfast. I was the chaplain of our group, so it was my responsibility to have devotions each morning. After our devotions, we worked on repairing the stoves. I tried to be positive, admitting it would only be one day, and we would leave that forsaken jungle in a few hours. I definitely was not enjoying myself while the other men seemed to be having the time of their lives. It was now afternoon, and we had finished our assignment. I was excited about escaping the jungle. We were waiting for the ladies on our team to come with dinner. All that was left to do was eat and say our goodbyes. I was ready to throw my sleeping bag into the truck and get out of there.

The trip leader said, "They want us to stay another night and work on the road tomorrow." My heart sank, and without thinking, I spoke up, "We agreed to come for one night only, and I don't want to stay for another." We talked back and forth for a few minutes. Everyone had to agree to stay another night, and I was the lone holdout. I finally said, "If I could at least take a shower and get the sweat off me, then I guess I could make it another night." The Calvary missionary leading the trip said, "I think we can find you a shower. If we can, will you stay?" I replied I would. He left and returned after a few minutes and said we could now go take our showers.

I imagined hot water, but we were taken to a muddy water hole in the ground. That would be my shower, but at least I could get wet and get some sweat off. I felt better afterward and resigned myself to sleeping in the jungle another night. I unrolled my sleeping bag back on the wooden bench. Scott joined me, and he took the mattress that was only the springs, and we both fell asleep. I was exhausted and fell into a deep sleep again like I had the night before. I made sure to put my flashlight in a different place to avoid the imaginary snake situation.

During the night, I heard the most awful screams, which sounded like it was right outside our window. My imagination went wild. Was it a lion coming to attack us? Was it some kind of jungle monster that took delight in eating missionaries? Was it a howler monkey coming to kill me? The screams grew louder and more intense. I covered my head in the sleeping bag, shaking in fear.

In the morning, we discovered the noise was a mare who gave birth right outside our window in the wee hours of the night. We finished our work for the day, and the ladies showed up in the afternoon with a nice dinner for us. We ate and said our goodbyes. I was the first one packed and the first one in the car, ready to go. I couldn't wait to get out of the jungle!

Another week we were scheduled to visit another ministry and do construction work. Didn't people know I was a city boy and didn't do "construction work"? What is wrong with these people? I remember a few things specifically about that week.

One day the men were to dig a hole in the ground to build a concrete wall. Each man took turns swinging a pickaxe to dig up the ground. With each ax swing, several inches of ground turned up. It was my turn. I had never seen a pickaxe before, much less actually used one. I picked it up and swung, using all my strength. The ax hit the ground with a "light thunk." I barely moved the dirt, but at least I tried, and I laughed and shrugged it off and said, "I told you I would be useless in construction."

A big tractor was being used, and I was asked to drive it from one location to another. I thought *this ought to be fun* as I climbed into the driver's seat. Gearshifts were everywhere, and each one did something different. I was told what to do, and I put it into gear and started moving. I evidently hit the gearshift, which caused the tractor bed to lift off the ground. People were chasing me and yelling directions to me, and I hit the gearshift again, which caused the tractor bed to level off. There is a video of me driving in circles with the tractor bed lifting off the ground and back down. It was a fun experience, and I was more than happy to provide entertainment for our group. I am still a city boy at heart!

The internship was coming to a close, and we would soon be going our separate ways. I was having devotions one morning, and the Holy Spirit whispered to me, "You will be on the mission field by this same time next year." I was stunned. I couldn't believe what I just heard. I returned to the United States with both excitement and heaviness in my heart as I contemplated the meaning of what the Holy Spirit had spoken to me.

Transitions

I was happy to return to the United States. The internship went well, but frankly, I was glad it was over. I talked to Mom a couple of times a week and kept abreast of what was happening. Mom's health had always been precarious, but she was pretty healthy despite her ongoing medical challenges. However, her health declined quickly when I returned from Guatemala, and she passed away on June 6, 2006. My nephew, Kory, had come to Nevada around the same time Mom passed away and stayed with me for several days. I remember fondly the long conversations we had each night; it brought such comfort to have Kory by my side.

Looking back, I can see God orchestrated everything while I cared for Mom. From Calvary International starting the Associate Missionary, to the Lord giving me a job that would give me thirty-five vacation days every year, to having someone care for Mom while I traveled on short-term mission trips, I was overtaken by God's goodness. I surely made mistakes, and I did not do everything right, but my heart was in the right place. I quickly learned how selfish I was when Mom came to live with me, but just as quickly, I learned about sacrificial love. I experienced God's love and grace in a greater measure while being her caregiver, and I am so very thankful.

Scouting out the Land

I had been praying about returning to the mission field and developed ministry plans. The Lord gave me a vision to be an itinerate Bible teacher for our Calvary Bible schools throughout Southeast Asia. I had planned to move back to Manila, but after praying and seeking the Lord for direction, I realized being based in Thailand would be the most practical. Bangkok was less than a four-hour flight from many countries that housed our schools

I had the opportunity to join Craig and Sandra Kuehn on a trip to Thailand, and I jumped at the chance to spy out the land. We were in Khon Kaen for a couple of days, just long enough to see the Acunas and tour the city. It was six hours by bus to Bangkok, so flying in and out of the country would be relatively convenient. There was also a McDonald's, so I could at least get a burger when I needed one.

When I returned to the United States, I gave a report to Scott and Susan Oldaker. During the internship, they talked about their plans to move to Thailand and join the new team in the process of being planted there. They were excited to hear what I learned about the city. I jokingly said to Scott, "There isn't a Starbucks, though. If the Lord really wants me to move to Khon Kaen, He will have to open one there." We both had a good laugh.

Preparing for Thailand

I set my financial goals for the ministry and the set-up budget I needed to raise. Once I returned to the United States, I had everything I needed to impart vision for my plans, so I built my financial partnership base once again.

It was incredibly easy to reach my financial budget goals. Most previous financial partners I had while I was in the Philippines quickly rejoined. All the financial partners who had given toward short-term mission trips while I took care of my mom also became monthly financial partners. I had my sails up, I caught the wind, and was sailing effortlessly toward the destiny the Lord had for me. I worked diligently, and by January 2007, I was officially released to move to Thailand.

PART V

Second Missions Assignment: Southeast Asia

CHAPTER

19

New Beginnings

Thailand has the longest constitutional monarchy of any country, and the Thai people love and deeply respected the king. Thailand is affectionately called "the land of smiles," and the Thai people are friendly and relationship-oriented. Many times, when I met a Thai person, they would ask, "How long are you going to be here?" When I would answer, "For a long time," they would let out a sigh of relief, knowing they would have plenty of time to develop an intimate relationship with me.

As I prayed for Thailand, I continuously saw a scene play out in my mind. I saw a Thai man standing in a field harvesting the rice. He wore a conical-shaped hat typical to Thailand. He would raise his face and look at me with sad eyes because he was working so hard but not getting a good harvest. I felt the Lord speak to me during those prayer times that there was a famine in the land for His Word.

Statistically, Thailand is considered an unreached nation, with less than 2 percent of the population being Christian[1]. The northern area, the Isan region, is the least reached, with less than 1 percent being Christian[2]. In Khon Kaen, there were about twenty churches and three different pastoral fellowships, and it was challenging to find unity within the churches since few pastors worked together.

The Oldakers moved to Thailand a few months before I arrived. About two weeks before my departure, I got a call from Scott. "You are not going to believe this," he chuckled. "I went by the mall today, and they are opening a Starbucks! It should be open for business by the time you get here!" We both had a good laugh as we remembered my comment, "If the Lord wants me to be in Thailand, He will have to put a Starbucks there!"

I purchased my airline tickets, departed for Thailand on May 5, 2007, and arrived in Khon Kaen two days later. The first thing I needed to do was to secure a place to live. I stayed in a hotel for the first few days while searching for a place to call home. I was put in contact with an Australian missionary couple going on furlough, and I talked with them about staying in their condo while they were gone.

The couple proposed charging me 5000 Baht a month (about $150 USD) for their place while they were gone. I agreed and moved my stuff into their home and felt settled temporarily. They were gone for several months, so I had time to learn the city's layout and find a place to live. I soon discovered they paid 2500 Baht monthly for the condo. Not only were they charging me double their rent, but I also paid an extra fee to sit on their couch and use their forks and knives.

That was my first experience doing business with another missionary. It left a bad taste in my mouth for future dealings with other Christian workers. Even though I was upset a fellow missionary took advantage of me, I stayed in their place for a few months. I figured if they were so desperate for money, the least I could do was be a blessing to them.

There was a small expatriate community in Khon Kaen. I thought we would be welcomed by other missionaries with open arms because we were on the same team, working for the same Jesus to reach the Isaan region. It is difficult to explain the reception we got from the expat community. While most of them outwardly welcomed us, inwardly, they were wary and kept us at arms-length. Most missionaries at that time had been in Khon Kaen for more than twenty years, and they were skeptical of new missionaries. They were protective of *their* people, and their attitude was, so you think you will come into my territory and try and do something for God. I was stunned and made a mental note to not have that same attitude toward other new missionaries. The pastors in the city could not and would not work together, and in many cases, the veteran missionaries added to that division by their attitudes and actions. Our work was cut out for us.

Stories from the Field

It was wonderful and exhilarating to be back on the mission field. God had promised me it would be better than my previous missionary experience, and I was determined to enjoy every minute. Every experience was new and exciting, and I kept my sense of humor in every situation. I had plenty of opportunities to be discouraged, but I found irony and humor in those situations as well. Culture shock hit me in waves, but I handled it better because I could identify when it was happening to me.

I noted things about my everyday life I found humorous and wrote them down and had a collection of random experiences from being on the mission field.

My New Haircut

One day I decided it was time to get my first haircut in Thailand. I don't have much hair, so usually, I get my hair cut using clippers set on #5. Well, I take that back. I *used* to like the clipper set on #5. I found a barbershop this afternoon and inquired about a haircut. I should have known I was in for a treat when I saw plastered on the wall the different cuts they did, complete with stick figure people. Even though I don't speak Thai, I was sure I made myself clear on how I wanted my hair cut by pointing to the appropriate stick figure and saying, "like that."

I should have known what would happen by the lady's expression when she was handed the clippers. You know the look, it's that *deer in the headlight* look—that glazed-over look in the eyes one gets when they have no idea what is going on. I don't think she had ever seen a set of clippers, much less used one. She kept trying to put the #5 clip on and couldn't, so I helped her put it on. When the correct clipper was finally on, the woman got eye-level to the back of my head, closed her left eye, and stuck her tongue out of the corner of her mouth. At this point, I knew this would be a unique experience, but I was okay with that. I just wanted my hair cut. However, when she took her first swipe with the clippers, I thought, *oh, my, this isn't going to be pretty.*

Getting a haircut is much like getting pregnant. Once the process has begun, you are committed to delivery, and I thought, *I'm committed now. I can't leave looking like this.* After she took her first swipe, she really went at it. My only thought was she was going after the "Kojak" look and wouldn't be satisfied until there was no hair left. She took what seemed like ten minutes, going back and forth, back and forth, on the same spot. She was doing it with such force that she pushed my chin to my chest with each swipe. Then she worked on the other side of my head, and because of her force, the clipper guard fell off, and the razor got caught in my hair. She couldn't figure out how to get the razor unstuck from my hair and could not get the clipper guard back on. I helped her get me untangled, and I tried to fasten the clipper guard correctly, but I really wanted to take the thing from her before I got seriously hurt.

By this time, I was making plans to purchase a hat and make up the story of how this all happened. Then it came to the final touches, trimming around the ear and shaving off the neck hair. After another twenty minutes back and forth on the same spot, my entire head was on fire because I got sunburned the day before while out in the sun.

It was the last straw, though, when she pulled out a straight-edged razor blade she wanted to use on me. She had this evil gleam in her eye. I could almost see her twitch with excitement at the prospect of using that razor, quite possibly for the first time ever in her haircutting career. At that, I smiled and said, "No thank you," and paid for the haircut, which was $3.00 USD, and left. The funny thing is I will probably go back there when I need another haircut!

I "Misunderstimate" Myself

I am learning to speak Thai. Before you congratulate me, you should know trying to learn to speak Thai in mid-life is like trying to speak with your tongue pulled out of your mouth up over your forehead and wrapped around your neck. That being said, I recently wondered just how dangerous can I be armed with a little bit of knowledge? So today, I would practice speaking Thai.

First, I had to find friendly, unsuspecting Thais to speak with. I thought of going to Starbucks, where I do a lot of business, but most of today's staff were single women. I knew it was not a good idea to get into a long conversation with a single woman. I went to another business I often frequent, but they were closed.

I then remembered the mall's parking attendants. Whenever I park basement, they always talk to me as I enter and exit. In the past few days, they have asked me in Thai things like, "Where are you going? Are you eating?" So, I chose them to be my unsuspecting audience for the day.

After I parked my car, I approached the men handing out parking stubs to other cars wanting to park. I went to the booth and said, which I imagine sounded something like, "I Thai speak practice." The entire universe stopped. My wanting to "Thai speak practice" was enough for them to completely stop what they were doing. They cleared off a chair and sat down with eager anticipation to hear the knowledge that would soon roll of my tongue that is pulled out of my mouth over my head and wrapped around my neck! The only thing they were missing was popcorn and soda; however, they were ready for the show I would put on.

I have to say I didn't do too badly. I could ask things in Thai like, "What is your name? How old are you? Where do you come from?" Then, of course, I would answer them in Thai afterward with, "My name is Steve. I am forty-four. I come from America." They had much fun at my expense, and they laughed a lot. I went over all the little phrases I've been learning this week. In all, "I Thai speak practice" pretty well.

Being Clueless Can be Dangerous at Times

I usually think I am on top of things and pretty smart, but after this experience, I can see I can be just as clueless as anyone else. Let me share a small part of that day while at the same time poking a little fun at myself. After all, if you can't laugh at yourself, who can you laugh at?

I was in Bangkok taking care of business and had spent the whole day in traffic. That is after taking the midnight bus from Khon Kaen to get to Bangkok and getting three hours of sleep during the trip. At the end of the day, I was extremely tired, and I was just trying to get back to my hotel. It is 6:00 p.m., right smack in the middle of rush hour traffic. You haven't been in rush hour traffic until you have been in Bangkok with millions of people all trying to get home at the same time.

All the taxis were full, and when one stopped, I told the driver I was going in the same direction everyone else was going. He said no and drove away. After about a fifteen-minute wait, I got a taxi. The driver was trying to overcharge and negotiate a price because of heavy traffic. I smiled politely and said every day was heavy traffic while thinking, *dude, I'm really not in the mood for this.* We started our journey, and I am tired and a little steamed this driver wanted to overcharge me. I started a conversation with the driver and practiced the few Thai words I learned, thinking I could distract him from wanting to cheat me.

I am clueless as to what he is saying in Thai, but it goes something like this, "You Khon Kaen, then you Bangkok, and bop-bop-bop? I, being "fluent" in Thai, reply, "Yes, I live in Khon Kaen, and I come to do bop-bop-bop in Bangkok." He then covers his mouth with his hands and laughs. He giggles and snickers like a little child at whatever I just said to him in Thai. I think this seems to be working. At least he is not concentrating on trying to overcharge me, so I continue my conversation, speaking mostly English and mixing it with the Thai words I know.

He says to me in Thai, "You have friends in Bangkok"? I reply in Thai, "Oh, yes, I have many friends in Bangkok and in Khon Kaen as well." I want him to know I am not a tourist and I live here and have many friends, thinking he won't want to mess with me. At this, he giggles and snickers even louder, and I am wondering what is so funny. He then says, "You bop-bop-bop friends?" I am thinking he is asking me if I do business with my friends, so I reply, again in Thai, "Oh, yes, I bop-bop-bop with my friends all the time." When I said this, he just about drives off the road as he is laughing so hard.

I haven't quite caught on yet, so I asked him about his family after a minute or two. I'm just trying to get to the hotel after a long day without getting ripped off, so I asked him if he has a wife, and he says yes. I then asked if he has children, and this is when the lights finally come on for me, and I realize the conversation we have been having. He says, "Yes, I bop-bop-bop my wife, and we have two children," snickering and laughing at me while he is trying to stay on the road.

I have to admit I turned fifteen shades of stupid. I then realized our entire conversation revolved around the fact I had just told him I have sex with all my friends in Khon Kaen and then come to Bangkok and have sex with all my friends here. I thought, what do I do now? He thinks I am a stud muffin. I've never been a stud muffin before, and I wonder how I can get myself out of this conversation, or do I even try? I will probably never see him again. I mean, what are the chances? My solution was to say no to everything he said from the point on.

I was so embarrassed that I paid him and gave him a generous tip when we finally arrived at the hotel. Actually, it was *hush money*, but I couldn't figure out how to tell him in Thai that our conversation was to remain just between us. I mean, I have a reputation to protect, you know?

So, What Did You Do Today?

I have often been asked two questions by my friends and family since I have been living on the mission field, and they are:

1. What is your normal everyday life like?
2. Do you cook at home or eat out?

To answer both questions, I would like to share one of my *normal* everyday life experiences.

I am quite the crockpot kind of guy. Since I do not have an oven, I liked the *throw all ingredients together and cook for eight hours* meal plan. One day, I came across a recipe for beef stroganoff. It was so easy to make and sounded like it would be a delicious meal. It is Saturday, so I went shopping first thing so I can throw all ingredients together and cook for eight hours, then go about the rest of the busy day I had planned.

Saturday is the worst day to shop in Khon Kaen. But I hit the store as soon as it opened at 9:00 a.m. and figured I could get everything I needed and be finished by 10:00 a.m. The first thing I learned was the type of beef the recipe called for was not available. I got the other ingredients, most of which I will never use again unless I make beef stroganoff. I couldn't find beef broth cubes. I am looking at literally hundreds of cubes—chicken broth, pork, vegetable, but no beef broth cubes.

I asked someone about finding me beef broth cubes. This should be easy since *I Thai speak well.* However, I was getting a blank look from the employee leaning against the broth shelf. To make myself understood, I did what anyone else in my position would do. I asked again in my perfect Thai—which I had spent a lot of money on learning—that I was looking for beef broth. To add emphasis, I demonstrated what I meant by doing a great imitation of a cow. Yes, I did! I let out a loud MOOO! That got the attendant's attention, and he said, "Sorry sir, no have beef."

Another option was to use cream of mushroom soup instead of the beef broth, but I am on a quest, and I will not be denied, so I checked at another store. It was then eleven-thirty, and I hadn't had breakfast yet, and my *throw all ingredients together and cook for eight hours* meal was not going as planned. I arrived at the second store knowing I would find the ingredients I needed. However, that store was also out of beef, and again, I got to the broth aisle and saw hundreds of chicken and pork broth options but no beef broth. By now, the day could go either way. I could enjoy the rest of the day or continue my

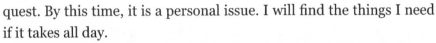

quest. By this time, it is a personal issue. I will find the things I need if it takes all day.

By three o'clock, I was hot, sweaty, and stinky, and I still hadn't found what I was looking for after going to all five grocery stores in Khon Kaen. I decided to go without the beef broth and substitute the cream of mushroom soup. I looked in the soup aisle, and they did not have cream of mushroom soup. There were hundreds of cans of cream corn soup, chicken noodle soup, every other kind of soup under the sun, but no cream of mushroom soup. At that point, McDonald's was looking like breakfast, lunch, and dinner. While I was venting to a missionary teammate, out of the corner of my eye, I spotted the cream of mushroom soup, grabbed a couple of cans, headed out of the store, and went to McDonald's.

On my way home, I remembered the propane tank for cooking was out of gas. I didn't know where to get the tank refilled, so I couldn't cook the noodles for my beef stroganoff. At that point, I did what every missionary learns to do. I adapted and overcame. Instead of having beef stroganoff, I called my new food creation the *I can't believe I got jerked around all day chicken stroganoff*. Instead of using beef, I used chicken, which was the only available meat that day. Instead of using all the ingredients I paid good money for, that I will never use unless I make beef stroganoff again, I substituted cream of mushroom soup. Seriously, I am a middle-aged man. What was I going to do with bay leaves, thyme, or oregano? Instead of using noodles like I was supposed to, I slopped everything over rice. Oh, how far my perfect meal has fallen! Beef stroganoff to *I can't believe I got jerked around all day chicken stroganoff*. I would eat my new creation because I spent every waking hour of my day preparing this meal.

That is the main reason I eat many meals out. It is so much simpler that way. That really was a *normal* day in the life of Steve Wheeler, missionary to Thailand. Just change the venues, and you have a typical day. Okay, not every day is that bad; sometimes, I just stay indoors with the curtains closed. But, seriously, what was I going to do with bay leaves?

CHAPTER

20

Early Experiences

I didn't have a vehicle when I moved to Khon Kaen, and public transportation was in its infancy stages. No taxi companies were in the city, so the only options for getting around were Tuk-tuks. These were motorcycle taxis and songthaews, which is like a large truck with two benches on each side for passengers.

I often had to walk quite a distance to reach the Tuk-tuk stand. However, someone on the team had bought a motorcycle for me to use. I never liked motorcycles and did not have much experience riding them when growing up, so I was hesitant to use them. After some time, I got up the nerve to borrow the motorcycle and used it as my transportation. Whenever I got on it, I prayed a hedge of protection around me and spent much of my time praying while I was in traffic. It was convenient, and I enjoyed having a little more freedom.

After being in Thailand for a couple of weeks, I was asked to teach on the power of prayer in the Calvary Bible School. I was excited about the opportunity. Late afternoon on May 23, 2007, I was finishing up the prayer course for that day. I shared with the class how I prayed a hedge of protection around me every time I got on my motorcycle.

Class ended, and I got on my motorcycle to go home. I had a prayer meeting at my house that evening, and I had just enough time to get home and have a quick dinner before my guests arrived. Unfortunately, it was rush hour, and the songthaew I was following stopped suddenly. I braked and swerved to the right to miss hitting it but was hit by a car.

When the car hit me, I fell backward and was thrown under the vehicle. As the back tire rolled over my head, I saw the vehicle's undercarriage raise, like it was going over a speedbump. I remember thinking *the tire just rolled over my head, and I am not dead.* The driver did not stop after they hit me. I laid in the street for several minutes, writhing in pain before I could get up and check for injuries. Many people gathered around, standing and watching but doing nothing to help. I managed to stand up, and as I took off my helmet, I heard loud gasps as the crowd realized a foreigner had been hit. Westerners are highly respected in Thailand, so the people then rushed to help me.

Suddenly, people shouting in Thai surrounded me, and I was disoriented and confused. Thankfully, I was wearing a helmet; otherwise, the tire would have crushed my head. I looked at the helmet and saw rubber marks where the tire went over it and scrape marks from where I was dragged on the asphalt. Nothing was broken, but I had several scrapes and wounds on my right side and severe pain in my ribs, elbow, and leg. I was shaking and scared by now. I had to get home, which was a few blocks away. I tried to start the motorcycle, but the thought of riding the motorcycle left me trembling with fear. I called Scott and told him about the accident and then walked the motorcycle home. I was stiff and sore for a few days, but I was thankful the Lord had protected me.

After I recovered, I knew I had to deal with the fear of riding the motorcycle. I took it out for a ride, but every time a car passed me, I panicked, and fear paralyzed me. I took the motorcycle out a couple of times to get over that trauma but never completely felt comfortable riding again.

Calvary Bible School

Calvary Bible School had already begun classes by the time I moved to Thailand. The Acunas were working with another Filipino pastor who had contacts with a church in Khon Kaen's slum area. The purpose of CBS was to network with the local churches in any given area to provide training for pastors and those in their congregations rising into leadership positions. Our schools are designed to be mobile, allowing us to go to where the need is. For that reason, Calvary Bible School has never had a stand-alone building but has always worked with the local church to bring the body of Christ together for training leaders.

The history of CBS over the years had been to go into an area and train pastors and emerging leaders. The need for the school usually lasted about three to five years. Once all the churches had been trained and equipped, we moved to another area. During that time, the Acunas traveled to Prakhon Chai to meet with pastors about doing a CBS in their area. The meeting went well, and tentative plans were made to begin CBS the following year.

After they returned, Ariel asked Scott and me to attend a meeting the Filipino pastor he had been working with had scheduled. We talked about the meeting's purpose, and Scott and I agreed to attend for moral support. To say the meeting was intense was an understatement. The pastor fired off questions to Ariel like he was a prosecutor, demanding to know why he had met with pastors without his permission or knowledge. It was obvious he was upset. He insisted on knowing whether Ariel would continue to work with him and his ministry exclusively. As he shouted that question, he slammed a file folder he was holding down on the table.

It startled me and caused me to jump out of my chair. I was shocked at that display and found it hard to believe it was happening. I had heard stories about pastors and missionaries in Thailand being territorial and controlling, but I thought they were just stories. It was a rude awakening that Christians could act like that, and I was concerned about what would happen next.

Calvary Bible School Prakhon Chai, Thailand

Calvary Bible School opened in Prakhon Chai in 2008. The classes would be held Tuesday through Thursday in the evenings from six to nine o'clock. That school would be unique in that the students were mostly from one church. I was the first teacher, and I looked forward to teaching. I traveled and taught in that school several times that year, and I became close with the missionaries and the church's pastors.

Several years later, I visited my friends there and spent the weekend with the church. It was during a low point in my life where I had been questioning if what I was doing was worth all the heartaches and suffering. I had been teaching but wondered if anything I taught impacted anyone? Was I effective? I was tempted to return to the United States and walk away from my calling. I had prayed and asked God to speak to me as I drove to Prakhon Chai. After preaching in the service, my friends and I had lunch together. It was good to be with them and get caught up on what was happening.

While we were eating, a church member came up to my friend and said something in Thai. My friend smiled and then turned to me and said, "You may not remember, but he was a student in the Bible school several years ago. He has something he would like to say to you." I looked up at the man, smiled, and said, "Okay." He said, "You changed my life, and you had such a great impact on me during school, especially the course you taught on Praise and Worship." He recited point by point several things I had taught. His words hit me with such force, and I tried to blink back the tears as I thanked him for his words. God answered my prayer at just the right time. It was a turning point and prevented me from walking away from my calling.

Home Cell Group

One of the first ministry opportunities I had occurred just after arriving in Thailand. I was introduced to Pastor Nueng and his wife Ruth, a young married couple who were assistant pastors of the church where we were conducting the Bible school. The Australian missionaries whose home I stayed in were discipling Nueng and his family through a weekly cell group. I was invited to take their place while they were on furlough. I spent the first year in Khon Kaen meeting weekly at the home of Pastor Nueng and his family. It was a wonderful experience and one of my fondest memories of my time living in Thailand.

The cell group consisted of Pastor Nueng and Ruth, their two children, Nueng's brother Pitak, their mom and dad, and one or two other friends. Pitak was sick with a cough the first several months of our weekly meetings. We would pray he would receive healing, and he would be healed for a short time, but the cough would come back. That cycle went on for several months before he went to a doctor, who diagnosed him with HIV. Now that we knew what was causing the problem, we prayed specifically, and Pitak was completely healed. When he gave his testimony of healing, he exclaimed, "I will serve the Lord for the rest of my life." The Lord continued to move in Nueng's family, and his mom, dad, and brother grew in their faith. It was wonderful to see God heal Pitak, and I had a front-row seat as I watched God move in Nueng's family.

Pastor Nueng and I had coffee one day at Starbucks, my *unofficial* office. He told me his family wanted to be water baptized. He planned to have a baptism service at a small lake nearby and invited me to help baptize his mom, dad, and brother. I was thrilled to be a part of this special event and quickly accepted the invitation.

It was early morning when we got to the lake. The water was green and slimy and full of waste. It looked like raw sewage to me, and I was apprehensive. Mist was rising from the water. I thought, *was it fog? Was it from the pollution in the lake?* There was a worship service on the lakeshore and then a short teaching on baptism. After the teaching, everyone quickly jumped into the lake and got ready to be baptized. I was the last one to get in. I saw Pastor Nueng, his mom, dad, and Pitak all in the lake waving for me to get in. They all had big smiles and were splashing each other. As I walked to the shore, I thought, *are there any scratches or cuts on my body that will become infected by the lake sludge?* I then saw the excitement on their faces, and I was suddenly overcome with joy. As I stepped into the water, my toes sunk into the squishy sludge, but I didn't mind. The joy I felt to be part of this significant milestone in the lives of Nueng's family outweighed my concerns about the lake water's condition. It was an honor to assist Pastor Nueng as he baptized his family. After everyone had been baptized, they played in the water while I made my way back to dry land.

Starbucks

Starbucks had opened shortly before I arrived in Khon Kaen, and it soon became my office. I visited several times weekly for coffee, and I often scheduled my meetings there. I got to know most of the staff personally, and they would greet me by name when I entered the store. One morning I approached the counter, and when I asked for coffee, the girl behind the counter said, "No. I won't make your coffee until I hear you order it in Thai." She then taught me how to order my coffee in the Thai language, and from that day forward, I had to use my Thai knowledge whenever I visited the store.

I learned several things about foreigners during the first few months of living in Thailand. I quickly discovered Westerners in general—and Americans especially—talked loudly compared to the Thai people, who are usually soft-spoken and rarely raised their voice. I tried to use a soft tone whenever I talked with a Thai person but often found myself loud and probably overbearing.

The expatriate community was small in Khon Kaen. I presumed every Westerner was a missionary doing ministry to reach the Thais. That assumption was quickly shattered over a two-day period at Starbucks. Since I was a regular customer, I had *my spot* I sat in every day. When I didn't have a meeting scheduled, my routine was to read the newspaper while enjoying my coffee. One morning, my routine was rudely disturbed when I heard a man with a British accent talking loudly with a young Thai woman. I couldn't help but overhear his loud, overbearing conversation. He was negotiating with this young woman to purchase a wife! I couldn't believe what I was hearing, and over two days, he completed the negotiations. The last thing I remember him saying to the woman was, "I will have her for six months, but when my wife arrives, she may not like having her around, and we may have to renegotiate our deal." It was a rude awakening to realize foreigners in Thailand were exploiting the Thai people. The rose-colored glasses from which I viewed Westerners were shattered.

21

Ministry Trips

I frequently traveled to Vietnam and Cambodia to teach in the Calvary Bible schools. In those days, those schools were taught simultaneously. Many trips included a week of teaching in Phnom Penh, Cambodia, then traveling to Vietnam for another week of teaching in Ho Chi Minh City. It was exhilarating to travel to these nations, and each trip had its own unique challenges and blessings. Even though many times I visited the same places to teach, it never got dull, as I always learned something about the people in those countries.

Ho Chi Minh City, Vietnam

I traveled to Ho Chi Minh City, Vietnam, to teach in the Calvary Bible School. My hosts were also missionaries with Go To Nations. They had arrived in Vietnam earlier in the week and were at the hotel when I arrived. We had a wonderful time being together that week.

I taught on the Blood Covenant, and I had a difficult time preparing for this subject.

It was dangerous to travel to Vietnam in those days. We always had to be on guard and alert of our surroundings wherever we went, and it was common for the secret police to follow us. One evening, my hosts and I met in their room to go over the week's schedule. I remember them saying in a hushed tone, "We have to be careful of what we say because the rooms may be bugged." We ordered coffee, and after a few minutes, there was a knock on the door. We got our coffee and continued to talk. I sipped my strong coffee and said, "I wish I would have asked for cream." A moment later, there was another knock on the door. When we answered, an employee was standing there with cream. I admit I was a little paranoid being in a communist country for the first time, with all I had heard about bugged rooms and being followed by the secret police. My voice quivered with emotion as I battled fear, and I said to no one in particular, "This room is bugged."

My hosts assured me everything would be okay as they continued to give me transportation instructions to the class the next day. I needed to be in the hotel lobby at 4:00 a.m., and someone would be there to pick me up and transport me to the class. Whenever I was in a foreign nation, the standard reply I got when asking about my transportation need is, "You won't know them. They will know you as you will be the only white person." I rarely had a name or photo to identify the person assigned to transport me. I usually waited until someone came and I left with them, trusting they were the person I was to go with. It was always a step of faith!

The next morning, I had my cup of strong Vietnamese coffee, and I felt good about the day. I was excited to be in Vietnam again. My previous trip had been in 1997 when I lived in the Philippines. It was now 2007, and I was beginning a new chapter in life as a missionary.

I was shaking as I skipped down the stairs, probably because of the strong coffee I had drunk.

I noticed a man sitting in the lobby with his head in the newspaper, engrossed in reading the daily news. He looked up at me as I sat next to him. I smiled politely, and he smiled back, and then we sat in silence. And I waited. The hotel check-in desk employee kept looking at us both strangely, but I thought nothing of it. My ride wasn't there yet, but I didn't panic because I was not in control. I was powerless to do anything about my situation. It was now five o'clock, and my ride still had not arrived. I went back upstairs and let my hosts know. They said, "Well, just go back downstairs and wait. Your ride will come." By now, the effects of the strong Vietnamese coffee had worn off, and the shaking had stopped. I thought as I bounded down the stairs that I could have another cup of coffee while I waited.

When I got downstairs, the man was still sitting on the bench reading the paper. He again looked at me as I sat next to him. Finally, the hotel employee looked at me and said in broken English, "Why you wait?" "My friend is coming," I replied. He then turned to the man sitting next to me and said to him, "Who you wait for?" "I wait for friend," he replied and put his head back into the newspaper. The employee let out a frustrated sigh and said to both of us, "You wait for each other." The man looked at me and said in broken English, "You from school?" When I replied I was, we all laughed as we realized we had spent two hours sitting next to each other, waiting for the other to arrive!

Even though we had left two hours past our scheduled departure time, we made it to the school's location safely. It was common for the secret police to raid the schools and cause the students to scatter, but the secret police left us alone, and we conducted the school in one location.

I was invited to preach on Sunday morning, and I gladly accepted. Being with my Vietnamese brothers and sisters was amazing. Their worship was restrained because they lived under communist rule and were constantly harassed by the secret police. They were conditioned by their circumstances to worship the Lord quietly, so they wouldn't arouse any suspicions. Despite that, their praises to the Lord were exuberant. Can you imagine trying to "shout" quietly?

Everyone sat on the floor, with the men on one side and the women on the other. When the worship service began, all the doors and windows were closed, the curtains were drawn, and the people quietly clapped their hands and sang in a hushed manner. But after a few minutes, they couldn't contain themselves anymore, and they shouted their praises loudly to the Lord. It was an incredible experience I would never forget.

I preached a short message on healing entitled, "The power of the Lord is present to heal." After the message, I extended an opportunity for anyone who needed healing to come and receive prayer. No one moved. I felt uncomfortable as I waited for someone to move. After waiting for what seemed like an eternity, I again encouraged anyone needing healing to come to the altar and receive prayer.

In the back of the room, a woman sitting on the floor was trying to stand up. Two women beside her were helping her get to her feet. As she tried to stand, she cried out in great agony. She slowly made her way to the front, and with every step, she cried out in great pain, "Oh, Jesus help me." The cries got louder the closer she got to the front. When she finally stood before me, she was weeping and wailing loudly in great pain. Whatever faith I had for healing had left me, and I thought, *oh, my God, this is terrible! What am I going to do? I don't even think I can pray for her, much less have any faith the Lord would heal her.* She sobbed because of the great pain she was experiencing, and I was looking for a way to escape the situation. I was trapped and scared, and I had to do something. After all, I was the man of God.

I was thinking, *Lord, couldn't we have started this healing service with something simple like praying for healing of a headache? Or maybe a sniffle? Couldn't we start with something easy?* However, that woman was standing in front of me, so I had to ask her what the problem was. I sheepishly said to her, "Uh, what would you like prayer for?" She replied, "I have two vertebrae in my back that have been fused together wrong, and I cannot stand or walk on my own." I could feel the color draining from my face, and I thought, *this is bad.*

Then in an instant, I remembered past times when the Lord used me to heal backs. I testified and said to the woman, "Just listen as I talk." I told story after story of how I had seen the Lord use me to heal backs. With each story I told, faith rose within me. I laid hands on her and prayed a simple prayer. After I finished praying, I said to the woman, "Now, do something you couldn't do before." She bent down and touched her feet. When she stood, she raised her hands and praised the Lord. After a few minutes, she said, "I could never bend over, much less touch my feet. I am healed!" Many people experienced miracles and were healed instantly as they came to receive prayer. We saw a mighty move of God that healing service.

Phnom Penh, Cambodia

It was my first trip to Cambodia. Like most of my other trips, I had no idea who would be at the airport to pick me up. I just knew "they would know who I was because I would be the only white person around." In those days, you obtained a visa after you arrived at the airport in Phnom Penh, Cambodia. As I disembarked from the plane, I immediately had to fill out the visa application and wait in line to get my visa. If you can imagine two hundred people getting off an airplane, then filling out visa applications, you can guess how long it would take to clear the airport.

By the time I obtained my visa, I had already experienced culture shock. I was the only white person amongst a sea of brown-skinned people. On top of that, I had facial hair and hairy arms, and most Cambodians were smooth-skinned and had no facial hair nor hairy arms, so I was a curious novelty to everyone I came across. People rubbed my arm hair and said the same thing I always heard wherever I went, "Oh, you're hairy. Hairy, like a dog." By the time I made it to the hotel, I was so frustrated. When I approached the check-in counter, the young woman behind the desk looked at me with big eyes, and her mouth dropped open as she stared at my hairy arms. Then she said those horrible words, "Oh, you're so very hairy." I tried to be polite, but I was tired of being petted like a dog and having my arm hair pulled out.

I got my room key and took the elevator to the fourth floor. When the elevator doors opened, I was greeted by a security guard sitting in a chair next to the door. He asked me questions and then said, "Do you want a girl? I can arrange a girl for you, cheap." I couldn't believe my ears, and I thought, *what kind of hotel is this?* "No, I don't want a girl," I replied incredulously. "If you change your mind, I can arrange a girl for you anytime," the guard said as I passed by him.

I got to my room and threw my suitcase on the bed and opened it. I looked for the most important item I needed right then. I rummaged through my shower bag and pulled out my beard trimmer. I turned it on and promptly shaved off all my arm hair. When I finished, a huge ball of hair was in my sink, and my arms looked funny without hair, but I didn't care. I shaved off my beard and mustache and remembered the joke Eric played on my first trip to Vietnam. He told me I needed to shave my arm hair off and how everyone laughed at the prank Eric pulled off on me. However, in that hotel room on my first trip to Cambodia, I decided to make shaving my arm hair part of my pre-departure routine in the future.

Later that afternoon, I met my host, the director of the Bible schools in Cambodia and Vietnam, in the lobby. We hugged each other, and then I asked, "Is this a brothel? The security guard offered to bring me a prostitute." She couldn't believe what I said, and she approached the hotel desk and inquired of the woman behind the counter. However, the woman did not understand the word prostitute, and after a few minutes of back and forth, we dropped the matter and went out for dinner.

The rest of the week went well, and I enjoyed my teaching time in the Bible school. Every day when we returned to the hotel, I would take the elevator to the fourth floor. As I exited the elevator, I was greeted by the same security guard who sat in the same chair and greeted me in the same way, "You want a girl? I can arrange a girl to come to your room, cheap."

Degrees and Debt Accumulation

I completed my bachelor's degree while I was living in the United States. After graduating from Logos Christian College, I enrolled in a master's degree program through Logos Seminary. Since my plan was to teach in a Calvary Bible school, the degree program I enrolled in had an emphasis on theology. I was fortunate I could bring all the necessary course books to complete the program when I moved to Thailand in 2007. I enjoyed the discipline of studying and had a regular time set aside each day to read and write.

I had been granted a 50 percent discount on my bachelor's degree program. When I enrolled in the master's degree program, I received a 40 percent discount! I was so blessed and encouraged by how the Lord provided the finances for my education. I remembered years

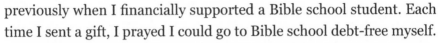

previously when I financially supported a Bible school student. Each time I sent a gift, I prayed I could go to Bible school debt-free myself.

I learned a valuable lesson during that time about sowing and reaping that serves me well to this day. When you plant a seed in the ground and continue to water it, you will receive more than just one harvest from that seed. That seed will continue to produce a harvest for years to come. Because I was faithful to obey the Lord those many years ago, not only did I go through Victory Bible Institute and Victory World Missions Training Center debt-free, I also completed my bachelor's degree without incurring debt.

I completed my course work and was scheduled to travel to Florida to graduate from Logos Seminary with a master's degree in New Testament Theology. I flew to Jacksonville, Florida, graduated and received my degree on April 15, 2008, and then spent a few weeks in the United States before returning to Thailand to continue ministry. During that season, I had a good financial base that enabled me to travel to Cambodia and Vietnam to teach in our Bible schools and pay for my tuition without incurring any debt. It was normal for me to put a charge on my credit card for airline tickets, etc., then pay the credit card bill off each month. However, that changed when I returned to Thailand. Several things happened that began my downward spiral into accumulating debt as I developed bad financial habits that would entangle me for years.

In 2008, a convergence of events along with unsound financial practices on my part caused me to get buried in debt. When I returned from the United States after graduation, I did not have the money to completely pay my credit card balance, so I only paid off part of that debt. I thought that since it was only around $2000, I could take two or three months to pay it off. Shortly after that, my annual medical insurance premiums came due. Medical insurance was mandatory for every Go To Nations missionary. My insurance company did not offer a monthly payment option, so I had to pay in full every year. That added another $2500 to my credit card balance. In just two months, I went from being debt-free to having over $4500 in credit card debt. Now, instead of paying my credit card bill off each month, I paid as much as I could and carried the remaining debt over to the following month.

At that time in life and ministry, I needed to travel. I was asked to teach in Vietnam and Cambodia several times throughout the year. It was difficult to decline the invitations coming my way. After all, traveling and teaching in our Bible schools throughout Asia was why I went to Thailand in the first place. A few months later, a special event was happening at our World Headquarters in Florida, so for the second time in 2008, I visited the United States. I should not have made the trip, but I failed to think of the long-term effects of my actions. My debt increased with each trip. I thought I could manage my debt and mistakenly believed I could pay off my credit card balance in the following months. It would be several years before I realized the consequences of my financial mismanagement and dig myself out of debt.

22

Transition and Change

When I moved to Thailand and began to travel and teach, I discovered International Victory Bible Institutes in several places I visited. I had a good relationship with the director of IVBI, and I was recruited to be an IVBI teacher. I was thrilled for the opportunity to teach in the Bible school that powerfully changed the trajectory of my life. I also desired to work more closely with Victory Christian Center, my home church at that time.

The IVBI director based in Penang, Malaysia, reached out to me. We discussed the possibility of my moving to Penang to help with the IVBI. We talked back and forth for a few months before I traveled to Malaysia to spy out the land. A conference was scheduled in Kuala Lumpur. I made plans to attend and spend time in Penang afterward.

The conference was a little different for my tastes. We arrived for a meeting a couple of hours early for prayer. However, I had never been in a prayer meeting like that before. As the person leading the session told the people to pray for one specific thing, a roar of prayer would arise. That wasn't unusual for me, so I joined as well. Then people all around me shook and contorted their bodies and flopped around the floor. I wondered what kind of conference I was attending. It was distracting, so I moved to another location in the back of the room. I sat down on the floor, crossed my legs, and quietly prayed. Another prayer item was issued, and people wailed loudly. A young couple was sitting in front of me praying. They looked at each other as if to say it was time to flop around, and then they both shook and contorted their bodies. The woman threw herself backward, and her head landed in my lap! I looked at my friends and rolled my eyes as I tried to figure out how to get disentangled from this girl. It was definitely the strangest conference I had attended!

The director over all the IVBI's lived in Tulsa, Oklahoma, and made plans to visit Penang, and we flew to Cambodia together. There was an IVBI in Kampong Thom, which was about a four-hour drive from the capital. We met the family running the ministry in that area. They had an orphanage and were conducting an IVBI in that location. We stayed for a couple of days in Kampong Thom, and when our tasks were completed, we departed for Phnom Penh in the evening.

There had been torrential rain that day, but the skies had cleared as we departed. The van driver was driving fast, and we were making good time. It was late in the evening, and because there were no streetlights, everything was pitch black. Suddenly, we hit a flooded portion of the road with a loud thud and spun. The force of the water caused us to sway as the vehicle slowed. I was almost asleep, and I woke up shouting, "Holy!" We made it through the deep water, and when we got out on the other side, we all patted the driver on the back and congratulated him on his driving skills. He had been driving about eighty miles per hour when we hit a ten-foot wall of water in the road, and we lived to tell about it. Once again, I was in a situation where I could have died, but the Angel of the Lord protected and delivered me.

I had many things to consider when I returned from Malaysia. On the one hand, I had been in Thailand for about two years and was established as a missionary. Considering the ministry vision the Lord had given me, I was walking out God's will for my life. I was traveling throughout Southeast Asia, teaching in Bible schools and training leaders. I was accomplishing what I went to Thailand to do. But, on the other hand, I desired to work more closely with my home church in the United States. My life had been transformed when I went to Victory Bible Institute. I wanted to be connected with the school that had impacted my life in such a powerful way.

I spent several months in prayer and sought counsel while I contemplated the pros and cons of moving to Malaysia. The Thailand team consisted of two married couples and me. Cultural differences within the team created challenges. I wanted to make sure I would move because of the Holy Spirit's leading and not because of the challenges. It would be a huge change, and I had reservations about being seconded to International Victory Bible Institute. I had not had a long-term relationship with the leadership in Penang. While I would continue to be a Go To Nations missionary, the spiritual oversight over my day-to-day life would shift to them. Naturally speaking, moving to Penang just didn't make sense. But I had a deep abiding peace in my spirit that I was supposed to move.

23

A New Season of Ministry

When I moved to Penang, a shift occurred in the ministry I was engaged in. I continued to teach in Bible schools, developing leaders; however, the International Victory Bible Institute curriculum was different from our Calvary Bible School. During the time I lived in Malaysia, I traveled frequently to Cambodia to teach in the International Victory Bible Institute and got to know my way around the country.

Penang, Malaysia

I arrived in Penang on January 6, 2009 and entered into a new season of life and ministry. I rented an apartment on the twenty-first floor in a complex near a grocery store, and yes, I lived right around the block from a Starbucks! My first impression of Penang was the extreme heat which took a while to get used to it. The team I joined consisted of two married couples, and once again, I was the only single person. So far in my missionary experiences, I had been part of three teams where I was the only single person.

Malaysia is a Muslim nation, and I discovered five calls to prayer happened daily. The call to prayer usually was broadcast over outdoor speakers. I wasn't aware I had moved into an apartment complex with three mosques nearby. When the call to prayer came, I heard it broadcast in surround sound! It took time, but eventually, I stopped being roused from sleep in the pre-dawn hours. The daily calls to prayer became background noise, and I hardly noticed them.

It was exciting to discover English was spoken by the vast majority of the population. I could finally speak without using my hands! Thai is a tonal language made up of five different tones. Many words can have several meanings depending on which tone is used—no more stressing over saying a word with the right tone. By using the wrong tone, I could call someone a cow by accident, but in Malaysia, I could be understood.

Malaysia in general, and Penang in particular, has an interesting mix of cultures. The country was made up of ethnic Malays, Chinese Malays, and Indian Malays. Each culture had its section of town with ethnic restaurants and shops. The men on the team met every Monday in the section called Little India at one of our favorite restaurants, where we could enjoy coffee and naan.

The public transportation system in Penang was fairly good and much more advanced than in Thailand. Busses ran along specific lines, and there were taxis and tuk-tuks as well, so getting around town was simple and convenient. I used public transportation for the first six months while I got settled. I had left my truck in Thailand with my GTN colleagues while I explored the possibilities of importing it to Malaysia. After researching, I discovered it would be much more convenient to sell my truck in Thailand and purchase another vehicle in Penang, which I did.

International Victory Bible Institute

I moved to Penang the week before IVBI classes began, and I was excited to teach in the first module of the new academic year. The schedule for IVBI was different than what I was used to with Calvary Bible School. CBS was taught in modules, and each module consisted of classes from Monday–Friday from 8:00 a.m. to 4:00 p.m. With that schedule, we graduated students in one year. Classes for IVBI were every Tuesday evening from 7:00–10:00 p.m., and with that schedule, a student would need six years to complete the IVBI first and second year.

On the first Tuesday of IVBI, the two missionary couples and I gathered in the foyer and waited for the students to arrive. The office décor was dated, but three separate classrooms were available. We would have a short worship time before we broke into the different classrooms. Although the IVBI and CBS curriculums were similar, I was apprehensive as it would be the first IVBI subject I would teach. When the time came for the class to start, there were no students. That was the first night of the Bible school, which would set the tone for the upcoming academic year, and *there were no students!*

The following week we had two students show up. One was enrolled in IVBI first year, and one student enrolled in IVBI second year. After worship, I taught one student for the remainder of that evening. Another IVBI was in Ipoh, which was about a four-hour drive from Penang. That school would start classes again, and I was asked to teach there. I would ride the bus to reach Ipoh on Thursday afternoon. I taught from seven to ten that evening and then returned by bus on Friday morning. There had been a networking relationship with an orphanage in Ipoh, and IVBI was training two orphans who lived there. My weekly schedule was to teach three to four students in Penang on Tuesday evenings, then travel to Ipoh to teach two students on Thursday evenings.

Those first few weeks in Penang were perplexing as I tried to understand what God wanted to do in me. I spent much time in prayer before moving. It did not make sense for me to move there in the natural, but I had a deep abiding peace I was walking out God's will for my life. Even though I had peace in my spirit, I grew frustrated with my situation. The information I was given about the IVBI schools was misleading, and teaching two or three students in a class was not what I signed up for!

Reaching and Impacting the One

I knew God was doing something in me, and He had a purpose for my life, so I asked Him why He brought me to Penang. I prayed, "God, the ministry was successful in Thailand. I was teaching in CBS schools with twenty-five pastors, and I felt I had a great impact there. Now, I am here in Penang, teaching two or three students who are not even in the ministry. Why am I here? What are You doing in me?" He lovingly responded to my anguished cries, "Son, if My plan for you is to have an impact on just one person, would that be enough? If you never preach to large crowds again, would knowing you are walking in My will be enough? Will I still be enough for you?"

I needed to learn God was just as interested in me reaching *the one* as He was in me reaching *the multitudes*. I don't know why He sent me to Penang to learn that important lesson, but through that experience, I learned God will go to great lengths to shape our lives and impart His character in us. I spent the first year in Penang impacting only a few people, but my soul was at peace and rest.

I had several opportunities to learn the importance of reaching *the one* during that season. I listened to a sermon from my church one Sunday about living the difference that struck a chord in my spirit. The next morning, I was reading in the Gospel of Luke, chapter six, verse thirty, and these words jumped off the page, "Give to everyone who asks." I was challenged as I meditated on this Scripture. Just give *to everyone who asks.* Period. No questions asked, no strings attached, just give. I then prayed one of those *dangerous* prayers: "Father, let me live the difference. Allow me to apply this Word into my life today, Amen." I got ready to start my day and decided to do grocery shopping. Of course, this would include a trip to Starbucks across the street from the grocery store. By that time, I was a regular Starbucks customer, and everyone knew my name and what I liked to drink. As I drank my coffee, I meditated on the words I read earlier.

After finishing my morning coffee, I was walking to my car when I heard someone calling from behind me, "Mister, Mister." I turned to see a beggar approaching me, saying, "Give me money." Because I was a foreigner, beggars constantly approached me asking for money, so I responded in my usual polite way and said, "No, thank you," and walked away. In my spirit, I heard *give to everyone who asks,* and my heart sank as I realized I missed an opportunity to live the difference. I repented to the Lord and asked for another opportunity.

The next morning, I was coming out of the store, and again I heard someone calling me. "Mister, Mister," the man called out. I turned around to see a man who was obviously in distress. He was shaking and was bloody. "What can I do for you," I asked, and he told me the story of what happened to him. After listening to him for several minutes, I asked him, "What is it you need from me?" He replied, "I need ten dollars." I reached into my wallet, and all I had was ten dollars, so I gave it to him. "Thank you, thank you," he sobbed as I said goodbye.

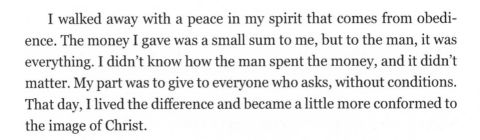

I walked away with a peace in my spirit that comes from obedience. The money I gave was a small sum to me, but to the man, it was everything. I didn't know how the man spent the money, and it didn't matter. My part was to give to everyone who asks, without conditions. That day, I lived the difference and became a little more conformed to the image of Christ.

Covington Theological Seminary

The Holy Spirit spoke to me about being a Bible teacher during a trip to India. I began my studies in theology in 2004. I completed my bachelor's degree in 2006 and my master's degree during my first stint living in Thailand in 2008. Shortly after receiving my master's degree, I contemplated furthering my studies and working toward obtaining a doctorate degree. Several GTN missionaries had received their degrees from Covington Theological Seminary, and the school was highly recommended. I looked at the programs they offered and enrolled in the Doctor of Ministry program. I paid cash for the program at the beginning of my studies and graduated summa cum laude on July 31, 2009.

I invested many years studying and building a solid foundation for the work the Holy Spirit had called to my attention during that trip to India. I incurred no debt while doing so. I had no idea when I began to financially support that Bible school student back in 1991 that those seeds I sowed would continue to produce a harvest in my life. I stopped going to school in the eighth grade and never graduated from high school, but years later, I completed Bible school, missions school, and received my bachelor's, master's, and finally, my doctorate, all debt-free. God has been incredibly good to me! Despite many obstacles, I am the first person in our family history for generations to have a degree. To God be the glory!

Have You Heard the One about the Haircut?

I traveled throughout Southeast Asia while I lived in Penang. I spent most of my time teaching at Calvary Bible School in Vietnam and the International Victory Bible Institute in Cambodia. I developed a pre-travel routine of getting a haircut and shaving my arm hair off before each trip.

I found it difficult to get a good haircut in Penang. There was a barber right around the corner from the IVBI office the men on the team often frequented. When one of us would get our hair cut, usually one side was cut down to the skin, while the other side was fluffy, and you had to tilt your head to one side to make it look even. The conversation amongst us afterward usually went something like this, "You got your hair cut?" "Yeah, I did." "I can tell. It is uneven." "Yeah, I know." "We should find another barber." "Yeah, we should. But this place is convenient." "Yes, it is, but we look horrible." Even though we always got bad haircuts, we continued to frequent that barbershop! One day, one man shared with us excitedly, "I found a good barber! Look at my haircut. It is even on both sides, and I don't have to tilt my head anymore!" I was getting ready to travel to Cambodia the next day, so I asked where the shop was and went to get my first real haircut.

I entered the barbershop, sat in the chair, and told the barber how I wanted my hair cut. He didn't understand my English, but I kept talking anyway. He was of Indian ethnicity and kept shaking his head from side to side as I talked. In India, shaking your head from side to side is how you say "yes," so I was satisfied he understood what I was saying, and I would get the haircut I wanted. He began cutting, and inwardly, I was ecstatic as I was finally going to get a decent haircut. He finished my haircut, and I must admit it was good.

He gave me a neck rub, which wasn't unusual for that culture. He then grabbed my head and massaged it while moving it side to side in

189

his hands. I was relaxing and enjoying the massage when suddenly, he became a ninja chiropractor and cracked my neck! I jumped up out of my seat and shouted, "No! No! Stop that! What are you doing?" I pointed my finger at him and said sternly, "I never want you to crack my neck again for as long as I come and get my haircut here." He just smiled and shook his head from side to side without speaking. When I sat back down in my chair, he grabbed my head again and was going to crack the other side of my neck! "I don't want you to do that," I said and got up out of my chair and reached into my wallet to pay. I left the barbershop with a good haircut and a stiff neck because he only cracked one side of my head. It took several days for my neck to pop back into place, but hey, at least I got a decent haircut!

Cambodia

While I lived in Penang, I traveled several times to Kampong Thom, Cambodia to teach in the International Victory Bible Institute. I taught there frequently and got to know the ministry directors and many students well. On one occasion, I was scheduled to teach at the IVBI in Cambodia. I then received invitations to teach at the CBS in Vietnam and two locations in Thailand. As I planned my schedule, it made sense to combine all those opportunities into one trip, and I coordinated my schedule with those schools' directors. I intended to spend the first week in Cambodia, then travel to Vietnam for a week, and then spend two weeks in Thailand. Because I planned to be gone for a month, I canceled my teaching engagements at the IVBI in Penang and cleared my schedule.

As my departure got closer, I still had not confirmed my teaching schedule in Cambodia. I wrote several emails to the school's director but never got a response. At the same time, the directors in Vietnam and Thailand wanted me to confirm my arrival and departure dates, which I couldn't provide. I had written one last email to the IVBI director in Cambodia. I explained I needed to purchase my airline tickets for Cambodia, Vietnam, and Thailand before a specific date. Because I had not heard from him, it was impossible to confirm the rest of my itinerary. I waited until the last moment but canceled the entire trip. A week after canceling, I received an email from the Cambodian IVBI director, welcoming me to come teach!

It was a challenge to know how to respond to his email. I wanted him to know his lack of response had affected every part of the trip. I couldn't do my scheduled ministry for that month because he failed to communicate effectively. I talked with my leaders in Penang and the Tulsa IVBI director about how I should respond. Everyone agreed I needed to lovingly challenge him on the importance of communication. I wrote down my thoughts and submitted my response to my leaders in Penang and Tulsa for approval before sending it out. Looking back now, I could have canceled the Cambodia portion of the trip and continued with Vietnam and Thailand, but I had not done that. I never forgot the lesson I learned about the challenges that come from working and communicating cross-culturally.

Several months later, I heard from a GTN colleague that a new Calvary Bible school had started in Kampong Thom, Cambodia, and I was invited to teach in the school. It seemed odd both an IVBI and a CBS were in the area. I was scheduled to teach on the Power of Prayer and was excited to travel to Cambodia again. When I arrived in Kampong Thom, I discovered the new CBS and the IVBI had many of the same students!

I had just taught about the power of agreement in prayer and stopped to take a break in between sessions. When the students came back from break, one pastor spoke emotionally. He told the class his backpack had been stolen. He was constructing a building for his church. All the money for the materials, along with the permits and official government papers, were in that backpack. That was a great opportunity to practically apply the teaching on the power of agreement! The class prayed together the backpack would be returned, and the Holy Spirit would convict the person who stole it. We finished teaching for the day and sent the students home.

The next morning this pastor had a big smile as he held up the backpack someone stole the previous day. He testified that when he got home after school, he received a phone call from the person who had taken the bag. The thief said he felt bad about taking the backpack when he looked inside and discovered it belonged to a pastor. He returned the backpack, and nothing was missing! It was a powerful testimony and practical demonstration of the power of agreement in prayer!

CHAPTER

24

I Will Not Live Through the Night

In March of 2010 things were going well. I was teaching in IVBI in Penang and Ipoh and traveled internationally throughout Southeast Asia. I had returned from a trip to Cambodia and was resting and recuperating. There was nothing unusual, and I had no inclination I would soon face the most difficult trial and dangerous threat to my life I had ever experienced. The events that followed took me completely off guard and would lead me *through the valley of the shadow of death.*

It was a Saturday morning, and I wanted coffee at one of my favorite coffee shops. I hopped into my car and drove toward the town's main tourist area. It was a bright, sunny day, and it was already pretty warm, even though it was only nine o'clock. It would be another hot day, I thought. I felt like something had gotten into my eye, so I blinked a couple of times. After I blinked, I couldn't see clearly and had double vision. It startled me, so I braked and pulled off the road and continued to blink, thinking something was in my eyes. It seemed to disappear. Even though nothing like that had ever happened, I

193

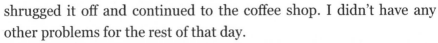

shrugged it off and continued to the coffee shop. I didn't have any other problems for the rest of that day.

When I awoke the next morning, the double vision had come back, and it was far worse than the previous day. My speech was slurred, and I had lost feeling in my lips, cheeks, fingers, and other areas in my body. I was showing the symptoms of having suffered a stroke. I had never experienced a major health crisis and had always been healthy. Being in a foreign nation, I was unsure of the medical care standards, and I was extremely frightened and didn't know what to do.

I drove to the emergency room, and I remember I had to drive with one eye closed to see clearly! After I was admitted, they ran tests. I was sure I had suffered a stroke, and it was scary to be in a foreign hospital. A doctor came into my room to talk with me about my symptoms. After a few minutes, the doctor outlined the procedures that would be taken. He said, matter-of-factly, "First, we will do a blood test, and after that, we will do a cat scan. If both of those tests come back negative, our next step will be to do a spinal tap. If a spinal tap is necessary, you will have to sign a release form waiving your right to sue the hospital if something goes wrong." He shook my hand and walked out the room, leaving me alone with my thoughts.

A nurse came and took blood, and then I was wheeled off to have the cat scan. The doctor came back to my room to discuss the test results. "The blood test and cat scan both came back negative," he said as he sat down at the edge of my bed. "Our next step is to do a spinal tap," he continued as he placed the consent form into my hands. I adamantly refused to sign the form giving my consent for the spinal tap and refused to sign waiving my rights to sue the hospital. I wanted to check out of the hospital and tried to get up and get dressed to leave, but the doctor refused to let me. "Sir, you are very sick. I cannot allow you to leave the hospital," he said. "You cannot keep me here, and I am leaving right now," I replied, raising my voice. We went back and forth, and finally, the doctor agreed to release me from the hospital. I had to sign a form saying I was being released against doctor's orders, but I didn't care. The doctor was upset with my decision, and he urged me to return quickly if I needed to.

I called the Thailand ministry that had previously provided me with a work permit when I got home. I talked with a nurse about what was going on. I described my symptoms, and she asked questions. "It sounds like you may have meningitis," she said. "The symptoms usually take about fourteen days to manifest," she continued. "And you should get better in about a week or so, but if you don't, you need to go to the hospital right away to get checked." We talked about where I could receive medical care that would be comparable to the United States, and she suggested I fly to Bangkok. However, I was too sick to fly.

I had not improved and, in fact, steadily declined over the next few days. The IVBI team leader convinced me to go back to the hospital, and he agreed to take me the following morning. Later that night, I got worse quickly and felt the life draining from me. I was going in and out of consciousness, and I knew I was dying. So many thoughts raced through my mind as I laid in bed. The front gate to my apartment was padlocked, and the front door was locked as well. No one else had keys, and someone would have to break the lock off the gate to retrieve my body. I thought if I died that night, it would be days, possibly weeks before anyone noticed I was missing.

I needed to do something, so I called Stan and Equilla Hicks, who were friends and prayer partners in the United States. When Equilla answered and heard my voice, she knew immediately something was wrong. "What's wrong?" Equilla asked. I cried, and through my tears, I replied, "Equilla, I'm not going to live through the night. I wanted someone to know Pastor Benny has a copy of my will, and I have repatriation of remains coverage with my medical insurance, so my body can be flown home for burial." "Wheeler, are you finished with your assignment?" Equilla asked sternly. "Have you done what the Lord sent you to do?" she asked again. "No," I replied through my tears. "Then you are not dying tonight," she said as she prayed over me. When she finished praying, she told me Stan would call later.

An incredible peace came over me when I hung up the phone. Wave after wave of peace flooded me. I had never experienced such peace as it washed over my entire being. Suddenly, nothing else mattered. I knew death would soon come, and I would see Jesus face to face. I lifted my hands and worshiped Him, who was worthy of all praise. There was such excitement and anticipation that rose in my spirit as I waited for Jesus to take me home. I finally fell asleep, and when the morning came, I was both disappointed and grateful I had lived through the night. I was grateful to be alive, but at the same time, I was disappointed I hadn't seen Jesus face to face as I had anticipated.

I was taken to a different hospital the next morning. The attending doctor severely rebuked the team leader for not bringing me in sooner. "He is in very bad condition, and it's amazing he's still alive," the doctor said sternly. An orderly tried to put a pic line in and missed my veins several times before she finally succeeded. I was taken to a room, and they ran the same tests as the other hospital did. The doctor gave me the same speech I had heard from the previous doctor. "We will do blood tests, then a cat scan, and if both come back negative, we will need to do a spinal tap," he said.

I needed a spinal tap, and reluctantly, I signed the consent form. The doctor came and explained the procedure. He said, "When the needle goes into your spinal cord, you will feel something like an electric shock, but try to stay completely still." He then pulled out the needle, and I noticed it was about eighteen inches long! I rolled on my side, and they inserted the needle. When the needle was inserted into my spinal cord, I felt an electric shock, and my body jerked uncontrollably. The doctor told me to stay still as I was screaming, "Pull it out! Pull it out!" It was the most excruciating pain I had ever experienced, but at last, the test was completed.

I was diagnosed with meningitis. The doctors couldn't determine if it was bacterial meningitis, which could be deadly, or viral meningitis, from which I would recover. I spent fifteen days in the hospital, drifting in and out of sleep. I had my laptop with me, and worship music played continuously. Eventually, I was strong enough to go home. As I was released from the hospital, the doctor warned me I was still sick, and I needed to stay in bed and rest. "Do you have family who can come take care of you?" the doctor asked. I whispered in reply, "No, I am alone." The doctor told me it would take up to six months or longer to completely recover.

I was extremely weak and sick and desperately needed help. One staff member of the church I attended picked me up from the hospital. I gathered my things and waited at the hospital's main entrance for him. I lost so much weight during my stay that I had to cinch my pants in my fist to keep them from falling down.

I was happy to be back home. My friend bought me groceries to last for a few days. I was supposed to stay in bed and rest, but as soon as I got home and settled, I drove around the block to Starbucks. I still had double vision, slurred speech, and trouble walking in a straight line, but I didn't care. I *needed* to get out and do something. When I walked up to the counter to order my coffee, the cashier looked at me with a shocked expression. "I have been in the hospital and have been very sick," I told her, trying to calm her down. "I am okay now," I assured her as I grabbed my coffee and sat down. Unknown to me, one pastor of the church I sometimes attended had seen me walking into Starbucks. When I saw him several months later, he told me he saw me that day but thought perhaps I had been drinking. I laughed and told him I had been sick and disobeying the doctor's orders to stay in bed and rest.

It took me a long time to recover, and I became discouraged because I looked and talked like someone who had suffered a stroke. There were days when I would cry out to God, "Is this how I am going to be for the rest of my life?" I couldn't see correctly, my speech was slurred, and the numbness had not left. Over time, I got better, but it was several weeks before I could see clearly.

Even now, I still am not sure if I had been diagnosed correctly. In foreign nations, the available medical care is not on par with what you would expect if you were in the United States. But the end of this story is God led me *through the valley of the shadow of death,* and I am still here.

I made a one-year commitment when I moved to Penang in 2009, and in January 2010, I agreed to stay for another year. I went into the hospital at the end of March of 2010, and it took me several months to recover. I physically could not do any ministry during my recovery. I didn't teach in IVBI again, and the remainder of my time in Penang was difficult.

As I recovered, I made concrete plans to return to Thailand. I decided the best way to move my stuff was to pack my car and drive. I was scheduled to teach in CBS in Mae Sai, the most northern part of Thailand that borders Myanmar. I would also return to Khon Kaen and look for a place to live. I was apprehensive about moving back to Thailand. For the fourth time in my missions' career, I would be the only single person amongst a team of married couples. There would be new responsibilities, and I wasn't sure if I could handle my new assignment.

One way the Lord has spoken to me throughout my years of walking with Him has been through dreams. During that transition season, the Lord spoke clearly and powerfully to me through several dreams.

One dream I had during that time has stayed with me. I was sitting on a chair, and people were gathered around me who were ready to lay hands on me and pray. I heard the Lord's voice whisper into my ear, "You can do whatever I ask you to do because I have already placed inside you everything you need for success." As I heard those words, the people laid hands on me and prayed, and I woke up. The Lord's tangible presence had flooded my room, and I lifted my hands in worship. I had received a Word of the Lord through that dream, and the revelation I received is still as fresh to me today as it was back then. *Anything* the Lord has spoken to me to do, any *assignment* He gives me, I can do because He has already equipped me and anointed me for that thing. *I can do all things through Christ who strengthens me* (Philippians 4:13 NKJV).

Near the end of 2010, I traveled to Thailand. Craig and Sandra Kuehn were visiting Thailand, and they wanted to meet with each of us individually. The Acunas, the Oldakers, and I were together in one place for the first time since 2009. I communicated by email with Craig and Sandra about moving back to Thailand, and my desire was to be based in Chiang Mai. I had great relationships with the Christian Outreach Center founders. I had my work permits and visas with their foundation when I had lived in Thailand. The foundation leaders were pleased to have me work more closely with them and had developed several ministry opportunities for me. They had developed ministry in Mae Sot along the Myanmar border. They were in the process of starting an office there. One opportunity I had was to move there and be the office manager.

When I met with Craig and Sandra, they suggested I return to Khon Kaen and continue to work with the leaders there. I remember Craig saying, "Your gifts complement each other so well, and it would be beneficial to each of you if you could learn to work together." I was disappointed that moving to Chiang Mai to work with Christian Outreach Center was not what Craig and Sandra had in mind. The Acunas and I had a long conversation about returning to Khon Kaen. We all agreed I would move in January of 2011.

When I returned to Penang, I had a concrete plan and started packing, giving away items, and saying goodbye to the wonderful friends I had made. I wondered if being a missionary meant moving to a country, buying furniture and appliances, living in a home for about two years, then selling and giving everything away, only to move to another country and start the process over.

That would be the third time I had moved in four years of being a missionary. I decided when I returned to Khon Kaen I would rent a furnished home and eliminate some set-up costs. That would save me the hassle of selling furniture if and when I moved again. I realized being a missionary came with a certain amount of uncertainty, which meant constantly whittling my worldly goods down to two fifty-pound boxes and a carry-on suitcase. I enjoyed the freedom of moving around, and I enjoyed seeing the world, but I also longed for the stability that always seemed just out of reach to me.

----------- CHAPTER -----------

25

Return to Thailand

My car was loaded with boxes of books, and I was headed to the northernmost part of Thailand. I had never driven across the border between two countries, but I had been assured it was relatively easy. I mapped my journey out and studied maps, deciding how many hours I would drive each day and marking where I would stop and rest each night. I was satisfied I had a good plan and excited for the adventure that awaited me. I had never taken such a long road trip in Asia before, and I was looking forward to passing through some of the most picturesque parts of Thailand.

I arrived at the Malaysia/Thailand border right on schedule. It took me longer than I anticipated to gather the necessary car insurance and permits to take my car into Thailand. Once my paperwork was in order, I crossed the border and continued my journey. The skies had turned cloudy and dark, and it rained. I had driven into a storm that would follow me for the rest of that day's drive.

The rain soon became a torrential downpour and was coming down so hard my windshield wipers could not clear my windows fast enough for clear visibility. My car's defroster wasn't working properly, so the windows fogged up, making it even more difficult to see. The Thailand region I was driving through was densely populated, and there were no large cities where I could stop for the night, so I kept driving. It was late afternoon, and I realized I wouldn't make it to the destination I had marked on my map. Some roads were flooded, which I couldn't see until I came upon them because of the blinding rain. The rain hit the windshield with such force that I thought it might break. I was in unfamiliar territory and could only safely drive at about 25 MPH. I sat forward in the driver's seat, my fists clenched around the steering wheel, and prayed in the spirit while I drove for several hours.

The southern part of Thailand was dangerous and had been a hotbed of terrorist activity. Muslim rebels had taken over parts of the south and had been fighting the government to gain autonomy. There had been several bombings by the rebels in the town of Hat Yai, where they targeted areas frequented by foreigners, and I was warned to bypass that town. It was evening when I reached the outskirts of Hat Yai, and it was too dangerous to continue driving. The storm didn't seem to let up, so I adjusted my plans and spent the night there. I found a safe hotel and settled into my room, physically spent from the anxious drive.

I enjoyed my road trip through Thailand and met many wonderful people along the way. I finally arrived in Mae Sai and joined the Acunas, who were conducting a module at Calvary Bible School. I spent a week teaching in the school, put my boxes into storage, and started my journey back to Penang. I would sell my car, settle my accounts, and pack my remaining things in two boxes and a carry-on, and fly to my new home in Khon Kaen, closing that chapter and opening another season of excitement and adventure.

Khon Kaen, Part II

Khon Kaen is known as the gateway to the Northeast and experienced considerable growth while I was in Penang. A new shopping mall had opened, and several high-rise condos were being built. The city's population was exploding as more people moved into the city from the villages. Public transportation had improved greatly while I had been gone, and now relatively inexpensive taxi cabs were available.

The first order of business was to secure a place to live. I asked friends to look for a place for me before I arrived, but they didn't have any leads, so I stayed in a hotel while I looked. One thing I appreciate about Thailand is the wide variety of available hotels. It is possible to find clean, safe hotels for about thirteen dollars a night. I found such a hotel centrally located near the city center and booked a room for five nights. I unloaded my boxes and searched for a place to live.

One day, I greeted a foreigner I saw sitting in the hotel foyer. We made small talk for a few minutes. I assumed he was from an NGO (Non-governmental Organization) or a missionary. When I asked him what he did in Thailand, he replied in a thick Australian accent, "Well, I just bought a wife today." I blinked in disbelief. *What did he just say?* "You did what?" I replied. "I bought a wife. The woman who runs this hotel has a side business that helps people find wives. I found this wife through the computer, and today I made my payment. I think the hotel owner said it was a dowry or something like that," he continued as if it was completely normal for someone to purchase another human being. "I just flew into town today and have come to pick her up and meet her family and make my final payment." I could hardly believe what I heard and shook my head in disbelief as I went to my room.

The ministry I had been engaged in changed once I moved to Khon Kaen. The leaders planned to start a Calvary Bible School, and responsibility for the school would be handed over to me. I had been an itinerate teacher previously in my missionary career, but now my international travel would be curtailed to concentrate on directing the school. I was hesitant about stepping into this new role and continued to have doubts about living in Khon Kaen.

I desired to be in Chiang Mai, and even though I willfully submitted to my leaders, inwardly, I felt I was forced to do something I didn't want to do. The attitude of my heart was to do my time and stay out of people's way for the following year and then make my move to Chiang Mai. Even though I spiritually submitted to those in leadership over me, I felt exposed and unprotected. I wondered where God was in all this.

One night I had a dream similar to what I had when I was preparing to move back to Thailand. In that dream, I was sitting on a wooden chair, and several people were standing around me. I felt the Lord standing behind me, and He leaned into me and whispered into my ear, "I have called you to walk in this season. I will not leave you, and I will help you. Now get up and walk." As I heard this, I found myself on my feet. The Lord stood behind me and helped me walk. At first, I was like a baby taking my first steps, I was wobbly and unsure of myself, but then I walked confidently. I immediately woke up, and the tangible presence of the Lord filled my room, and I knew I was where I was supposed to be. I had the assurance God was with me. *For He Himself has said, "I will never leave you nor forsake you." So we may boldly say, "The Lord is my helper; I will not fear. What can man do to me?"* (Hebrews 13:5–6).

Getting Settled and Reconnecting

The house I rented in Khon Kaen was fairly new and completely furnished. It had three bedrooms, and the yard was nicely manicured.

It was in a quiet neighborhood not too far from the center of town, and it was the nicest place I had lived in since I had been on the mission field. I was on friendly terms with my neighbor across the street, and we would stop and talk with each other from time to time. With his broken English and my broken Thai, we managed to have short conversations.

I remember a funny story typical of my cooking experiences in a foreign country. I had a craving for beef and broccoli and searched the internet for a quick and easy recipe. I found one and made my grocery list. The ingredients I needed seemed straightforward: beef, broccoli, corn starch, fish sauce, oyster sauce, and soy sauce. I ventured out to the store early one morning to purchase the necessary ingredients to prepare the dish. Approaching the meat counter, I glanced across the meat selection and did not see any beef, so I asked the man behind the counter, "Do you have beef today?" "No have beef," he replied in broken English. The store was also out of broccoli, so I pondered what I should do.

Remembering the shopping experience I had with the "I can't believe I got jerked around all day" beef stroganoff, I skipped my plan to make beef and broccoli for that day. I would buy what I could that day, then get other ingredients as they became available. The next day, the store had beef, but they were out of broccoli. The following day, fresh broccoli was available, but no corn starch. It took three days to gather all the necessary ingredients. By that time, the craving for beef and broccoli had passed, but I was determined to make the dish anyway. It was supposed to be quick and easy, and I had to push that challenge of not finding the necessary ingredients.

I finally had everything I needed to make that quick and easy meal. I have since learned when something says "quick and easy," it often ends up being long and drawn out. I found a wok and started cooking, listening to the sizzle of the beef cooking as I chopped the

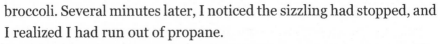

broccoli. Several minutes later, I noticed the sizzling had stopped, and I realized I had run out of propane.

I considered my options, then asked my neighbor friend if I could borrow his propane tank to finish cooking. With my less than perfect Thai language skills, I explained my situation, and he seemed to understand, but he said in his broken English, "Tank big." We walked into his kitchen and saw his propane tank was too tall to pick up and move, so I said, "No problem. Can I just bring my stuff over here and finish cooking it on your stove?" Without waiting for an answer, I went across the street and brought my stuff to his house. It took me three trips to get everything. I took over his kitchen, pushed his wife—who had been preparing a meal and using the propane tank—out of the way, and finished cooking my meal without even considering I was drastically imposing on my neighbors. When I finished, I left about half of what I cooked with them as a way of expressing thanks for their hospitality and went home and enjoyed my meal.

Reconnecting

I met Pastor Nueng and Ruth when I moved to Khon Kaen in 2007 and spent that first year in Thailand leading a cell group in their home. I became good friends with them and their families. He was helping in the church where our first CBS in Thailand was held. While I was living in Malaysia, they had started their church in Khon Kaen and had a congregation of about twenty people. Pastor Nueng and his brother Pitak, who had been healed of HIV, had also started a church within the prison and held weekly services. I had an open invitation to minister in the prison and would join them from time to time to share the Word of God and encourage the new believers. The vision for the church in the prison was to disciple the inmates as they completed the final phase of their incarceration. Once the inmates completed their sentences and were released, he continued to help with their rehabilitation into society. Many inmates became church members, serving in various capacities while they looked for work and started over in life.

I went with Pastor Nueng and his brother one day to minister in the prison church service. After the service was over, Pastor Nueng introduced me to an inmate. "This is Piterd, he will be released from the prison next week, and he will be a student in Calvary Bible School." I shook his hand and talked with him for a few minutes before we left. I know nothing about him or why he had been in prison, but I felt the Holy Spirit strongly urging me to tell him God would restore all he had lost and had been taken from him.

I had lunch with pastor Nueng after the service, and he told me the story of how Piterd ended up in prison. Many years earlier, he had been out drinking at a bar, and while he was drunk, he got into a fight and killed a man. He was arrested, and at the trial, he was found guilty of murder and sent to prison. He was married and had a young daughter. Once he was incarcerated, his wife left him, and his daughter was given to relatives to raise. Piterd truly lost everything as a result of one night of drinking. As he neared the end of his sentence, he was transferred to the Khon Kaen prison, where he met Pastor Nueng and gave his life to Christ. Over the next year, I would have a front-row seat as I saw the Lord radically change and transform Piterd's life.

26

Calvary Bible School

Chiang Yuen, Thailand

The leaders had done much of the preliminary planning for the Calvary Bible School I would direct when I returned to Thailand. That would be my first time to direct a CBS, and there was so much to learn. We worked with the local churches where our training was needed. The students came by the recommendation of the pastors. We entrusted the pastors to choose wisely their church members who they wanted to train to become leaders. We often would have a mix of pastors, assistant pastors, and leaders in the church and those who would become future leaders.

Up to that point, my involvement with CBS was traveling internationally to teach. I flew into a nation and spent a week teaching, and then went to another place. I rarely formed relationships with the students I taught and didn't see first-hand the resulting fruit from my teaching endeavors. From time to time, I heard testimonies about our graduates, but because I taught in so many different schools, I could not put a name with a face and hardly ever remembered any students specifically. When I accepted the responsibility of directing the CBS in Chiang Yuen, that would change. Over the school year, I got to know each student personally. I had the privilege of watching them grow in their relationship with the Lord as they heard the Word and put it into practice in their lives.

Five churches were represented in the school. Pastor Nueng and Ruth sent five students they wanted to train for church leadership positions. Piterd had been released from prison the week before CBS opened, and he was among the students from their church. As the date approached for the school's opening, the pastors and I met to go over the student applications, and I learned two students had been in prison for committing murder. I considered it a great testimony that two convicted murderers had given their lives to Christ and would be in Bible school and trained for the ministry.

Piterd's Testimony

Piterd changed and grew in his relationship with the Lord while attending CBS, and he became a leader in Pastor Nueng's church. While he had been in prison, his wife left him, and he lost all contact with his daughter. He knew his relatives were taking care of his daughter, but he didn't know where they were. He wanted to reconnect and locate her and approached his relatives, asking to see his daughter. The relatives refused for a long time, but he persisted, and finally, they granted permission. By that time, she was about fifteen. He could only visit her when the relatives were home and only for an hour. He did that faithfully for several months, and eventually, they relaxed their restrictions, and he could go see his daughter any time he wanted.

Piterd's family were strict Buddhists, and they were not happy he had become a Christian. One day, when he was visiting his daughter, his Buddhist grandmother, who had been blind for several, years called out to him, "I hear the God you serve heals. Do you think your God would heal me?" Piterd laid hands on her and prayed the prayer of faith, and when she opened her eyes, she cried and shouted, "I can see! I can see what looks like trees!"

He continued to visit his daughter on the weekends, and one day, he asked his relatives for permission to take his daughter to church. "We are Buddhists. We don't want your daughter to change religions," they replied. "Why do you want to take her to church?" Piterd replied, "Jesus has changed my life, and I want my daughter to know the One true God and to have the opportunity to have the life I have." The relatives responded, "Yes, we can see your life has changed," and they allowed him to take his daughter to church on Sundays. Eventually, she gave her life to Christ. They served together in the church, and she became a leader in the youth group. God was faithful to His Word, and He restored to Piterd an important relationship he lost during his years of incarceration.

Unique Challenges

I had to deal with unique challenges during the school year we had not observed in other schools up to that time. I met regularly with the five pastors who had sent students to the school to discuss different issues that popped up. It was a learning experience to navigate between our culture and the Thai culture, and I often felt pressure to lower the school's standards.

When I wasn't teaching, my habit was to sit in the back of the class and do paperwork while the classes were in session. One day, we had a guest teaching on praise and worship, and I had my computer out and was working on student grades. I wasn't paying attention too much to what the teacher was saying until I heard these words, "God gave my wife Bell's Palsy to teach me a lesson." I couldn't believe what I just heard and looked up at the teacher in disbelief and shock. "I wasn't doing what the Lord wanted me to do, so He gave my wife Bell's palsy," he continued.

That statement created a problem that needed to be addressed, and I wasn't sure how to handle it. I firmly believe, and Scripture proves, sickness and disease came as the result of man's fall in the Garden of Eden. God never intended His creation to experience sickness and disease, and God doesn't make people sick. The guest teacher left town immediately after the class was over, so I didn't have the opportunity to speak with him. The following week, I addressed the class and gave a short scriptural explanation on why we believe sickness doesn't come from God. It was the first and only time in all my years of teaching I had to stand in front of a class and correct something taught that didn't agree with Scripture.

As the school's director, it was my responsibility to handle any student problems or challenges. One student wasn't adhering to the school's policies and procedures. I met with the pastor to discuss how we should handle the situation, and we scheduled a meeting with the student. Four of us were in the meeting, the student, his pastor, our interpreter, and me.

I prayed beforehand that whatever was hidden in darkness would be brought out into the light. As we talked with him about his school challenges, he looked at me and said through the interpreter, "I have committed murder." I knew he had been incarcerated for murder, so I replied, "Yes, I know you had been in prison before for murder." I could tell by our interpreter's facial expression the next thing the student said wasn't good. I looked at the interpreter in shock as he said, "He just said he has killed four other people since he has been out of prison, and he is wanted by the police." *Unbelievable,* I thought, as I silently thanked the Lord for answering my prayer. I discovered afterward the pastor knew the student killed four people and was wanted by the police when she recommended him to be a student. The pastor willfully harbored a fugitive. The student vanished after that meeting, and we never saw him again.

My relationship with the pastor was strained from that point forward, as trust was broken. We always assumed the pastors who sent students to our schools had been properly vetted and were ready to pursue God's calling on their lives. It was hard to grasp someone would knowingly harbor a murderer while sending them to Bible school. The pastor put the entire class and me in an incredibly dangerous situation, not to mention our entire ministry in Thailand. I praise the Lord that He protected us from what could have been an unbelievably dreadful situation.

As I write, I am still friends with Pastor Nueng and his family, and I talked with him recently. He said that out of the five students he sent to the Bible School in 2011, four are still with him and are leaders and pillars in the church.

Calvary Bible School Mae Sai, Thailand

An opportunity opened to do leadership training among the Akha Tribe in Northern Thailand. Our Regional Director for GTN, Craig Kuehn, had met a young Akha woman named Deborah when she was a student at Christ for the Nations Bible School. After Deborah graduated, she moved back to her home in Mae Sai on the Thailand-Myanmar border, where she married Arthur, who is also Akha.

The Akha people live in China, Myanmar, Laos, Vietnam, and Thailand. In Thailand, they are considered one of the six hill tribe people groups in the forests between Thailand, Laos, and Myanmar.

We began a school in Mae Sai, targeting the Akha living across the border in Tachileik, Myanmar.

The schedule for the school was grueling, with classes Monday through Thursday from 8:00 a.m. until 9:00 p.m. We taught our modules every two months, so I frequently drove from my home in Khon Kaen to Northern Thailand. Mae Sai is an eight to ten-hour drive through several mountain ranges, and it was always a beautiful but somewhat dangerous drive.

I soon became great friends with Arthur and Deborah. It was a unique teaching experience, as many times, our words and phrases did not have meaning in the Akha language. When that happened, Arthur and the class had to interpret the meaning into Akha, which would take several minutes. Arthur was the sole interpreter for the school, which meant he stood on his feet for twelve to thirteen hours a day, every day, as he translated for the different teachers. Many times, as a treat after the training module was complete, Arthur and I would get foot massages. It was a wonderful way to unwind and get to know each other.

Whenever we traveled to Mae Sai, we passed through a small city named Chiang Rai, which was about thirty miles from the Myanmar border. I didn't know it then, but I would spend the remainder of my time in Thailand living in Chiang Rai and working exclusively with the Akha tribe.

Preparations for the Future

I continued to have a great relationship with Christian Outreach Center, which had its main office in Chiang Mai, Thailand. Obtaining proper work permits and residency visas was complicated, and I had maintained my legal missionary status under that organization. The founders of COC, Jonathan and Judy Vickers, had become great friends over the years I lived in Thailand. They, unlike many other organizations, gave me the freedom to fulfill the calling on my life. Working with other organizations in Thailand was difficult as many ministries would use their work permits and residency visas to manipulate and control those who worked under their ministries, but COC didn't operate that way.

When I moved to Thailand in 2007, the team was made up of Ariel and Paz Acuna and their family, Scott and Susan Oldaker and their family, and I. We had our work permits and residency visas with different organizations with their own restrictions and requirements. The Khon Kaen team grew, and as new missionaries came to Thailand, we explored options for obtaining work permits and residency visas with various ministries.

During that time, COC desired to open a Khon Kaen office, and Jonathan approached me about helping them establish it, which would be a win-win situation for everyone, as COC would have a presence in Khon Kaen. The new missionaries who came to Thailand to join our team would have an opportunity to obtain their legal status in the country. It would be a lot of responsibility for me, the office manager. I would have to make sure all the missionaries kept their legal status current and follow through with all the Thais government obligations. I was hesitant, but Jonathan and I agreed we would take one step at a time.

We worked closely in finding a building to rent for the offices, and I found a small room to rent big enough to make into an office. When the government officials inspected the building, they rejected the site as an official office, so we had to make other arrangements. In the end, Jonathan Vickers and Pastor Nueng and Ruth agreed to put the COC office in their church. Pastor Nueng became the office manager, and I believe the COC office in Khon Kaen is still in Pastor Nueng's church.

I had made several trips to Chiang Mai. It was always good to get to the big city with many foreigners and western amenities you would expect in the United States. I had several favorite restaurants, and I would enjoy a cheeseburger (my favorite food) at each one during my stay. I enjoyed going to Chiang Mai and visiting Jonathan and Judy and the church called House of Praise.

On one particular trip, I spent eleven days in fasting and prayer. When coming off a fast, I had always been encouraged to begin eating food slowly and in small amounts. I would usually start by eating soups, broth, and then adding solid food slowly. When I broke this fast, I decided my first meal would be a cheeseburger and French fries, and oh, and it was delicious! It was smothered with grilled onions, bacon, and avocado, and I topped off the meal with an ice cream sundae at one of my favorite ice cream parlors. Since it was early, I figured if my stomach had any problems, I would have all day and the evening to smooth things out before departing for Khon Kaen the following morning. I knew it wasn't wise to eat all that greasy food for my first meal, but the heart wanted what the heart wanted. I made it through the day and evening without any problems. As I left Chiang Mai the following morning, I wasn't expecting any difficulties.

I was about halfway through my trip when my stomach grumbled. I was in an isolated area deep into the mountains, and soon my stomach was churning, and I desperately needed to find a bathroom. I was in the middle of nowhere with no gas stations, hotels, or houses anywhere, and I was in trouble. I thought I would have to pull off the road and go out into the bushes. I was frantically looking for a spot wide enough to safely pull off, but there was nothing but winding, curving roads. I regretted my decision to eat that cheeseburger and fries, but it was too late for that, I needed to find a bathroom now, and I prayed for God to intervene.

I came around the corner and spotted a small house and what looked like an outhouse in the distance. I pulled over and looked in the glovebox for tissue. The only thing I had was one Starbucks napkin and my handkerchief. I grabbed it and said to the woman in my broken Thai, "Is that a bathroom?" She looked at me as if I was the first white person she ever saw and said yes as I walked to the outhouse. I closed the door and discovered I was in a squatty potty. If you have never seen a squatty potty, it is just a hole in the ground. I quickly surveyed the situation, and it would be best if I took off my clothes. I was extremely happy to have found a bathroom to use!

I looked between the wooden door slats and saw several Thai people surrounding my vehicle, trying to open the door to take what I had in the vehicle. There was absolutely nothing I could do as I was being held captive to the previous night's greasy cheeseburger. I had locked the car doors, so even though I was in a helpless situation, the contents of my vehicle were safe. After that experience, I made sure to carry toilet tissue wherever I went.

27

Chiang Rai, Thailand

In 2012, the operations base for the Go To Nations team relocated to Chiang Rai. We continued to train Akha leaders on the Thai/Myanmar border. Another Calvary Bible school had started about an hour east of Chiang Rai. The team had grown, with new missionaries being added. I was the last missionary to move to Chiang Rai. I had planned a trip to the United States and still had several months left on the lease for the house I was living in, so I waited until after returning from my trip to move. It was difficult to say goodbye to my friends in Khon Kaen, but I was also looking forward to not having to make the long mountain drive to teach in the Bible school at the Thai/Myanmar border. By the time I moved to Chiang Rai, the newly built mall was open, and it was the largest mall in the region. Of course, a Starbucks in that mall had opened, and I would continue to enjoy having morning coffee there a few times a week.

The difference in the spiritual climate between Khon Kaen and Chiang Rai was like night and day. Khon Kaen was an unreached area with only about twenty churches in the city. Moving to Chiang Rai was like a breath of fresh air, as there were about a hundred churches in the city. It was nice to be so close to the Myanmar border where we were doing leadership training, and I spent more time with Arthur and Deborah, who lived in Mae Sai. Many times, Arthur invited me to preach at the church he started in the mountains where his mom lived. It was just a three-hour drive to Chiang Mai, and I visited the Christian Outreach Center and the House of Praise church often while I lived in Chiang Rai.

When I transitioned to Chiang Rai, it took me time to find a place to live. Every place I looked at was either massively too big for one person or rented before I had a chance to decide. Several homes were two-story, five-bedroom homes, and I recall the person helping me find a place would say, "Pastor Steve, this would be a great place to start a church," but I had no intention of starting a church. My home was to be my sanctuary, and I didn't intend to entertain or conduct ministry there.

After what seemed like weeks, I finally found a small house in a neighborhood just outside of town. The house was run down and dirty and not in a great location, but the rent was inexpensive. It was a two-bedroom house, and I paid one hundred dollars a month for rent. It was a shock as the home I previously rented in Khon Kaen was fairly new and beautiful and was the nicest place I had lived in so far in my missions' career. The house in Chiang Rai was unfurnished, and I didn't want to hassle with buying furniture again. However, I bought a bed and other odds and ends, but other than that, I lived in an almost empty house for two years. I didn't have a couch or chairs for the living room, and when it was my turn to host our weekly team meetings, I used a stack of plastic chairs for people to sit on. I would never be happy in that home and always regretted signing that lease. As new missionaries joined the team and moved to Chiang Rai, the majority found homes on the other end of the city, so I was far from the rest of the team, which added to my sense of isolation.

During my many drives from Khon Kaen to Mae Sai to train Akha leaders, I developed a good relationship with Arthur and his wife, Deborah. When he discovered I would be moving to Chiang Rai, he was happy to have me near him and his family. One night after the CBS module was completed, as we were having our usual foot massages, Arthur and I talked about my upcoming move to Chiang Rai. "When you get settled here, I want to introduce you to one of my friends who lives in Chiang Rai. He is Akha as well, and I think you would like him very much. A couple of his pastors have actually been trained in our CBS here on the border," he said. We talked about what we would do together once I moved, and although he never told me the name of his friend, he mentioned introducing me to him from time to time. I didn't think too much about it then, but behind the scenes, God was working on my behalf and positioning me for the next few years of ministry.

My Life Is a Blank Canvas

Once I got my living situation settled, I fasted and prayed. I was in a new location, and I wanted to hear from my Father what His plans for my life and ministry would be. I didn't have any preconceived ideas of what ministry would look like. Although I had been teaching in Calvary Bible schools, I didn't take it for granted I would continue. Over the years, the ministry philosophy I had developed has been simply to pray, "God, my life is a blank canvas. What picture do You want to draw on it? What do You want to do in me right now?" It has always been an exciting way to live my life, as I gave up control over my destiny and submitted to the will of my Father.

As I prayed, I felt the Holy Spirit speak to me to begin developing good relationships with the local pastors and within the expatriate community. I would soon discover various ministries and organizations were based in Chiang Rai. There was a higher unity level within the body of Christ than in Khon Kaen. I felt the Holy Spirit had given me a specific direction, so I created a plan of implementation.

One day a week on Saturday, I got in my car and drove around the city to learn the lay of the land and see what was available in the city and surrounding villages. I chose a road to drive and sometimes I got lost. When I discovered a church, I wrote down the name and location and attended services the following day. I usually greeted the pastor after the service and then would meet with them during the following week for coffee. That was the ministry that took place during the first several months of living in Chiang Rai. I wasn't teaching in Calvary Bible School or preaching in many church services; I just drove around the city, found churches, and met with pastors.

God was taking the blank canvas I had given Him, and He was drawing His picture on it. As I followed His leading and allowed Him to control the colors, He built a beautiful tapestry, weaving all the different parts into one cohesive picture. Those first few months of obedience set the course for the entirety of the ministry I would do during my remaining time in Thailand. I asked the Lord what He wanted me to do. I then obeyed His prompting, which led me on a beautiful journey and years of fruitful ministry.

Blessing Stream

I frequently visited Arthur and Deborah in Mae Sai. On the drive to their house, I noticed a single building—a big church—about twenty minutes outside of town in the middle of an open field. Every time I passed that church, I felt prompted to visit, so I determined to attend a Sunday service, not knowing then how God would use me in the future. Neither did I know God would use the connections I made in the church to launch me into the valuable ministry that would take place over the next few years. God continued to work behind the scenes, ordering my steps, painting His picture on the blank canvas I had given Him.

I soon discovered this church was affiliated with Campus Crusade for Christ, and I was pleased to learn the pastor had a heart and vision for missions. The church was near the major university in Chiang Rai, so the congregation was mostly college students and foreign missionaries. Even though it was quite a distance from my home, I attended services there faithfully for over a year. In that time, I developed a close relationship with the pastor and his wife. The church culture in Thailand is unique in that part of the Sunday church experience is having a meal together after services. Many Sundays, I stayed after services, had lunch with the pastor and several leaders, and soon got to know several church members.

Will You Train Our Worship Team?

One ongoing conversation the pastor and I had was about his worship team. One day, he said, "Will you train our worship team and teach them how to flow with the Holy Spirit in worship?" I was stunned and not sure how to answer. That was an evangelical church, and he was asking me to teach his team how to flow with the Holy Spirit! I was honest about my thoughts on releasing the prophetic ministry in worship. My definition of flowing with the Holy Spirit in worship was most likely different from his. My experience in worship was more charismatic, whereas worship in his church was more evangelical and traditional. If he was asking me to train his team, I could only impart what was in me, and it would be in that vein. He simply said, "That is okay with me, as long as what is happening is of the Holy Spirit and not manufactured." I couldn't believe what I was hearing! The pastor trusted me with a vital part of his ministry.

We continued talking about what things I would teach. I committed not to teach anything he hadn't personally approved of beforehand. Each week I sent my teaching notes to him to read, and I talked with him about what I planned to teach. I told him if there was anything he didn't agree with or didn't want me to teach to let me know. He never disagreed with anything I wanted to teach, and I had the freedom to work with his team. I spent about two months doing worship workshops each week. I taught from the Scriptures, as well as by impartation and demonstration how to allow the Holy Spirit to move in their private times of worship, which eventually spilled over into their ministry of worship as a team. Over time, the church's worship took on a more charismatic tone and dynamic.

Can You Train These Future Missionaries?

The pastor approached me during the meet and greet time one Sunday several weeks after I completed the worship workshops and asked me if I could talk with him after service. After we had lunch together, we went into his office, and he asked me to have a seat. He left me by myself, and after several minutes, he came back with two young women, who sat across from me. The pastor spoke for a few minutes to the young women and then leaned over to me, "Pastor Steve, are you ready to share something?" I had no idea what was going on, so I smiled and whispered to him, "Pastor, I do not know what's happening." He replied, "These two young women are preparing to be missionaries, and we will be sending them to China in six months. I want you to talk with them about what it will be like on the mission field and help them with all they need to know about being missionaries."

It was such an honor the pastor respected and valued our relationship so much he would entrust his future missionaries to me for guidance and training. The two students had notebooks and were ready to write as they looked at me intently to speak. They asked questions about cross-cultural missions, carrying the anointing, overcoming language barriers, and dealing with false expectations. As we talked, I learned they were from the Lisu tribe and were planning to go to the Yunan Province in China to be missionaries.

We talked for several hours that afternoon. I gave them Calvary International's Missionary Preparation Orientation training that all new missionaries go through as they become part of the Go To Nations family. I opened my heart to them and taught them about culture shock and how to work together with other denominations to expand God's kingdom. I talked about raising finances and believing in the calling God placed on them. They asked several questions, and each question led to a lengthy conversation as I shared from my heart. They wrote everything down in their notepads and listened intently to everything I said. It was nearly dark by the time I answered all their questions. As we ended, I said, "I will help each of you financially when you are ready to leave for China, and if there is anything else I can do to help you in your calling, please let me know."

I went home amazed at all that happened. I had no idea that morning when I went to church what the Lord had planned for me that day. I had no idea the pastor had such respect for me to seek me out to help his future missionaries. God was filling the blank canvas with a beautiful tapestry. I allowed God to control my destiny, and He was using my life in ways I had never anticipated.

It was such a joy to my heart when the pastor brought the two women before the congregation several months later and presented them as the church's missionaries to China. The pastor asked me to come and pray over them and commission them into the ministry. I kept my word to the women and gave substantial financial gifts to each one as they embarked on their exciting adventure on the mission field.

Akha Outreach Foundation

I heard there was an expatriate church that met twice a month in Chiang Rai. I found the location and attended a service. Many missionaries attended, and I recognized a few faces, so I felt comfortable, and it was nice to hear different missionaries share the Word at each service.

At the first service, I met a Thai leader, Pastor Aje Kukaewkasem. I didn't realize it then, but God was ordering my steps and orchestrating events that would lead me into the most fruitful ministry season I would do in Thailand. Pastor Aje and I talked for a while after service. I discovered he led the Akha Outreach Foundation ministry. Pastor Aje intrigued me as we talked about our ministries. There was something different about Pastor Aje, and I felt drawn to him. Over the next several months, we continued to talk and develop a friendship. When he asked what ministry I was involved with, I casually mentioned I mainly taught in our Calvary Bible Schools. That is when I discovered he had several leadership training levels for the Akha people. As we got to know each other better during those Sunday evening services, Aje talked with me about teaching in one of his leadership schools. I was happy to help however I could.

We made plans for me to visit his campus and go for lunch to talk specifically about my teaching at Akha Bible Institute. When I arrived at the compound, I saw Aje talking with two men, who recognized me as I approached them. They had just graduated from the Calvary Bible school we conducted in Mae Sai on the Thailand/Myanmar border with Arthur and Deborah. It was kind of funny we were all connected, but none of us knew we knew each other. It was good to catch up with our graduates, and I was pleased to hear they were faithful pastors in the Akha Outreach family. It was also ironic Pastor Aje was the person Arthur kept telling me about who he thought I should meet.

When we talked about my teaching in his schools, I encouraged him to properly vet me before allowing me to teach. I said, "Don't just take my word I am a good teacher. You have two pastors who attended our school; meet with them and ask them about me. You know Arthur and Deborah very well. Ask them for a referral. Do your due diligence to find out from others what my character and reputation is before you open your school to me." I continued, "I am doing the same thing now. A Thai pastor wants to work with me, and I discovered we have mutual friends, so I am asking them about this pastor's character before I make any commitments." Aje replied, "Thank you for that, Pastor Steve. I haven't seen Arthur and Deborah for a long time, but maybe I will call them. I am going to a baptism service tomorrow at the home of one pastor we met today. Maybe I can talk to him later," and with that, we finished our lunch, and I went on to the other meetings I had scheduled for that day.

During our meeting, we talked about my teaching the subjects of the blood covenant, the Holy Spirit, and divine healing. The following day, I visited the Akha Outreach Foundation to drop off those course syllabi for Aje to look over. When I greeted Aje, I could tell he was excited about something. He told me, "Arthur and Deborah came to the baptism service last night out of the blue. We talked, and they told me all about you. I want to tell you our entire ministry is now open to you. You can come and teach in our Bible Schools. You can go to our villages and do ministry. Everywhere we have ministry is open for you!"

The following day I attended his weekly staff meeting and met several pastors who led various parts of the ministry. Pastor Aje introduced me to Yawtha and Buti, two of his key leaders, and we exchanged phone numbers. Yawtha and I became friends over the next year as we worked together doing ministry in various Akha villages. Buti and I worked together in the Akha Bible Institute as she interpreted the classes I taught. God had arranged for Arthur and Deborah to be at that baptism service. God had also arranged for those two pastors who graduated from our Calvary Bible school to be at the Akha Outreach Foundation offices the same day I met Aje there. It was amazing to see how God worked and fit all the pieces together.

After that conversation, I taught at the Akha Bible Institute, Aje's foundational leadership school for emerging leaders. The small classes made it an intimate setting and allowed time for good conversations, and I got to know the students fairly well during that first year. The following year I taught in his advanced level leadership school. That school consisted of pastors being trained every month. The pastors came from Thailand, China, Laos, Vietnam, and Myanmar. They stayed at the Akha Outreach Foundation base for a week. The school was large, with over one hundred and twenty pastors attending, and I spent three years teaching there.

I was so impressed with the way graduations for the different levels of leadership schools were conducted. Seven different leadership schools graduated at the same time. Everything was done with excellence, and it was always a big celebration. Graduation was the biggest event of the year. Usually, more than fifteen hundred Akha gathered to celebrate. It was such an honor and privilege to be a part of the training and graduation ceremonies.

Aje and I met once or twice a month to have coffee and a time of fellowship. One morning while we were having coffee, Aje told me about how the Akha Outreach Foundation started. When he started the ministry, the Lord directed him not to emphasize the Holy Spirit, even though he was what some would classify as charismatic. Aje wanted to reach across denominational lines. He worked together with Baptists, Methodists, Lutherans, and other denominations. Over time, he would have many pastors leading evangelical Akha churches.

About the time I met him, he had slowly begun introducing the Holy Spirit to his pastors, and a revival had broken out amongst them.

As we talked, Aje said, "Many pastors on staff are not filled with the Holy Spirit. Maybe you can come to a staff meeting and teach on the baptism of the Holy Spirit?" I readily agreed, and we made plans for me to attend his staff meeting the following week. About twenty-one pastors were at the staff meeting. After the teaching, we prayed for everyone, and several pastors received the Holy Spirit!

Aje has been instrumental in translating the Bible into the Akha language and has been working on the translation for several years. He has also written several books and training manuals that have been translated into Akha to be distributed throughout the different countries where the Akha people are. His ministry continues to flourish, and we continue to be great friends.

CHAPTER

28

The Storm: Struck Down, but Not Destroyed

I didn't know I would soon walk through the most difficult season of my life. The attacks I experienced were physical, mental, and spiritual, and it was a constant, everyday relentless battle. It felt like the enemy used every weapon he had to destroy me and the calling God had on my life. The storm lasted for about two years, which tested and shook my faith to the core.

By that time, the Chiang Rai team had grown and become the largest team in Asia. I was surrounded by people, and yet I was isolated and felt alone. My teammates often misunderstood me, and I found it difficult to reach out to anyone for help. My emotions were a roller coaster. One minute I was happy, and then just as quickly, I would be depressed and cry, and it wasn't something I could control. Every "bent" toward iniquity I had dealt with in the past was thrown at me. I constantly dealt with suicidal thoughts. I was frightened because I couldn't understand what was happening, and in the back of my mind, I wondered if I was having a nervous breakdown.

The oppression and pressure I felt were unbearable, and every day I begged God to let me leave the mission field. I often felt like running away, and many times I did. Most times, I would just disappear without telling anyone. I wrestled with the thoughts that clouded my thinking, and in my mind, I constantly heard, *go ahead and leave; no one will even notice you are gone because no one cares for you.* Sometimes I just needed to get out of town, and I would hurriedly pack clothes and drive to Chiang Mai and stay a few days. Once I left Chiang Rai, all the pressure, stress, and oppression would lift off me, and I could think clearly, only to hit me with a vengeance when I returned home. Every time I begged God to let me leave, He always told me, "My grace is sufficient for you" (2 Corinthians 12:9). So, I stood and weathered the onslaught coming against me.

I often talked with my friends Eric and Therese Nehrt about what I was experiencing, and they constantly prayed for me and gave me counsel. Because of my wild emotional swings, I had tests done to check my thyroid and testosterone levels, both of which came back normal. The next step was to have a complete physical, as it had been quite a few years since I had a check-up.

The hospital I went to was thorough. They had several types of physicals available, and I chose the "50 years and older" check-up, which included several blood tests, an ECG, and a complete MRI. After I completed the physical, I returned a couple weeks later for a follow-up. As the nurse discussed the results, it felt like my world shattered. "The MRI shows you have a gall stone, which is not serious. However, there is a spot on your liver we are concerned about," she said.

I felt the blood drain from my face as I struggled to comprehend what I had just heard. The words repeatedly echoed in my thoughts, *there is a spot on your liver; we are concerned about.* The words hit me with such force that I felt like I had been punched in the stomach and couldn't breathe. The nurse didn't give me time to digest that news as she followed up with the next sentence, "the test results also show you have tested positive for hepatitis B." *This can't be happening,* I thought, *not to me; I am a Christian. I've given my life to serve God on the mission field.*

The nurse continued talking, but her words were drowned out by the voices in my head. It seemed I heard some words she said, off in the distance, "Hepatitis. Unprotected sex. Sharing a needle. Mr. Wheeler, Mr. Wheeler, are you listening to me?" the nurse said, bringing me back to reality. With panic rising in my voice, I said, "There must be some mistake. It is impossible for me to have hepatitis B. I haven't had sex in twenty-six years, and I haven't shot up drugs for even longer than that." I pulled out my vaccine records, showed them to her, and said, "I have had vaccines for hepatitis B. Here, look at my shot records."

The nurse looked at my shot records, and in a calm voice, replied, "Mr. Wheeler, you may have had hepatitis B even before you were vaccinated. Were you tested to see if you had hepatitis B before you received the vaccine? I'd like to do another blood test to see how much hepatitis B is in your blood. This will help us determine what treatment we can prescribe, or if there is any treatment we can administer." I had the blood work done and was asked to return in two weeks to get the results.

It was extremely difficult to wait for the test results to come back. What was the spot on my liver? Was it cancer? Why is this happening to me? I struggled to control my thoughts and tried to keep myself busy, but at night when I laid down in bed, those thoughts came rushing back, playing over and over in my mind. I felt I *had to do something, anything,* but I didn't know what. Waiting for the results and not knowing what was happening became unbearable.

One evening I researched hepatitis B and looked at several websites to gather information. What I read scared and shook me to my core. One website stated, matter-of-factly hepatitis B can be dormant for decades, and once symptoms appear, it was usually fatal. My thoughts raced, *I've had this for over twenty-five years, it's been dormant until now, and I'm going to die.* Oppression hung over me as I walked through those two weeks while I waited for the results.

I received a call one day from the hospital, "Mr. Wheeler, we have your test results. Can you please come in today to discuss them?" When I arrived, I was ushered into a small office and asked to wait for the doctor. After weeks of turmoil and uncertainty, fear and anxiety, I had this unexplainable peace that suddenly flooded my spirit, and I felt at rest.

The doctor greeted me, and we made small talk for a few minutes, then she said, "Mr. Wheeler, the tests did not show any hepatitis B in your blood." "What do you mean?" I asked. She explained in some cases, test results can be wrong. She said there may have been a mix-up when the tests were done, or maybe they were done incorrectly. I noticed she wouldn't look me in the eye while she talked, and I wondered if she was trying to cover up a mistake. Were my tests accidentally switched with someone else's?

We had all the blood tests taken over, and again I had to wait two weeks for the results. Those second results came back as normal. Somehow a mistake was made with the original tests, and I did not have hepatitis B. When I asked about the spot on my liver, she replied, "We don't think there is any concern for that."

To this day, I am not sure if my tests were accidentally switched with someone else's, if they were a false-negative, or what happened throughout that health scare, but that season eventually ended. Those two years were extremely difficult as I weathered the storms that came against me physically, mentally, and spiritually and walked through the valley of the shadow of death. The Lord never forsook me nor left me, and He walked through it with me. The devil threw everything he could at me, but I refused to quit.

With the benefit of hindsight, I can clearly see the enemy was trying to stop what God would do with me in the future. I learned some valuable life lessons during that season. I learned in Jesus, I was much stronger than I thought. When everything was coming against me, and God would not allow me to leave the mission field, I stood. I didn't leave. I didn't quit. When the winds of adversity blew with such force, I discovered I had built the house of my life on the Rock and not on sinking sand. My roots in Jesus went deep, and even though I bent beneath the weight of the storm I faced, I did not break.

The other thing I learned is the enemy works with smoke and mirrors. He takes things and distorts them, making them seem real when they are not. When I was a child, we went to the state fair every year. One fair ride was called the House of Mirrors. A house of mirrors is a maze-like puzzle. The mirrors were obstacles that kept you from parts of the maze you could not get to. They were arrayed at different angles to confuse the path you were on. Many times, those mirrors distorted your view of yourself, and you had to distinguish what was real and what was a false reflection to help you find the path that would eventually lead you out of the house.

The health scare I experienced, even though it seemed serious and life-threatening, wasn't real. The enemy used it to distort, distract, and try to knock me off the path the Lord had been leading me on. Those last years in Thailand were incredibly fruitful and painful at the same time.

29

Crushing Debt, Transition, and Change

I sensed a season of transition about to happen in my life, so in March of 2014, I set aside time to fast and pray. In my missions' experience, I learned the one constant thing in my life was transition and change. It's ironic because my personality type thrives on stability and consistency, the two things missing since I became a missionary. I had moved frequently since I had been on the mission field. Whenever I moved to a new place, the posture of my heart was to put down roots as if I would never leave, but at the same time be ready to go somewhere else whenever the Lord led.

I had been unsettled in my spirit, but I couldn't put my finger on what was happening. As I sought the Lord for wisdom and direction, He spoke to me. It was my seventh year on the mission field, and I felt the Lord say He was bringing things to completion and would birth something new in me. There had been a death, burial, and resurrection, and I sensed the Lord was saying that ministry was winding down for me in Thailand. As I entered my eighth year of ministry, a change would come. I had no idea what that would entail or how radical that change would be.

After that fasting and prayer season, most of my Thailand ministry ended, except for partnering with the Akha Outreach Foundation and teaching in their leadership schools. I wasn't invited to preach in other church services as I had often done, nor was I scheduled to teach in Calvary Bible School from then on. However, I received invitations to travel internationally.

I was drowning in an overwhelming sea of debt. In my early years in the mission field, I had accumulated credit card debt. This debt had a snowball effect and soon affected every area of my life and ministry. I hadn't been a good steward over the things the Lord had placed in my hands. I didn't know how to say no to people, so I took several international trips I could not pay cash for. I charged airline tickets, hotels, and visas to my credit card, and when the bill came, I would only pay a portion, leaving the remainder to roll over to the next month. Those bad financial habits took me on a downward spiral of debt.

By 2014, I had accumulated $26,000 in debt. I owed $5,500 from a vehicle loan when I returned to Thailand in 2009, and I had $20,500 in credit card debt. I was sinking further and further into debt and couldn't see a way out. Missionaries were required to have medical insurance. I opted to pay my premiums once a quarter with my credit card because I couldn't pay in one lump sum. Each month I could only make the minimum payments on my credit cards. Even though my monthly budget was adequate, the monthly credit card and car payments took a big chunk of my finances, leaving me little wiggle room to make extra payments to pay down my debt. Then every three months, another $400 was added to my credit card for my medical insurance. Little by little, I was sinking deeper into debt, and I realized I was in over my head and didn't know how to stop the cycle.

Out of desperation, I talked with my friend Eric and told him about my financial situation. The Bible talks about the benefit of confessing your sins to one another (James 5:16), and as we talked, I felt relieved. I had kept my debt a secret, and by telling Eric, I brought darkness into the light. I didn't know it then, but the process of becoming debt-free began that night. My financial situation was not sustainable, and as we talked, he asked pointed questions about my debts. I gave him a detailed account of my credit cards, what I owed, what my minimum payments were, etc. We talked about what expenses I could cut from my life that would enable me to make extra payments. We discussed at length what I could do to alleviate the financial stress I was under.

I considered filing for bankruptcy but decided that was not the answer. I concluded I needed to come off the mission field for a season to focus on getting out of debt. I thought maybe this was the new thing the Lord had spoken to me about during my fast earlier in the year.

Eric was the missions pastor at his church, and he mentioned the church had made a push for individual members to get involved and support their missionaries. They previously presented five missionaries to the congregation for consideration. Each missionary received new financial partners from the congregation members. It had been so well received that Eric told me they would profile another five missionaries to the congregation. He asked me to send a short video about my ministry that he could present to the congregation. He was sure there would be new financial partners that would be added to me. I was happy to make a short video and sent it to Eric and didn't think too much of it afterward.

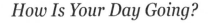

How Is Your Day Going?

Several weeks later, I got a text from Eric asking me to call him. I had had a particularly rough day, and when Eric asked, "How is your day going," I unloaded on him and told him about my bad day. Eric listened patiently, and when I finished, he said, "Well, let me see if I can make your day better. We presented five missionaries to the congregation to consider supporting financially, and I have a list of over twenty people interested in partnering with you. So how is your day going now?" he asked. I jokingly replied, "It's better, but I think you could do more." "Okay, I will," he continued without missing a beat, "I talked with our missions counsel, and we want to pay off your car loan. How does that make you feel?" I could hardly believe what I was hearing and replied, "I don't know what to say, Eric." He continued, "I also talked with the pastor about your situation, and during the service on Sunday, he talked about you. He told the congregation we needed to make sure you stayed on the mission field. Then he received a special offering for you to go toward your debt."

I was in shock as Eric continued, "The church historically has never helped pay off credit card debt. We have helped a missionary purchase a vehicle from time to time, but this is the first time I know of that we received an offering for debt. The church only does four special offerings during the year, so it is unique the pastor took an offering for you." Eric then jokingly asked, "So, how is your day going now?" We continued our conversation, then he said, "We want you to follow some conditions. First, we do not want you to charge anything else on your credit cards. Second, do not take any other trips you cannot pay for with cash. Third, we want you to communicate regularly to let us know how you are paying down your debt. Can you agree to those conditions?" I was happy to agree to those conditions, and we discussed ways I could pay extra on my credit cards.

I would be tested on the commitment I made to Eric and the church right away. I was scheduled to go to India in June and preparing for that trip when I had that call with Eric. Looking over my budget, I realized I was short several hundred dollars and wouldn't have the money to pay for that trip. I faced a dilemma. I had committed to travel to India to teach in the Bible school, but I had also committed to Eric and the church I wouldn't take any trips I couldn't pay for upfront. I tried to raise the needed funds by asking fellow missionary teammates to help me financially, but I still lacked what I needed. I talked with Eric, thinking he would extend grace to take that trip, especially since it was already in the works when we had that phone call. "I understand your dilemma," he said, "but trips get canceled, and schedules get rearranged all the time. It is not the end of the world."

After I hung up, I realized this was a test, and how I responded would set the course for years to come. It was not difficult to cancel the trip and keep the commitment I made to the church, although I suffered greatly for that decision. When I told the team leader I couldn't make the trip, he was upset. That entire school module had to be canceled and moved to another date as I was the only teacher scheduled. The team leader told me I would never teach in one of his Bible schools in India again. Although we talked again after the dust settled and agreed about future trips to India, I never had the opportunity to return. With the offerings I received from the church, I paid off my car loan and could pay extra on my credit card. In two months, my debt was cut in half, and the road to financial freedom had begun.

PART VI
Africa

Africa. Sometimes even now, it baffles me. How in the world did I end up in Africa? It wasn't in my five-year ministry plan, and it surely wasn't part of my long-term missions' goals. My stomping grounds had been in Southeast Asia. It was all I had ever known in ministry, and I planned to live there for the rest of my life and eventually be buried there. *But then came Africa.* Everything radically shifted and changed in ways I could not fathom.

How did I end up in Africa? Like so many other times in my life, *I simply said yes.* That one "yes" would lead me on an amazing journey, full of twists and turns. That one "yes" would indelibly change my life in unimaginable ways. God's ways are much higher than my ways and unknown to me, God was leading and directing my path to the place where I would have a rendezvous with destiny.

30

Shifting

I had sensed a change coming, but I had no idea what it was, what it would entail, nor how radical it would be. I was used to a certain amount of uncertainty and instability as a missionary. Other missionaries I knew seemed stable and put down roots, but that wasn't my experience, and I didn't know why. Maybe it was because I had said many years ago on that first Mexico mission trip, "Wherever You want me to go, Lord, I will go. Whatever You want me to do, Lord, I will do." Or maybe I just got restless after I had been somewhere for a year or two. Nevertheless, I was ready for a change, and I was open to something new.

I heard about Global Pathway through Dr. Jim Oxendine. He and his wife, Sherry, have been Go To Nations missionaries for many years. We had worked together on different leadership development projects over the years. He came to Thailand to talk about the upcoming Global Pathway training in the Philippines. Global Pathway is a practical, step-by-step training tool to assist pastors in building

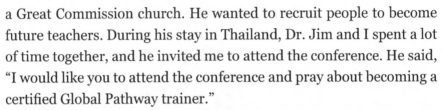

a Great Commission church. He wanted to recruit people to become future teachers. During his stay in Thailand, Dr. Jim and I spent a lot of time together, and he invited me to attend the conference. He said, "I would like you to attend the conference and pray about becoming a certified Global Pathway trainer."

The conference was in November 2013, and it was the catalyst that launched me into the next season of life and ministry. Being at the conference was incredible. Several of my fellow Go To Nations missionaries attended, as well as a large group of area pastors being trained. Dr. Jerry Williamson, the President of Go To Nations, and Dr. Jim, were the main conference teachers. We stayed at the same hotel, and it was wonderful to spend time with both men. The hotel was convenient, and the rooms were fairly decent. The hotel owner also owned a Dunkin Donut shop, so instead of having eggs and toast for breakfast, we had donuts every day! After a few days, we asked for eggs and toast because, eventually, you tire of eating donuts for breakfast.

At the end of the conference, several of us received our certificate of completion. When we got back to the hotel, Dr. Jim pulled me aside to talk. "Dr. Jerry and I have been invited to go to Arusha, Tanzania, in January of 2014. We will do our first Global Pathway conference in East Africa, and we'd like you to come be a part of this historic event. Dr. Jerry and I feel East Africa is ready for a global missions' movement that will start in Arusha and touch the nations. You could have a role in what the Lord will do in that nation." I felt honored to be invited and quickly said, "I'd love to go, but that gives me just one month to raise the $3000 for the trip, and I'm not sure if that is possible."

When I returned to Thailand, I opened a map to find Tanzania, as I had never heard of that country. I wasn't familiar with Africa, and I surely knew nothing about Tanzania. I contacted some ministry partners, and by a miracle of God, I raised my entire budget in just a few days. *I was going to Africa!*

Tanzania

The trip to Tanzania was pleasant. I arrived in Arusha in the early afternoon. As I disembarked, I realized most everyone on the plane needed to apply for their visa, so it took a long time to obtain my visa and clear customs. I don't remember who was there to greet me, but I vividly remember the hot air blast that greeted me as I exited the airport.

There was one main highway, if you could call it that. Once you exited the airport, if you turned to the right, you would head toward Mount Kilimanjaro. If you turned to the left, you would head toward Kenya, passing through Arusha on the way to the Kenyan border. Part of the highway was under construction. The closer we got to Arusha, the pavement gave way to dirt and potholes, which took time to navigate. There were no police to guide traffic, so cars were tangled and snarled together with vehicles going in the wrong direction and drivers yelling at others to get out of the way. I finally arrived at the African Tulip hotel and checked in. *I'm in Africa,* I thought as I settled in my room. Who would have ever thought that someday I would be in Africa?

I had only been in Africa for a couple of hours, but I had already discovered differences between Thailand and Tanzania. While the cultures were similar, with outgoing and friendly people to foreigners, Thailand's infrastructure was much more advanced than Tanzania's. In Thailand, most roads were paved, but not so in Tanzania. Thailand was considered a second-world country and Tanzania a third-world country. The differences were stark, making me appreciate the blessings I had living in Thailand.

Global Pathway

The rest of the team arrived from the United States, and we had one day together before the conference started. Anticipation hung in the air as we discussed Tanzania's future ministry possibilities. It was an honor and privilege to be on the ground floor of what God would do, and I was thankful I said yes to go to Tanzania. Although I didn't know it then, God would use that experience to lay the groundwork for the future.

Dr. Jerry, Dr. Jim, and I had lunch at the hotel. Dr. Jerry talked to us about the importance of the Global Pathway training we were to do and the potential ripple effect of that first conference. That was when I first heard about launching missions' movements within a nation that would affect the world. That first conference *put a stake in the ground* for Go To Nations in East Africa. As Dr. Jerry talked about the strength of the Tanzania church, I caught the vision of what we could accomplish in the future.

Calvary Temple
Tanzania Assembly of God

The conference was hosted by Calvary Temple Church in Arusha, part of the Tanzania Assemblies of God denomination. Bishop Wilson, who was in his early eighties and pastored the church for many years, led the church. We expected about three hundred bishops and pastors from the Tanzania Assembly of God to attend, with many coming from the surrounding region.

I had only recently become familiar with the Global Pathway material. I had sat through one conference just two months before traveling to Arusha. It would be my first time teaching the material. On top of that, I would be teaching in front of Dr. Jerry, who not only wrote the material but also happened to be the Go To Nations president. To say I was nervous was an understatement! I felt pressure to do well, as Dr. Jim recommended me to teach, and I wanted to live up to his expectations. I must admit I secretly hoped that when it came time for my session, Dr. Jerry would be called away and not in the room when I taught.

I remember the first day of the conference very well. The sanctuary was large, seating about one thousand people. To the right of the stage was a seating area where the leaders and dignitaries would sit. Our team arrived at 8:45 a.m., and the conference would start promptly at 9:00 a.m. We expected to see the church full of leaders sitting in their seats and eagerly waiting for the conference to start, but when we arrived, our team made up most of the people in the church! We were ushered into the upstairs office, where we had snacks and fellowshipped with Bishop Wilson and some of his pastoral staff. Soon the delegates arrived, and we started the conference. That first day was powerful as Dr. Jerry challenged the mindsets of those in attendance who had held the African church back from stepping into their God-given calling for the Great Commission. It was a historic day, and I felt like a fly on the wall witnessing something great taking place.

As my teaching session approached, I was glad Dr. Jerry and Dr. Jim were sitting to the side, so I wouldn't see them looking directly at me as I spoke. I was anxious as I approached the podium, but once I grabbed the microphone, the anointing set in, and it was like I turned into a different man. Once or twice while I was teaching, I glanced out of the corner of my eye and saw Dr. Jerry and Dr. Jim huddled together talking with each other, but that didn't deter me. When I completed my session, they rushed up to me, and Dr. Jerry said, "Man, Steve, you just hit that out of the park! I just want to tell you that you can consider yourself a part of the Global Pathway teaching team!" I can't adequately describe the effect his words had on me. It was a high point of my missions experience to have Dr. Jerry's validation.

One day during lunch, I went downstairs to the sanctuary while the rest of the team remained upstairs talking with the bishop. I was visiting with the delegates when I heard, "Bishop Wilson would like to speak with you, Pastor Steve." I thought it unusual but obediently followed the pastor upstairs to the office. I sat across from the bishop and smiled. What he said next totally caught me by surprise as he prophesied to my future. "Brother Steve, is God leading you to move to Africa?" I tried to keep a straight face, but inwardly I thought, *there is no way I'm moving to Africa.*

Undeterred, the bishop continued, "We need you, Brother Steve. We need you and your gifting here. If God is calling you to move here, you are most welcome." I didn't know what to say or how to respond to the word the Bishop just gave me. "I don't have plans to move to Africa, but if the Lord says to come, I will come," I replied. *What just happened?* I thought as I walked out of the room. Did I just receive an invitation to move to Tanzania? I was shaken to the core as that was my first trip to Africa, and I had just received a word of the Lord about moving to Tanzania. *Unbelievable.* I didn't want to think about it. I just came for a trip and was not expecting to encounter a life change.

I vividly remember Bishop Wilson addressed the pastors and bishops on the closing day of the conference. He repented publicly to the other pastors and to our team. He said, "We never knew we had a responsibility for completing the Great Commission. We have always been taught missions were the white man's job. No one ever told us we could be part of fulfilling the Great Commission." He said he would implement the Global Pathway training for his congregation. They would send their people out to the mission field. It was a remarkable thing to witness, and it marked the beginning of an incredible journey for me.

The team had a couple of days together before everyone went their separate ways. Several meetings took place with Dr. Jerry, Dr. Jim, and the Tanzania Assembly of God leaders. I felt privileged to sit in on some meetings, and I knew enough to keep quiet and observe while the leaders of Go To Nations and the Tanzania Assembly of God talked and strategized. During those meetings, the plan to implement the Global Pathway training in all the TAG churches was born. God set an open door of historic proportions before Go To Nations, and God placed me there at the beginning to observe what He would do.

I found it difficult to sleep my last night in Tanzania as I thought about the previous week's events. Never in my wildest dreams had I ever planned to be in Africa, but there I was. I thought about the time I moved to Chiang Rai and told the Lord, "My life is a blank canvas, and I'm giving you the paintbrush. What do You want to draw with my life?" Why was I in Africa? Why would I be part of this historic trip? The only answer that makes sense to me is it was because I simply said yes.

I was thankful for the opportunity to be in Arusha, but I was looking forward to getting back to Thailand. The team got together one last time for breakfast, and Dr. Jim pulled me aside, and we talked for a few minutes. "I am going to need you to come to Arusha four times over this next year to help me with these upcoming conferences," he said. Without hesitation, I agreed, and we planned for the next Arusha conference. The new adventure of faith had begun.

Living in Two Worlds

From that point, I had my feet planted on two continents. I lived in Thailand but traveled to Tanzania every two to three months to teach in Global Pathway conferences. Every time I traveled to Tanzania, someone suggested I needed to move there, or someone would prophesy about ministry in Africa, but I didn't want to hear of it. I was happy to live in Asia and minister in Africa, and I enjoyed the new season. I particularly enjoyed being with Dr. Jim and Dr. Jerry as we traveled and taught together.

Unknown to me, God was busy working behind the scenes and setting amazing things in motion. He hid the bigger picture for what He wanted to do with me. I couldn't spiritually discern God's long-term plan for me yet—probably because my heart wasn't ready to receive what He was saying. My vision didn't extend any further than living in Asia and ministering in Africa, but each time I visited Tanzania, I met new people, made friends, and formed connections vital to my future.

One of the first couples I met was Timothy and Asumpta Muna, who were spiritual sons and daughters of Dr. Jim and Sherry Oxendine. At the end of one trip, they invited us to their new house for dinner, and afterward, they wanted us to pray over them. We had an enjoyable time, and when it was time to leave and say our goodbyes, we went around the room hugging each other. I approached Timothy and hugged him, and as I did, he grabbed me tightly and wept for several minutes. As I prayed over him, the rest of the team gathered around and prayed as well. That was such a tender, unexpected moment and was the beginning of a valued friendship that continues today.

Go To Nations had a connection with Pamoja Ministries. I wasn't familiar with them until I came to Tanzania. There I discovered they had translated the Global Pathway materials into Kiswahili and were responsible for printing and distributing the conference books. Their offices were about thirty minutes outside Arusha, and we visited the compound every time we came to Tanzania. There the seeds of a relationship were planted. I had no idea how instrumental Pamoja Ministries would become to me in the future.

One of the most significant relationships I formed in those early days in Tanzania was with Bishop John and Apostle Trice Shumbusho. They pastored Zion City Church in Arusha and were close friends of Dr. Jerry and Dr. Jim. I remember very well when we first met. Dr. Jim had preached in their church, and they had asked the team to come to their house for dinner.

When being with new people, I normally fade into the background and let others carry the conversations. However, as we sat at the dinner table, I sat directly across from Apostle Trice, making me nervous! She was sweet and soft-spoken, but it seemed she saw right through me and could peer deep into my soul and spirit when she looked at me. I felt like my life was laid bare before her, and she could see things in the spiritual realm about me.

The dinner table was elegant and formal, and I thought, *this setting is so nice, you better not break anything!* A huge vase filled with sparkling red soda was the table's centerpiece. After we finished dinner, Bishop John stated we would have communion together. He took the elements, blessed them, and passed that huge vase to each person. *Dear Lord, please don't let me drop that vase!* In my mind, I could see myself dropping the vase and spilling the sparkling red soda all over the nice white tablecloth! The closer the vase got to me, the more nervous I got. As Apostle Trice passed it to me, my hands shook as I grasped that vase. Once I received communion and passed it to the next person without dropping it or spilling the contents, I inwardly sighed with relief.

31

2014: The Year of Decision

I went to Tanzania several times in 2014. Each time the Lord spoke to me about moving to Arusha, my heart softened little by little toward the idea. Most of my previous teaching trips had been packed with ministry. I only went to the conference and back to the hotel, which afforded me little time to explore the city. On future trips, I arrived a few days earlier than the rest of the team. I then stayed after everyone departed to learn to get around town and see more of the city and what it offered. Outside of taking part in the first Global Pathway in East Africa, other significant developments occurred that made 2014 a monumental year for me.

Dr. Jim had told me one church we worked with had a vision for leadership development and desired to start a Bible school to train their leaders. Zion City Church was pastored by Bishop John and Apostle Trice Shumbusho. Dr. Jim had frequently ministered in their church, so I was familiar with their ministry. I had extensive experience teaching in Calvary Bible School, and Dr. Jim thought it would be a good idea to meet with them. Until that point, my peers and Thailand team members had not seen me as a leader. That meeting forced me to step out of my comfort zone. I was comfortable with being in the background and working in a supporting role in an established ministry. In that instance, I was seen as a leader working together to start a ministry, and I was not accustomed to that.

As I talked about the Calvary Bible School, I realized I was in a room with spiritual giants of the faith. Who was I, and what was I doing in that room? *I'm not a leader,* I thought. Bishop John and Apostle Trice sat across from me. They listened attentively as I explained the vision for the school and our training's core values. *You don't know who you are talking to; I'm just a helper, I'm not capable of starting a school.* Those were some of my thoughts as I talked. But they looked to me as a leader, and as I talked, it felt like a mantle had been placed on me, and I spoke as someone with experience and authority. At the end of our conversation, they expressed a desire to begin a Calvary Bible School in their church. We didn't have a starting date, but we agreed we would continue to talk and plan for the school in subsequent Arusha trips.

Over the next year, as we discussed my leadership, I committed to starting the school, getting it established, and laying out a three-year plan to turn it over to the church. The plan was to nationalize the school as soon as feasible, allowing me to focus on other projects. As I contemplated how this could be accomplished with me living in Thailand, I envisioned two scenarios. The first allowed me to continue to live in Thailand and travel to Tanzania every two months to oversee the school. The second was to temporarily move to Tanzania for one year to establish the school. Once it got established, it would be turned over to the national leadership and, I would move back to Thailand. While both scenarios were plausible, neither included a permanent move to Tanzania.

Whenever I visited Arusha, I was invited to preach in the same church. I became good friends with the pastor. One Sunday service, as he introduced me to the congregation, he said, "Pastor Steve is no longer a visitor; he has become part of our family." We had lunch together after the service, and we talked about my next Arusha trip. "Pastor Steve, I want you to come to do a five-day leadership conference for our church network." As he talked, I thought, *you don't know who you are talking to, I'm just a volunteer. I'm not capable of leading a conference. I am not a leader.* That thought echoed over and over in my mind. *I am not a leader. I am not a leader.* I suggested he work with one of my friends who would come on that next trip, but he wanted me to do the conference for him.

When I got back to the hotel and thought about our conversation, the Holy Spirit revealed I needed to change a defect in my thinking. Merriam-Webster's dictionary defines a defect as a shortcoming, an imperfection, or a flaw. A stronghold in my thinking hindered me, and I needed to tear it down and replace it. To advance in my walk with Christ, I needed to look at myself through a different set of lenses. I never thought of myself as a leader or aspired to leadership. My *sweet spot* had always been in a supporting role, working behind the scenes, not out in front leading.

A war began inside me as I struggled to work through what the Holy Spirit had spoken. Faith had been ignited in my spirit at the Word of the Lord, but my mind refused to believe. I wondered why I constantly thought I was incapable of doing great things for God. Where did that faulty thinking come from? How did it get there? How could I break free from the shackles that held me in captivity?

As I lay in my bed staring at the ceiling, the Holy Spirit reminded me of a dream I had many years ago when I lived in Penang. I was about to transition back to Thailand, and I didn't have confidence I could do what the Lord was asking me to do. In that dream, the Holy

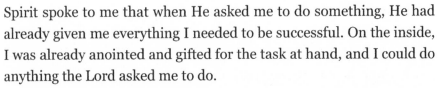

Spirit spoke to me that when He asked me to do something, He had already given me everything I needed to be successful. On the inside, I was already anointed and gifted for the task at hand, and I could do anything the Lord asked me to do.

In that hotel room, I discovered some keys that would break that defect in my thinking. In Romans 10:17 (TPT), it says, "Faith, then, is birthed in a heart that *responds* to God's anointed utterance of the Anointed One" (Emphasis mine). One significant key was hearing. I heard the Word of the Lord, and that sparked faith. A second key was to believe. I needed to believe God had put everything I needed inside me. I already had every gift and anointing I needed. The third key would be obedience. I needed to respond and take a step of faith. Would I allow God to do what He wanted to do in my life? Would I believe and trust? Would I take steps of obedience?

I contacted the pastor before I left and told him I would be delighted to do a Global Pathway conference for his church when I returned to Arusha two months later. Slowly, my thinking changed, and that stronghold crumbled. A Global Pathway conference had been planned for that time, and two team members agreed to stay an extra week to assist me. That trip would be significant in my development as a leader, and that conference would be the first I had planned and led. A shift had occurred in my life as God stretched me. The season God was leading me into required more of me, and I saw myself as a leader.

Looking back, I can see 2014 was a significant year in my life and ministry. I'm reminded of Psalm 119:105, which says, "Your word is a lamp to my feet and a light to my path" (NKJV). Although what the Lord had in store for me wasn't clear, I was walking in obedience the best I knew how, with each step of faith leading me closer to the greatest blessing of my life. Little by little, the Lord was preparing and positioning me for the next season. I had made my plans, but God was the One directing my steps.

Yes, Lord!

The Lord was leading me to a place of decision. In my heart, I knew He was asking me to move to Tanzania. I saw the open doors set before me, and I saw the possibilities of what could be accomplished. Why would the Lord lead me out of Asia? Asia was comfortable. It was what I knew and was familiar. It was home. Would I lean on my understanding, or would I trust Him? Would I step out in faith, or would I shrink back?

I struggled with the prospect of moving to Africa. I didn't want to move halfway around the world to another continent. Throughout my travels in Africa, I realized Thailand was a nice, safe place to live. In all my years of living in Thailand, I had always felt safe and secure. I never had to look over my shoulder to see if anyone was following me, nor did I ever worry about my safety. I was a single man, and Thailand had things available for me to do. There were restaurants, coffee shops, and movie theaters to frequent. Thailand was lush, green, and vibrant even during the dry season when there was no precipitation.

Tanzania's spiritual climate was different. During my frequent visits, we were urged to avoid being outside after dark by ourselves. Even when our team walked one block to a restaurant, we had an armed guard escort us. I never felt safe in Arusha. Every time I went out of the hotel, I had a feeling I would be robbed, or worse. I had to be aware of my surroundings constantly in public, always looking over my shoulder to see who was behind me.

As far as I knew, there were none of the amenities I was accustomed to in Thailand. I didn't know of any coffee shops, restaurants, or movie theaters in Arusha. Arusha was a tourist hotspot with many people coming from around the world to climb nearby Mount Kilimanjaro.

The expatriate community was large with many foreigners in the area, but Arusha was a small, dirty, dusty, third-world city. Thailand was an enjoyable place to live, but Tanzania would be challenging.

The battle between my head and my heart continued throughout the summer of 2014 as I counted the cost of moving to Africa. *Africa*. Africa was once known as the missionary graveyard, and that was where the Lord wanted me to go. I had made a mental list of the pros and cons of moving and went over it daily, and the cons far outweighed the pros. I was conflicted. The words I had spoken to the Lord on my first mission trip to Mexico rang in my spirit, "Wherever You want me to go, Lord, I will go. Whatever You want me to do, Lord, I will do." Those were words I lived by, words that defined my spiritual walk with the Lord. *I will go. I will do.* Yet, it was difficult to find the courage to say yes.

I visited the United States in the fall of 2014. I spent a couple of weeks in Jacksonville, Florida, at our Go To Nations world headquarters. Our home office scheduled a Leadership Development Forum I had been invited to attend. I was looking forward to seeing my missionary cohorts from around the world. It would be a week of intense leadership training and impartation from the leadership of Go To Nations into the lives of its missionary force.

October 13, 2014, will remain etched in my memory. The Leadership Development Forum was coming to a close. It had been a wonderful week, and I had received so much from the Lord. One of the last sessions was a time of prophetic prayer. We were instructed to find a secluded place to pray and seek the Lord. I found a place in the sanctuary, knelt down, and immediately wept uncontrollably before the Lord as He spoke to my heart. *Will you go for Me? Will you go for Me?* Those words repeatedly echoed in my spirit as the battle for the destiny God had for me was being waged.

As I had done so many times previously, I submitted my will to the Lord. *"Yes, Lord, I will go. I will go for You."* It was finished. The surrender of my will had taken place. I said yes to the Lord. As that time of prayer and consecration closed, I looked up and saw I was kneeling beneath a large photo on the wall. It was a photo of an African man with a big smile. Such joy was in his eyes, and as I gazed at the photo, I felt at peace. *I was going to move to Africa!*

That picture still hangs on the wall in the sanctuary at the Go To Nations headquarters. Every time I see it, it reminds me of that pivotal time of saying yes to the Lord. Clearly, God wanted to do something with me in Africa. He was working behind the scenes setting things up and putting me in a position to receive the greatest gift of my life. As 2014 rolled over into 2015, God would shake my world and speak clearly and powerfully to me.

--------- CHAPTER ---------

32

I Have a Gift for You

I arrived back in Chiang Rai shortly after 2015 began, and life set-tled into a normal routine. I had said yes to the Lord, so I knew change was coming. I just didn't know how radical that change would be. I wasn't sure what the next step would be, but I knew it would include moving from Asia to Africa in the distant future. In the meantime, I would continue to travel to Arusha to help with the Global Pathway conferences and work toward starting the Calvary Bible School.

March 5, 2015, started like every other morning with nothing out of the ordinary. I had no great expectations other than to begin my normal routine, having coffee and reading emails. But God had cho-sen that day to break forth into my world unexpectedly and dramati-cally to express His desire for my life.

As I was reading my emails, I noticed I had a message on social media from the mom of a missionary teammate. I was surprised to see a message from her, as we had only met once or twice when I was in the United States. She wasn't someone I communicated with regu-larly. It was out of the blue.

I opened the message and read these words, "I feel like God gave me a message for you. I feel in about a year's time, there could be a special lady in your life, but only if it is the desire of your heart and you enter into declaration and agreement about it." The words leaped off the page, and I could hardly believe what I was reading. I read the message over and over again, staring at my computer in utter disbelief. It was troubling; I had settled in my heart years ago I would never marry and have children. I had vowed to serve the Lord as a single man. It was not something I focused my attention on or thought about; until God broke through that morning.

The message shook me, and I wondered if it was from the Lord. I didn't know anything about my teammate's mom, so one day as we were having coffee, I asked him nonchalantly, "Is your mom prophetic?" He was surprised by the question but answered, "No, not at all. My mom doesn't have a prophetic bone in her body," and asked why I wanted to know. When I read him the message, he was shocked and said, "That is not like my mom at all. It's not like her to give a prophetic message like that." We finished our time together and went our separate ways, and I contemplated what it all meant.

For the next several months, I thought about that word and wrestled with it. *If it's the desire of your heart.* Was it a desire of my heart? Was that what I wanted deep down? I had put the desire to have a wife and family in a box, wrapped it tight, and put it in the back part of the closet in my heart. I tried my best not to think about that box. Now, it seemed God had brought that box out and wanted to open and air it out. As I struggled, the Lord lovingly and tenderly spoke to me, "I have prepared a wonderful gift I want to give you because I love you." As always with the Lord, He was patient with me as I wrestled, and the choice was mine. God had something amazing He wanted to give me, but only if it was my desire and only if I would trust Him.

After struggling inwardly for several months, I took a chance with God. I prayed and came into agreement and said to the Lord that if He had a woman for me, He could bring her to me. But I attached a lot of conditions to my agreement. I would not waste time looking for her, date anyone, or look at every woman and wonder if she was the one. I would continue to focus on the ministry like I had been doing since I became a Christian. He would have to bring her to me supernaturally, and He would have to do it in such a way I would know it was Him and not someone playing matchmaker. I wouldn't do anything to make that happen in my strength.

I was in Tulsa, Oklahoma, and I wanted something to remind me of my agreement with the Lord. I was in a Christian bookstore one afternoon, and I came across a silver ring with 1 Thessalonians 5:17 written on it in Greek, "Pray without ceasing." I slipped it on my finger, and it fit perfectly. That was the only ring with that Scripture on it. I took it as more than a coincidence. I bought that ring so that whenever I looked at it, I would remember God's Word, His promise to me, and my agreement with His will. Although I wore that ring every day, I didn't think about having a wife and quickly put it out of my mind as I continued to focus on the ministry and serve the Lord. It just wasn't at the forefront of my thinking. Life returned to normal as I continued to make trips to Tanzania, but behind the scenes, God was working.

April 17, 2016

A Global Pathway conference was scheduled for April of 2016 at Zion City Church in Arusha. That would prove to be the most pivotal week of my life. Over the previous year, Bishop John, Apostle Trice, and I continued talking about starting the Calvary Bible School in their church. During that conference, we planned to announce the school's starting date in July, and we would register students. The conference would begin on Monday. I arrived on the Friday prior, which gave me a couple of days to adjust to the time change and be rested and refreshed when the conference started.

April 17 fell on a Sunday in 2016, and as I dressed for church, I had no idea what was about to happen. It was just another church service, and I expected nothing out of the ordinary. Our team entered the sanctuary after the worship service started, and I sat near the back while Dr. Jim and the rest of the team were escorted to the front row.

As I entered into worship, the Lord's presence surrounded me, and the Holy Spirit gently whispered to me, "You will find your wife here in this place." I wept as the Spirit of God washed over me. It was as if a thunderbolt came from heaven and knocked me off my feet. Could this be? I had completely forgotten about what the Lord had spoken to me about the gift He wanted to give me. I heard the Holy Spirit gently whisper again, "You will find your wife here in this place." As I wept before the Lord, I prayed, "Lord, if this is from You, I need you to confirm it." I was stunned, and I found it difficult to pay attention to the message preached.

On April 21, Dr. Jim pulled me aside to talk with me when we got to the hotel after teaching at the conference. He looked a little strange and had a serious look on his face as he said, "Brother, I have something I need to tell you, and I don't know how you will take it." *That's always a great way to start a conversation,* I thought as he continued. "Bishop John and Apostle Trice have been praying for a wife for you ever since they met you two years ago, and Apostle Trice thinks she may have found someone." I tried to hide my excitement at the Lord confirming so quickly what the Holy Spirit had said to me the previous Sunday and said noncommittedly, "Hmm, okay." I walked away and went to my room and thanked the Lord for His confirmation. They wanted to arrange for us to meet that week, but I refused, as I wanted to pray.

I met with the bishop and the apostle after the conference was over. Apostle Trice gently said, "Pastor Steve, we are not saying 'thus saith the Lord' on this. But we have been praying for you for a long time, and we know your gifting, and we know her gifting, and they are compatible with each other, and it just seems the Lord may be in this." I found out her name was Veronica, and Apostle Trice sent a photo of her to my phone. The face I saw in the photo was familiar, as I had seen it several times in a vision as I had prayed over the past several months. In that vision, I saw a picture of my newsletters. On the top of the newsletter was a photo of my wife and me, standing behind me, resting on my shoulder. The woman in that picture was Veronica. I had plans to return to Arusha in July to start the Bible school, so I said, "Let us pray separately and seek the Lord. When I return in July, Veronica and I can meet face to face and talk then."

For the next three months, I prayed. Every afternoon I took a twenty-mile ride on my mountain bike, taking the winding back roads through the mountains to a local waterfall. The ride was beautiful and serene because there wasn't any traffic. Nobody else was along the route that took me through the wilderness. It gave me plenty of time to think, pray, and talk to the Lord. Whenever I prayed, I had an incredible, unexplainable peace that flooded my spirit, but when I thought about it, my mind thought it was crazy, and it just didn't make sense.

During a bike ride, the Lord brought to my remembrance a prayer I prayed when I was a young boy. I must have been about twelve or thirteen. As the scene played out in my spirit, I saw myself kneeling down, and with my hands clasped in prayer, I said, "Lord, if I ever get married, let it be to someone named Veronica." Veronica had been my favorite name ever since I can remember. As a boy, I prayed for a wife named Veronica.

It's interesting that many years later, on the other side of the world, in a remote Tanzanian village, lived a young thirteen-year-old Iraqw girl named Lohi, which in Kiswahili means *road*. She was given that name because she was born while her mom was going to the hospital. She had become a Christian and wanted a Christian name and chose Veronica. Only God could orchestrate something like me praying for a wife named Veronica at around age thirteen and a young girl changing her name to Veronica around the same age!

July 2016: My Birthday Weekend

We decided Calvary Bible School would start on July 11, which just happened to be my fifty-third birthday. The bishop and apostle agreed to continue praying and said they would arrange a time for me to meet Veronica when I returned to Arusha, since all I had was her name and photo, but I had a peace the Lord was leading us to each other.

A Global Pathway conference was scheduled for that week. Dr. Jim and a United States team would come to do the conference, held in the morning and afternoons. The Bible school would also start that week, with evening classes. Dr. Jim would kick off the school by teaching the first class.

I arrived in Arusha in the afternoon of Friday, July 8. I had just gotten to my room and was unpacking when the phone rang unexpectedly. It was Bishop John who said, "The only time we can meet with you and Veronica is right now. I'm coming to the hotel to pick you up in twenty minutes." I hung up the phone and walked out the door to wait in the lobby for him. I didn't have time to change my clothes or shower. I had butterflies in my stomach. We would meet at a nice restaurant near the hotel.

When we arrived, Apostle Trice and Veronica were already there and seated. Veronica was a vision of beauty in her green dress. Veronica sat across from me, and we stared at each other the entire time, saying little. I was glad the bishop and apostle were there. Veronica and I were both so nervous! Near the end of the meal, I finally worked up the courage to speak, "You have been praying for three months, Veronica. What do you feel the Lord saying?" She replied, "When I pray about it, I have a deep peace in my spirit. But when I think about it, it doesn't make sense." To which I replied, "That's funny because when I pray, I have a deep peace in my spirit too, and when I think about it, it doesn't make sense to me, either." We all laughed. We finished dinner and took a photo of ourselves together. I asked Veronica to come to the hotel the next day to talk, and she agreed.

The team from the United States had arrived, and I desperately wanted to have our meeting without anyone knowing about Veronica and our connection. They had a luncheon appointment that day, so I asked Veronica to come to the hotel when they would be gone. That was a good plan, or so I thought. I waited in the lobby for Veronica to arrive, nervously looking at my watch and the entrance. Then I saw the team returning from lunch, and Veronica was walking with Dr. Jim. *So much for my plan of having a private meeting with Veronica,* I thought as I greeted everyone and introduced Veronica.

We found a small table by the pool and sat down and talked. As she was talking, the Holy Spirit whispered to me, "I have created you to care for her." Before I knew what was happening, I heard these words coming out of my mouth, "Veronica, I think we should just plan on getting married." Veronica replied, "I think that is a good idea." It was shaping up to be a great birthday weekend!

Sunday morning, we went to church and had our first "date" later that evening. Our friends Timothy and Asumpta met us for dinner. Timothy looked at me during the meal and said, "Pastor Steve, I have a question. What is going on here between you two?" I remember looking at Veronica and saying, "Let me answer this, and if you have something to add afterward, you can." Looking at Timothy and Asumpta, I said, "Well, Veronica and I are planning to get married," then turning to Veronica, I said, "Is that about right, Veronica?" She smiled and replied it was true. We finished our dinner and went our separate ways. The following day would be my birthday as well as the start of Calvary Bible School that evening.

Calvary Bible School—Arusha

Calvary Bible School started, and I was excited. Eighty-one students were registered, one of the largest Calvary Bible School classes I knew of, and I was the director. I felt liberated by the past constraints I had lived under, and I was stepping into a new leadership realm. The strongholds in my thinking were being torn down, and I was looking at myself in a new light. I was becoming a leader.

Eighteen churches from different denominations were represented in the school, and people from five nations attended. Most students were pastors and leaders from the Zion City church network. At that time, Zion had planted about twenty churches in the region. Many of those pastors and leaders attended the school. Veronica was a student, and I made a conscious effort to treat her like the other students. We didn't want anyone to know we were courting, so I tried to keep my distance from her.

Dr. Jim was the first Bible school teacher. During his teaching, the Holy Spirit fell in the auditorium, and spontaneous praise broke out. It was an incredibly powerful night and a great start to school. During the teatime, I stood with Dr. Jim talking about the school when Veronica approached us with snacks. As she turned to me, she smiled, batted her eyebrows, and did a little curtsey as she gave me snacks, which tickled Dr. Jim.

As the school's first module came to a close and I prepared to return to Thailand, I wondered how a long-distance courtship with Veronica would work. How would we communicate and get to know each other better? I had planned to move permanently to Tanzania but wouldn't do so until January 2017. Veronica bought a phone which enabled us to communicate. As I boarded the plane and back to Thailand, I reflected on the previous week's events. I came to Tanzania to start school and surprisingly got engaged. The Lord said He had a wonderful gift for me. I just didn't know I would receive it on my birthday!

It was difficult when I returned because even though I was physically in Thailand, my heart was in Tanzania. It would be another two months before I traveled to Arusha and another six months before moving to Africa permanently. When I traveled to Arusha, I focused on running the school, which left little time with Veronica. I tried my best to keep our budding relationship separate from my running the Bible school. When classes were in session, Veronica was simply another student, and I said little to her other than hello, as we were not ready to announce our relationship publicly. We usually managed to have dinner together once the school module was completed. And I usually attended services at Zion City Church before departing Tanzania.

As I wrapped up my time in Thailand, a friend suggested I go through a debriefing before leaving Asia. It took several weeks to work through all the things I had experienced during my time there. I had been in Asia for ten years and had many things to work through. While there had been great victories over the years to celebrate, I had also suffered several hurts and wounds. Several life-threatening events had left their mark in my soul. I didn't want to carry any baggage into my new Tanzania assignment. I desired a fresh start, and I wanted to begin ministry in Africa with a clean slate.

As the debriefing closed, I felt in my spirit I was to write on paper all the things that had happened over the years—good and bad. I acknowledged my failures, repented where I needed to for the things I had done wrong, and praised and thanked God for the things He had accomplished in and through me. I felt there was a prophetic act I should do that would signify my break with the past and serve as a reminder I would be going to Africa with a clean slate.

I looked around hardware stores until I found a twelve-inch-long spike. I took those pieces of paper and that spike, went into the nearby mountains, and walked up to the waterfall. I went off the trail and found a secluded spot and prayed over each paper, then drove them into the ground with the spike. I nailed everything that had happened to me—every victory, every defeat, every hurt, and every sorrow—prophetically to the cross that day. I discovered a gift for painting, and I painted a picture of a spike being driven into the ground, separating the light from the darkness.

I still have that painting, and when I look at it, I remember what the Lord did for me, and I have left the past behind. I am reminded I am God's child, and He has taken me out of the kingdom of darkness and brought me into the kingdom of light. I am no longer a slave but a beloved son in God's family.

--------- CHAPTER ---------

33

Tanzania

Transition. Life as a missionary for me has always been one of transition. I had been on the mission field for ten years and had moved on average about every two years, except for my time in Chiang Rai, where I had lived for over three years. I faced another transition as I prepared to move to Africa. That would be the most difficult transition as all my previous moves had been in Asia and relatively close to each other. The upcoming move would be halfway around the world to another continent. I had grown accustomed to the Asian cultures, but now I would embark on an adventure of a lifetime as I stepped into Africa and all the Lord had prepared for me there.

That transition season was complicated. I was moving to a new continent, a new country, and a new culture. How would I handle all the transition and change I was going through? On top of all that change, I was now engaged. Once I moved to Arusha, Veronica and I would begin pre-marital counseling. A few years later, I would joke our courtship was pre-marital counseling. I was responsible for directing the new Calvary Bible School at Zion City Church and would also be instrumental with Global Pathway. I was transitioning from being a behind-the-scenes support person, which I enjoyed, into a new leadership role.

I had no desire to be a leader, but that was changing. How would I handle that? I certainly didn't ask for the new role, but I had said yes to the Lord and did my best to follow His leading. Comparing my situation with a mama bird getting her chicks ready to fly, I felt all my comfort and security had been stripped away. I was uncomfortable and didn't feel ready to leave the nest.

As I prepared to move, I had possessions to sell and give away and goodbyes to say to dear friends I had made over the years. One difficult thing about being a missionary, at least for me, was the revolving door of people coming in and out of my life. Very few missionaries I met had ever stayed in one place for long periods. It always seemed just when I got to know someone and let them into my heart, they would move to another location. Over the years, I had said goodbye to many dear friends. While always promising to keep in touch, I knew deep down the goodbyes were a finality in the relationship.

I had volunteered for the Akha Outreach Foundation for several years, teaching in the Akha Bible Institute. I had become close friends with Aje and Nancy Kukaewkasem, who founded that ministry. One of my closest friends, Jeremy, who also worked at the Akha Outreach Foundation, threw a going away party on my behalf. It was difficult to say goodbye to Aje and Nancy, Jeremy, and their families. God truly blessed me by bringing them into my life, and I would surely miss them.

Another Calvary Bible School module started on January 9, 2017, and I booked my tickets to arrive in Arusha on January 6. Sharon Williams, who founded Go To Nations with her husband Daniel in 1981, would bring a small team of women to teach the module. It was crazy to make a major move across the world just three days before

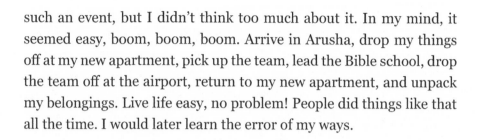

such an event, but I didn't think too much about it. In my mind, it seemed easy, boom, boom, boom. Arrive in Arusha, drop my things off at my new apartment, pick up the team, lead the Bible school, drop the team off at the airport, return to my new apartment, and unpack my belongings. Live life easy, no problem! People did things like that all the time. I would later learn the error of my ways.

Arusha and My New Environment

I arrived in Arusha on Friday, January 6, 2017, and went straight to the Pamoja ministry base. I stayed there just long enough to put my things in my new apartment and spend the night. I picked up Sharon and her team at the airport on Saturday and then went to the hotel where we would all be staying. On Sunday, Sharon would preach at Zion City Church, and Monday, the Bible school would start. I don't remember much of that week, as it went by in a blur, but I remember Veronica made a great impression on Sharon and the team when she met them. Sharon made a good connection with Apostle Trice, and they tentatively planned for her to return to Tanzania to lead a women's conference for the church. As I escorted Sharon and her team to the airport, she prayed over me and gave me great advice about leadership and the role I was stepping into.

After saying goodbye, I went back to my new apartment. I had planned to unpack my belongings and get settled. However, the emotions and stress of moving across the world had finally caught up to me. The adrenaline of moving and directing the school waned, and I suddenly felt extremely tired. It seemed as if my body just collapsed as I fell into bed and slept. I slept continuously for the next six days, not even waking to eat or shower. I would sleep for what seemed like forever and then would wake up for a few minutes, only to roll over and fall into a deep sleep again. I completely lost track of time and often didn't know where I was when I woke up. The other missionaries at the Pamoja ministry base worried about me, as I didn't answer the door, their texts, or phone calls. I eventually recovered, and things went back to normal, whatever normal was for me then.

I have never been a fan of change. I desire stability and predictability and love to have a schedule. I thrive on having a routine. However, being a missionary has meant a lifetime of continuous change, instability, and unpredictability. When I moved to Tanzania, it felt as if things were moving too fast, and I often felt like things were out of control. I wanted the merry-go-round I was on to stop and let me off, but that was impossible. Too much change was happening all at once for me to handle. Everything was new. I was in a new continent, a new nation, surrounded by new people I did not know well. There was nothing familiar I could cling to. I was engaged. I was directing a Bible school and becoming a leader. It was all too much, too soon, and I was desperate for stability that seemed just out of reach. My security had been stripped away. Too many plates were spinning in the air, and I felt I couldn't keep up, and they were all about to come crashing down.

Can We Slow Down, Lord?

When Veronica and I talked about a wedding date, I told her I wanted to have a long engagement—at least two years. But in her culture, that timeframe was too long. People just didn't have long engagements in Africa. I felt I needed time to adjust to the culture and my new surroundings. Veronica was gracious and understood, and we continued to talk about when we would have our wedding date as we went through pre-marital counseling.

I wanted to put the brakes on life, slow down, and regain control. It was all frightening. I frequently had the same puzzling dream during that season. The dream sequence was always the same. I would be driving a car and lose control of it. I would apply the brakes, but they would not work, causing the vehicle to go faster and faster. I would panic and continue applying the brakes, and then I would lose control of the vehicle. I usually woke up with a start and always felt as if I was in a tug-of-war and was physically exhausted.

I asked God what the dream meant. Because it occurred regularly, I knew there had to be a reason for that particular dream. A woman in a partnering church had a gift of interpreting dreams. I shared the dream with her, and as I talked, the Lord gave her insight into what was happening. The car represented the ministry. When the Lord wanted to do something new in me, I would put the brakes on or try to stop God's move on my life. Putting the brakes on represented being afraid, insecure, and unsure. When the Lord accelerated what He was doing in my life, I would try to stop the move of God from happening. Applying the brakes represented a fear of stepping out and allowing the new thing the Lord wanted to do in me. Yeah, I thought that was an accurate interpretation.

I settled into life and ministry in Africa and felt comfortable in my new surroundings. Even though I now lived in Tanzania and had gotten familiar with Arusha and its people, I never felt safe and never lost that feeling of being watched. I felt I needed to be aware of my surroundings whenever I was out in public. I always looked over my shoulder to see if I was being followed. I was continually on edge and could not relax. Living at the Pamoja ministry base proved to be a haven for me. It was tempting to stay under that safety bubble and never venture out of the compound, so I often forced myself to go into town.

When I lived in Thailand, I preached in different churches on most weekends, which did not allow me to be planted in one local church. Now that I lived in Arusha, Veronica and I attended Zion City Church, but we also ministered once or twice a month in other churches. The nature of my work required me to visit other congregations, which enabled me to form good working relationships with area pastors.

One pastor we formed a good relationship with was Philip Wilson. He pastored Calvary Temple, the first church where Global Pathway was conducted in East Africa. Pastor Philip had taken over the church from his father. The latter had prophesied over me and invited me to move to Tanzania during that first Global Pathway conference on my first African trip. Pastor Philip met with me at the hotel during one trip to Tanzania before I permanently moved there. There in the lounge area, he laid his hands on and prayed over me in place of his dad, releasing me into the ministry the Lord had for me in Africa.

Veronica was a teacher and had been teaching for about ten years before we met. We didn't see much of each other during the week because she was busy with work, but we spent time together on the weekends. We usually went out to dinner Friday nights. After dinner, I would drop her off at the church where she attended the overnight prayer service. On Saturdays, we had our pre-marital counseling sessions, and then on Sunday, we were in church worshipping together. We did not sit together, as we still had not announced our engagement publicly.

34

Life Experiences

When I lived in Thailand, I exercised with a group of young missionaries starting a health and fitness ministry to reach the Thais, and their training was similar to CrossFit. I felt I needed to be physically fit as I got older, so I was lifting weights, running, and bike riding. At one time, my goal was to do a triathlon, which was an annual event held by a Christian school in Chiang Rai. I had developed a routine of working out and did Olympic weight training in the mornings. In the afternoons, I would run ten miles or ride my mountain bike for twenty miles.

I had a slight tear in my meniscus. The doctor I had seen about it recommended bike riding as one treatment, so I purchased a mountain bike from somebody I worked out with. That bike, like my books, soon became one of my most important possessions. When I moved to Tanzania, I felt it was important to take my bike with me, as I guessed that would be my main form of exercise.

After falling out of my exercise routine when I moved to Arusha, it was difficult to get motivated to exercise again. Life was hectic.

Even though I had searched for a group to exercise with, I found no one doing the Olympic training I did in Thailand, so I stopped lifting weights. Looking at my bike in the corner of my apartment, I decided I needed to go out for bike rides again. In Thailand, I took a secluded off-the-beaten-path route, which I preferred. That secluded route allowed me to think, pray, and hear from the Lord. However, I hadn't lived in Tanzania long enough to find a secluded route, so I rode along the main highway.

Angels Watching over Me

Tanzania traffic is disorderly. Vehicles and motorcycles often drove on the wrong side of the road, so I had to constantly look for vehicles coming at me. That's not to mention the busses and matatus that would suddenly pull to the side of the road without looking, blaring their horns to pick up and drop off passengers. Then the motorcycles were often riding on the sidewalk instead of the paved road, which I likened to mosquitos always buzzing around. They frequently went against the traffic flow and thought nothing of forcing me off the sidewalk as they looked for passengers. The portion of the highway I rode my bike on was in a dangerous construction area. The government was widening the highway into two lanes in each direction, so heavy tractors were tearing up the old asphalt and making way for the new traffic lanes.

One main road construction area was about five miles from our ministry base, where the road went down a small hill and crossed over a river. A construction crew was building another bridge to span that river, and the traffic went from two lanes down to one each way while crossing the old bridge, then returning to two lanes on the other side. I would ride my bike to that construction area, and when I came to the bridge, I would turn around and go back the way

I came. Depending on the time of day, if I got to the bridge and there was no traffic, I would quickly cross and ride for a few miles before turning around.

One day, I was riding in the early afternoon, and when I got to that bridge, the road was clear with no traffic in either direction, so I quickly pedaled across the bridge and extended my ride. I rode for several miles before turning around to trek back to the mission base. By then, traffic was heavy and congested. As I approached the bridge, I made a mental note of the traffic and wondered if I could get across.

I came down the hill where the bridge was. I heard the Holy Spirit whisper to stop and take a drink of water. When I got to the bridge where the two traffic lanes went to one at the most dangerous part of the road, I heard a shout within me, "Stop and drink some water!" I stopped and grabbed my water bottle, and just as I drank, I heard a loud horn blast behind me.

Just then, I saw beside me a huge greyhound-type bus going too fast. It was so close that if I stuck my right arm out, I would have touched the side of it. The horn blasted again as the bus careened down the hill. In front of the bus was a small matatu. I saw a woman seated in the back turn around and look with terror in her eyes as she saw the bus. She turned to the driver and screamed, "Go! Go!" The bus, which was going about sixty miles per hour, crashed into the back of the matatu, and the matatu slammed against a large concrete barrier. As the bus slammed on its brakes, it flipped on its side and hit the matatu again, causing both vehicles to flip end-over-end in the air several times before stopping. The matatu landed in the middle of the bridge, and the bus came to rest along the barrier wall.

Chaos ensued as people got out of the vehicles and rushed to the scene. I was dazed, shaking uncontrollably, and I didn't know what to do. I set my bike down and started to run over but decided that wouldn't be a good idea. Everything seemed to be in slow motion with people screaming and bodies pulled out of the vehicles and set on the side of the road. I remember looking at the bus and seeing the tires still spinning. I saw one young girl being pulled out of the bus who was alive in a state of shock. The whole scene was surreal and terrifying.

I needed to get out of there, but the accident had happened right at the bridge, and there was no way to cross over to the other side. I looked to the left and saw the new bridge under construction and discovered enough cement had been poured that I could walk across safely with my bike. As I crossed the bridge and started walking home, I realized if I hadn't stopped for those few seconds, I would have been riding my bike right behind that matatu as it crossed the bridge and would have been between the matatu and the bus. I am sure I would have died instantly in that horrible accident. As I walked, I shook uncontrollably as I relived the scene over and over again in my mind.

I have suffered from post-traumatic stress disorder because of that event. Every time I heard a horn blast, especially if it came from behind me, I would freeze in panic. Several months after the accident, I was in the passenger seat with friends riding together to dinner, and they took me back to the church where I left my car. It was late at night, and as we were driving, there was a loud horn blast from a truck behind us. I screamed, "Jesus! Jesus!" and tucked into a fetal position and tried to open the door to get out. I was frantically crying, trying to get out of the moving vehicle. My friend quickly pulled over and tried to calm me down, saying, "Pastor Steve, it is only a truck. You are okay." Still in the fetal position, I cried for several minutes until I calmed down. It happened so quickly, and it seemed I didn't have any control over my reaction. I hadn't told many people about that accident and thought I was over the trauma, but I realized then I wasn't. I have had counseling, but to this day, noises behind me can cause me to panic.

Dirt Roads and Health Care

It was incredibly dusty in Tanzania, and most dirt roads had only been paved in the past few years. Many Pamoja missionaries would tell me how blessed they were to have the newly paved roads to drive on. The Pamoja ministry compound was especially dusty, as dirt roads surrounded the base. If you didn't clean your counters, dust would accumulate and cover them quickly.

I had developed a cough that never completely went away and thought I needed to see a doctor. That is when I learned Tanzania's medical care was, well, sub-par, to say the least. I had often heard people say, "You'd better not ever have a medical emergency in Tanzania, and if you do, go to Nairobi if you need medical attention." It was unnerving that I lived in a country so far behind the rest of the world as far as medical care. When asking what I should do other than drive to Nairobi, it was suggested I go see a doctor in a newly opened medical clinic.

The first doctor I saw tested me for tuberculosis, which came back negative. Then, the doctor suggested I had a parasite in my stomach that traveled into my lungs and caused the cough. I was given antibiotics and sent on my way. What the doctor said sounded ridiculous, but I took the antibiotics, and the cough went away. However, it came back again after a couple of months.

Planning for the Future

Veronica and I continued our pre-marital counseling sessions, which we found helpful. After one session, we were asked to talk about

285

our expectations for a family. I was driving Veronica home as we planned for the future and talked about having children. I had never thought much about that since I had never planned to marry, so being a father was the farthest thing in my mind. While we didn't answer the question of how many children we wanted to have, we agreed it would be best if we started our family right away since we were both older.

We talked about communication and cultural differences frequently. Being from two different cultures, we would experience different issues than most married couples. We were encouraged to talk about how we would meld our two cultures into one happy family. We didn't know of anyone in our circle of friends like us, so we had no example to follow. However, we both realized communication would be one of the most important keys to our happy marriage and family life.

Calvary Bible School continued to flourish, and classes were going well. We started with over eighty students. However, as with most of our schools, some dropped out for various reasons. Most students were bi-vocational, both pastoring and working secular jobs. We had our classes at night, and many students came straight from work, so the schedule was grueling, even if it was only nightly for one week every two months. Despite students dropping out, we still had a large class, averaging between sixty to seventy students. Bishop John, Apostle Trice, and Pastor Sulley, one of the church's main pastors, were students and attended every class. The plan was for them to sit through the training to take over the school's leadership the following year. I would then release my responsibilities to them and ease myself out of the school.

35

Cultural Awareness: Events Leading Up to Our Wedding

2017 was a banner year as Veronica and I took steps toward getting married. So much was going on, and it seemed I had too many plates spinning in the air. Things were changing way too fast, but I was handling the changes better than I expected. Veronica and I met weekly for our pre-marital counseling sessions. We saw each other on weekends, and we continued planning for our wedding.

Calvary Bible School was entering its last modules, and we would have commencement in the upcoming months. I was working with the bishop, apostle, and Pastor Sulley to plan the ceremony details. It is our custom to make graduation a special day. For many of our students, it would be the first and only time they had graduated from school, making it an important day in their lives. In our pre-graduation ceremonies the day before graduation, we gather all the students for a time of praise and worship, then there is a short message, which Crain Keuhn would give that year. The United States teaching team would pray and prophesy over each student, which would take several hours over the day. The day before graduation is always the most powerful day of the academic year, as God breathes into the students' lives. It's also one of the most physically exhausting. As the Calvary Bible School ended, we graduated forty-two students.

One of the most efficient ways to get immersed fully into a culture is by planning a wedding and getting married! We needed to honor many cultural customs, some similar to those in the United States. It was a learning experience, and Veronica was great about helping me through all the different aspects of a Tanzanian wedding.

Veronica's family background is not uncommon in her culture. Her dad and mom had gotten married, and both their first and second babies were girls. In that culture, having boys was expected, and society did not value girls. When Veronica was born, her dad did what most men of that era did—he left with Veronica and took another wife. Veronica was raised by her dad and stepmom from a young age and never knew her mother. She was forbidden to contact her real mom and was often told she couldn't come back home if she went to look for her. Her stepmom treated Veronica and her siblings badly, and they were not considered part of the family. Veronica has told me when she was young, she wasn't allowed to sleep in the house but slept with the cows outside.

Several years later, Veronica and her dad both accepted Christ. That is when she changed her name from Lohi to Veronica. She and her dad had a few years of a good relationship and reconciliation before he passed away. Veronica also discovered her mom lived around the corner from her dad and stepmom all those years, and she developed a relationship with her. Although we didn't talk about our pasts often, I knew enough of her background that when it came time to meet the family, I had to keep my anger in check at how she had been treated.

By the time we met, Veronica had been gone from her village for quite a few years. She had lived in the big city of Arusha and didn't visit her relatives frequently. Because she was no longer under her parents' care, Veronica desired to have a modern wedding and wanted to do away with many cultural customs.

Getting married in her culture is a lengthy process and requires several steps. The first step is the introduction of the families. The groom's parents approach the bride's parents to state their intentions. During that meeting, the two families get acquainted with each other. The next step is the send-off, where the bride's family officially gives the bride to the groom and sends her off to start her new life. The final step is the wedding, which usually takes place a couple of days after the send-off.

Veronica wanted to do away with the send-off, however, when she broached the subject to her family, they were adamant the send-off must take place. Because she had been gone from home for so long, her family must have the opportunity to properly send her off into her marriage. Her family must be allowed to celebrate her upcoming marriage in the traditional way it had been done for generations.

The Introduction:
The Meeting of the Families

In Veronica's culture, one of the first things that happen when a couple wants to marry is introducing the two families. The future groom and his father approach the father and family of the future bride, the two families meet, and the groom's father states his son's intentions. In our case, I was a foreigner. I didn't have any family in Tanzania to represent me, and Veronica's dad had already passed away. Veronica's uncle would stand in her father's place, and Pastor

Sulley would stand in place of my father. Apostle Trice would represent the church and vouch for my character, and together, they would represent me to Veronica's family. I didn't know what to expect at that first meeting, and I was glad my colleague, Jacob—who was one of the Pamoja missionaries and had been raised in Africa—accompanied us to meet the family.

Veronica went to her village a couple of nights before the meeting. According to their culture, she needed to be there when the families met. On the morning of our meeting, Pastor Sulley, Jacob, Apostle Trice, and I made the four-hour drive to Babati, the village where Veronica grew up. Before we arrived at the village, we stopped and bought gifts of rice, sugar, and other items to present to Veronica's family. It would be an elaborate and formal meeting of the two families, and there was a protocol to follow. First, I was told I could not talk during the meeting. I was to be seen and not heard. Pastor Sulley would represent my father, and it was his responsibility to talk to Veronica's family on my behalf.

When we arrived, I noticed about twenty-five or more of Veronica's relatives were at her uncle's house. It was customary to greet each person, so Pastor Sulley and I did just that. We met Veronica's great-great-grandma, who was one hundred and five. Veronica's stepmom was sitting outside and was introduced to me, as were Veronica's brothers, sisters, and other relatives. It was a little uncomfortable to have both Veronica's mom and stepmom together in one place. I wondered if there would be trouble between them, but they held their peace. Veronica's uncle greeted us at the door and escorted us into the house. I was nervous and kept my mouth shut! There was small talk, and then the business at hand took place, most of which was in Kiswahili, which I did not understand or speak fluently. Jacob sat beside me and loosely interpreted.

Apostle Trice had an official hand-written letter on church letterhead to present to the family, vouching for my character. After Apostle Trice signed it, it was stamped with the official church seal in front of the family. Then it was presented to Veronica's uncle, who read the letter silently before passing it to Veronica's mom to read. After the letter was accepted, we presented the gifts of rice, sugar, and other items to Veronica's mom, who accepted them. Then there was more talking between Pastor Sully and Veronica's uncle. Pastor Sulley then asked me to give him the envelope with the monetary gift we prepared beforehand, and he ceremoniously presented it to Veronica's mom. Her uncle then said a few words, and when he finished, he asked Veronica to come into the room.

That was the first time I had seen her that day, and she looked beautiful and stunning in her gold dress. She came into the room, and her uncle asked, "Veronica, who is it you are here to see? Do you know the one who is here to see you?" Veronica replied, "Yes, I do." Then she walked over to where I was and sat beside me. Everyone clapped and gave their congratulations. We had a meal together, and after some time, Pastor Sulley suddenly stood and announced we were leaving and walked to the door. Of course, before we departed, it was culturally necessary to say goodbye to everyone. So, we said goodbye to each relative, got into our vehicle, and headed back to Arusha. It was a long day, but our meeting was successful. I had met Veronica's family and stated my intentions. Her family seemed pleased with the prospect of our pending marriage.

Calvary Bible School Graduation

The final module of Calvary Bible School took place in May of 2017, and there was so much to do to prepare for graduation. Veronica and

I had completed our pre-marital counseling and talked about what life would be like as a missionary. I wanted to prepare her as best as I could for the upcoming changes. During one conversation, I told her that for me being a missionary meant moving to a country, buying furniture and appliances, using them for about two years, then selling and giving away everything to move to start over again in another location. I wondered how my nomad lifestyle on the mission field would affect her.

A United States team came to teach the last school module and participate in the graduation. We decided the ceremonies would take place during the Sunday morning church service, which would allow the whole congregation to participate. It was a great way to end the school term and build momentum and excitement for the next class of students.

I planned to travel to the United States right after graduation, and I needed to accomplish several things before then. Although Veronica and I had talked about getting married and gone through pre-marital counseling, I still had not officially proposed, nor had I gotten her an engagement ring. I had asked Veronica if she wanted to go with me to choose an engagement ring, but she wanted me to pick one for her. She told me what she liked, so I had an idea of what to look for. I found the perfect ring and purchased it.

Now I needed to find the right time and place to propose and surprise Veronica. I had arrived on the mission field on May 6, 2007, and I celebrated that day every year, usually by myself, doing something special on that day. I called Veronica the day before and told her, "Tomorrow is my tenth anniversary of being on the mission field, and I want to celebrate it with you. Let's get dressed up and go out for dinner tomorrow night." I had arranged dinner for us at a nice hotel around the corner from the Pamoja compound. A nice table was set up outside for us, and I picked out the evening's menu. When I asked her to marry me, she said yes! I proposed to her on a Saturday, and the last module of Calvary Bible School began the following Monday. It would be a great week!

We wanted to announce our engagement to our church family, and we planned to do so during the Bible school graduation. That last week of classes went well, but it was hard to concentrate during such a momentous week. I would complete my leadership of the first Bible school in East Africa. I had proposed to the most beautiful woman the good Lord had ever created, and I would get married!

After graduation, I packed my suitcase and made my way to the airport to begin my journey to the United States. It was an exciting time, and I was looking forward to seeing my family, friends, and ministry partners. Word had gotten out we were engaged. We made a short video before I departed to introduce Veronica to my family and partners. We had not set an official wedding date, but we were thinking of fall. We would be separated for a couple of months, but with the miracle of modern technology, we frequently talked through the internet.

While I was itinerating in the United States, Veronica was making plans for her send-off. Although having a send-off wasn't what she wanted, her family's cultural expectations and wishes had prevailed. According to her tribal customs, she was responsible for covering the event's financial burden. I was a little concerned about how much control she would have over the affair.

There was much to do for the wedding when I returned to Tanzania, and time was short. We needed to fulfill several cultural customs before the wedding, so I hit the ground running. We had talked about handling the wedding planning and details ourselves before my trip to the United States. However, upon my return, we realized we needed help, so we formed a wedding committee.

I fought against the culture while also trying to honor Veronica and her wishes. Veronica wanted to avoid some cultural aspects in the wedding process. For example, she didn't want to have a send-off, but because of the cultural expectations, she found herself planning and paying for that event. Another cultural expectation was having a wedding committee responsible for the planning and finances, which Veronica wanted to avoid. I found it difficult to navigate through those circumstances.

The wedding committee turned out to be a great help, although not without its challenges. The primary challenge revolved around obtaining money for the wedding which the committee members were responsible for. Each member would have had to raise a certain amount from their circle of friends, and if they fell short of their goal, they would need to take out loans to cover the shortage. Veronica had been on a committee and knew the pressure of raising money, and she didn't want to put that burden on our friends.

We talked at length about it and agreed she would cover the send-off party costs, and I would cover the wedding and honeymoon costs. When we announced this to the wedding committee, it caused concern. One Tanzanian friend met me for lunch and asked me why I was forbidding the team from raising money. I explained that as her future husband, it was my responsibility to take care of her. I was simply trying to honor her wishes and make sure what she wanted happened. He seemed to understand, and in the end, everything worked out, but it was challenging, and I experienced culture shock during the process!

Veronica's Send-Off Party

The wedding committee was handling the wedding details, and the next event would be Veronica's send-off. This occasion would be all about Veronica, and I was frequently told to be seen and not heard.

By that time, I had gotten used to being told I wasn't to speak at these family events.

We arrived in Babati early in the morning on October 7. I wasn't allowed to see Veronica yet, and many people were milling about. I was amazed at how many people were there because the village wasn't large. I stood with Jacob outside the house and listened as he explained the day's events to me. Suddenly, we heard a distant noise. We both turned to see what was happening, and we saw a group of women in traditional dress, marching, singing, and hitting their drums with sticks! It was quite a sight. It took these women about twenty minutes to arrive at the house. I had never seen anything like it in all my life, and I was in awe as I watched the procession.

By that time, more people had arrived and filled the house's outside courtyard, and people were spilling out onto the dirt road and the surrounding land. Jacob and I continued talking about what would take place and the significance for the family when we heard more music from the opposite direction. We turned to see what was happening, and another group of people, again in traditional dress, were standing in formation, holding drumsticks, and singing and dancing their way to the house. Incredible! That group took a long time to reach the house as they chanted, danced, and sang. It was the most amazing thing I had ever witnessed!

The ceremony finally began, and I sat in the back of the room—seen, but not to be heard. It was Veronica's special day, and I didn't have a part to play until the end. The people who represented my family sat to the right of the stage, and Veronica's family sat to the left. Veronica and her maid of honor sat center stage. There were toasts between the families. It was an elaborate affair and well done.

At the end of the ceremony, Veronica brought me out from the crowd. After she gave me her gift, a pair of dress shoes, we stood in the middle of the stage and presented ourselves to the family. We were wrapped together in a shuka, a traditional type of cloth, and people were invited to come bring their gifts and congratulate us. That event was larger than our wedding, as the entire village came out to witness the send-off. It was estimated that over five hundred people came! We returned to Arusha in the late afternoon while Veronica stayed for a few days afterward. It was a unique cultural experience and one I will never forget as long as I live. Veronica looked stunning, wearing a long gold-colored dress, and she handled herself with poise and grace throughout the day. We were one step closer to our wedding day, which would take place just two weeks later.

The following week was Veronica's birthday, which was just five days before our wedding. A couple of my groomsmen had arrived by then, traveling from Thailand to spend the week to help me before the wedding. I wanted to do something special for Veronica since it was the first time we had been together for her birthday. We made reservations at a nice restaurant, and I gathered a large group of friends to come and celebrate. There were several of my Pamoja family and Bishop John and Apostle Trice, along with my groomsmen, Ryan and Jeremy from Thailand. I gave Veronica a nice Tanzanian stone with a pendant. The necklace was so small and delicate that it was all tangled and knotted when she opened her present. After being married for a couple of years, she told me that was the first birthday party she had ever had.

36

God's Promise Fulfilled

I was fifty-five years old, and I was getting married! I never imagined something as wonderful as that would ever happen to me. God
had clearly spoken that He had a gift for me, and I wanted all that God
had for me. At times, I had to pinch myself; was this really happening? Is it too good to be true? I was awed at God's goodness toward
me, and I was so thankful to the Lord for all He was doing.

With our wedding day quickly approaching, all the details had
been taken care of, and the cultural events had occurred. A lifetime of
being single was ending. My best man, Eric Nehrt, had arrived a few
days before the wedding, as well as Tim and Nancy Lovelace, leaders
from Go To Nations. Veronica and I had scheduled a safari for our
guests two days before the wedding. With our guests' international
travel, the rehearsals, and life's busyness, we thought it would be a
great way to relax and unwind. It was a long day, but the safari was
just the thing we needed. It allowed Veronica and me to spend quality
time with our guests and take our minds off the wedding planning.
We stopped at an elegant resort and enjoyed a nice lunch on the way

back. When we arrived in Arusha, one of our friends had prepared a lavish dinner for us. It was a perfect day!

Veronica had prepared me not to expect a large crowd for the ceremony. "People here usually do not think of the wedding ceremony as an important occasion," she said. "The important occasion for our culture is the send-off, which everyone usually attends. Few will attend the actual wedding ceremony, but everyone will want to come to the reception." While I thought it strange the wedding reception would be the day's big event, I was thankful Veronica had encouraged me to lower my expectations.

Time. To the western world, time is our most important commodity. We are on time. We keep time. Time is money, it is said. We like things to go like clockwork. We schedule our day. We "block out" and set aside our time. Time. Time. Time. However, for most of the world, the concept of time is vastly different from the typical westerner. Most of the world is "event-driven" and not "time-driven." The event drives the day. Today, we have a party, which will start at whatever time people arrive. You ask someone in Africa what the schedule is for the day, and they will say, "There is a party." When you ask what time the party starts, the reply most often will be, "Later." If an event is to start at 10:00 a.m., you can be assured people will not arrive until 11:30 a.m. or later. That is especially true for weddings.

Veronica and I had attended several friends' weddings. The first wedding we went to was to begin at 1:00 p.m. Since I am a westerner, my expectation was if the wedding started at 1:00 p.m., we needed to be there a few minutes early. Veronica and I talked about my need to be there at 12:45 p.m. so we could be "on time." She told me several times the wedding wouldn't start then, and the bridal party wouldn't even be at the church until at least 3:00 p.m. If we arrived when I wanted, we would be the only people there. We finally agreed we would go to the church by 1:30 p.m. Sure enough, when we arrived, we were the only people there, and we waited for over two hours before anyone else showed up!

It is customary in Tanzania to announce our engagement and wedding date in our church for four weekends before the big day. I'm not sure why that is, but it is a legal requirement for Christian weddings. With our wedding, it would be tricky because Veronica is Tanzanian, and her culture is "event" oriented, and I am a westerner whose culture is "time" oriented. In announcing our wedding, Bishop John continually let the congregation know the wedding would happen in western culture and not Tanzanian culture. We set the wedding for 10:00 a.m. and would start promptly at 10:00 a.m. and welcomed everyone to attend. Veronica and I wondered if we would be the only ones at the church when the wedding started, but we needn't have worried.

Our Wedding Day

The week before the wedding went by in a blur. When the morning arrived, I was ready. I have been to many weddings in my day, and it seemed one common characteristic was the groom's nervousness. Many grooms had to drink whiskey or beer before the wedding to calm their nerves, but I was calm, even though it was somewhat surreal I would be married.

Our church would stream our wedding live on their YouTube channel, which would allow many of my United States family and friends to watch and take part in the ceremony. I would go to the hotel where our guests were staying and hang out until Veronica and her bridal party arrived at the church. We had been at the hotel for some time, and I laid down on a lobby couch and napped. We received a call that Veronica had arrived at the church, and we got ready to go. The time had come! I had lived for fifty-four years alone, and in a short

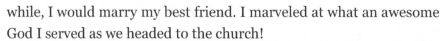

while, I would marry my best friend. I marveled at what an awesome God I served as we headed to the church!

When we got to the church, the worship service was underway, and I was asked not to look at the vehicle Veronica was sitting in. The ceremony soon started, and the groomsmen entered the sanctuary, followed by myself and my best man, Eric. When Veronica entered the sanctuary, I couldn't take my eyes off her, and I got giddy! All the rehearsals we had done of where I would stand, what I would do, and when I would do something, were completely forgotten as I gazed at my beautiful bride walking down the aisle.

Our wedding ceremony blended two cultures, interweaving each of our customs into one beautiful tapestry. We would write our wedding vows and recite them to each other. There is a funny story about writing our vows. Veronica and I are both introverts; at least, I claimed to be an introvert until I met Veronica. Over time, we have discovered that even though I may be an introvert, I am the one who has the most words to say in our family. Our first inkling to that came when we recited our vows to each other. I had many things I wanted to say, and many promises I wanted to vow to keep. I thought it would be a great idea to recite them to Veronica in Kiswahili when I began writing. However, I realized that would not be possible because my vows would be several pages long! I read my vows to Veronica first, and when I came to the end of the first page, Apostle Trice looked at Veronica and asked her to begin. I had to interrupt her to say, "There's more!" Veronica's vows to me were just as meaningful, but she said what she wanted to say in just a paragraph!

By western standards, the ceremony was long, and many of my family and friends watching on YouTube commented on its length. As the ceremony neared its conclusion, I sang the song "You Are So Beautiful" by Joe Cocker to Veronica. I sang that song to her when we announced our engagement to the church, and it seemed fitting to sing it to her on our wedding day as well. I wanted to finish the ceremony, so I could kiss my bride and kept interrupting to say, "Can I kiss the bride now?" Finally, that time came, and we kissed. It would be my first kiss in thirty years; that's 10,951 days! The reception that followed was one of the most fun events I had ever attended. It was truly an African affair, with the Tanzanian culture on full display.

One thing I most enjoyed was presenting the gifts. In our western culture, guests place their gifts on a table for the bride and groom, only to be taken afterward for the couple to open privately. In Tanzania, each person or group with a gift would line up at the back of the reception area and dance with their gift and present it to the bride and groom. It was a highlight of the reception to see all the creative ways various groups danced and presented their gifts to us.

Honeymooning in Seychelles

We had a few days after the wedding before we departed for our honeymoon. I had asked Veronica if she wanted to be involved in planning the honeymoon, but she chose to be surprised. My friend Jacob was part of the wedding committee, and he researched honeymoon places. He did a great job of providing me options to choose from. I decided we would have our honeymoon in Seychelles, which would require a six-hour flight.

We would depart Arusha at 3:00 a.m. When we got to the airport and went through Immigration, we had a hiccup and were almost not allowed to get on the plane. Veronica had been a teacher, and she had quit her job several months before the wedding. She was technically a government employee. When she presented her passport, the officer wouldn't let her on the flight because she didn't have an official government permission letter to leave the country, which we didn't know she needed. We explained our situation to the immigration officer, but he was adamant she could not leave the country. We appealed and were allowed to speak to the chief immigration officer, who gave her permission to leave. However, we had to agree to call him on his cell phone once we arrived back in Tanzania. We quickly got through Immigration, went straight to the boarding area, and got on the plane.

True to Veronica's wishes, I kept the destination secret; she only knew we would be flying on our honeymoon. When the plane descended, we saw the sandy beaches, and the look of awe and surprise on Veronica's face as I told her where we were is forever etched in my memory.

It's hard to describe the beauty of Seychelles. We were there for seven days, and it was just magical. We stayed in two different hotels on the beach, facing the west, which gave us wonderful sunsets to watch every evening. With all the wedding stress and busyness, we just rested the first couple of days, sleeping and relaxing. It was such a wonderful experience for both of us, and we sat on the beach every evening to watch the sunset. It was so beautiful and peaceful, sitting with our feet buried in the sand, listening to the waves gently crashing on the shore, as we watched the sky change with its radiant colors of oranges and reds as the day turned into evening.

We came back to Arusha, rested, and relaxed, and settled into our new home on the Pamoja compound. Once we were married, we moved into what was affectionately called "the corner house," which was somewhat secluded from the rest of the compound. That was where we started our lives and ministry together as husband and wife. Veronica and I were both involved with Global Pathway. Veronica had been through the certification process and was now teaching alongside me. Although she is usually quiet, I soon discovered she is an anointed teacher of God's Word.

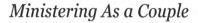

Ministering As a Couple

One of the first ministries we did together was to the youth. I was asked to teach at an overnight youth rally, and I felt I needed to talk about purity and abstinence. In Africa, youth groups are usually people from the age of thirteen up to thirty, so there was an opportunity to speak to many age groups on the importance of waiting until marriage to have sex.

After that experience, Veronica and I got invitations to speak about purity in different settings. We didn't plan to share our history in that manner, but God supernaturally orchestrated events and invitations came our way. People heard our testimony of how we both waited until we were married to have sex. Pastors wanted us to share our story about the steps we took individually to walk in purity. It was humbling to be asked to teach on that subject, and Veronica and I coordinated our teaching notes as we planned our teaching time. Veronica has always had a heart for young people. When she stood to minister, anointing came on her as she shared her heart, and she quickly became the favored speaker of our duo. We also received an invitation to teach in the university near our home, and for several weeks, we taught the evening classes. The students wrote down their questions, and we agreed to discuss them at the end of the last class.

Starting Our Family

Because we were both older, we planned to start our family right away. Soon after our honeymoon, we discovered Veronica was pregnant. We were thrilled the Lord had answered our prayer, and we were excited about having our first child. Our joy turned into concern as Veronica had challenges in the early stages of the pregnancy. Several times in those early days, we thought we would lose the baby, which caused unbelievable stress for us. We made several emergency trips to our doctor to have Veronica checked out.

On one particular doctor visit, we were sent to have an ultrasound done. When the doctor began the ultrasound, the baby was facing away from us. When she felt the doctor, she turned and, with both of her hands, waved as if to say, "I'm here! I am okay. I'm doing good, and you don't have to worry about me." After that visit, our hearts were soothed, and we never worried again about losing the baby.

We decided to have the baby in Nairobi. We welcomed Veronica Grace Wheeler into our world and lives on July 23, 2018. She was born at 11:01 p.m. and weighed in at 5.86 pounds, and she was 19.29 inches long. The song by Chris Tomlin, "God of Wonders," was playing on Veronica's phone as Grace was delivered.

There had been some back-and-forth between me and the hospital about staying in the room with Veronica and the baby. During one initial visit before Grace was born, the nurse in charge insisted I wouldn't be allowed to stay overnight. I insisted I would not leave my wife and newborn baby by themselves. I politely asked her if she would be paying the bill for the delivery, jokingly suggesting that since I would be paying the bill, I would be staying put.

Once Grace was born, and we got into our room, I climbed into bed with Veronica, which was a feat as it was only a single-sized bed. Possession is nine-tenths of the law, as they say, and I took possession of the room we were in, and no one bothered us for the duration of our stay. I slept with Veronica in that single-sized bed until we were discharged.

We had arrived in Nairobi about a month before Veronica's due date. We stayed for about four weeks after the baby was born before we traveled back to Arusha. In Veronica's culture, when a baby is born, a family member comes and lives with the parents to help take care of the newborn. Since we were in Nairobi, Veronica's mom didn't have the opportunity to come live with us.

Those first few weeks and months of family life were full of joy and anxiety. When we arrived back at our home in Arusha, we stayed secluded in our home for several weeks before taking the baby out in public. In African culture, normally, the mom and baby are not out in public for at least three months after the baby is born. When we went to church after we returned to Tanzania, some people were shocked Veronica had taken the baby out so soon.

37

New Opportunities

We continued our work with the Tanzania Global Pathway conferences as we learned how to be a family and parents. Before we had Grace, we talked about the vision for our family, and we set boundaries for our ministry and family life. We agreed to the best of our ability, we would do everything together as a family. If I had a ministry trip away from home, Veronica and Grace would accompany me, even if Veronica wasn't involved with ministering. Another thing we settled on was our evenings would be family time for us. We would not accept any invitations that would keep me out of the house at dinnertime and into the evening. We wanted to have dinner as a family and reserve the evening for ourselves, and I made a personal commitment to tuck Grace into bed every night.

Before we started our family, we talked about examples of ministers we knew who had put the ministry before the family and how that affected their children. We didn't want our children to grow up and turn away from God because Dad was never home or never had time for them. We desired our children to grow up loving God and people, so we set parameters to protect and guard our family life. By God's grace, we have lived by our convictions.

One day we drove into town, and we saw several large banners throughout the city that read, "God Loves Arusha." They announced the venue and time for a city-wide event that would take place the following weekend. I had never heard of a church doing a city-wide event for the city and asked Veronica about it. She had never heard of any church doing something like that either. While we were curious about the event, we didn't think too much about it.

Soon after that, I received a call from our friend, Pastor Philip of Calvary Temple. He called and asked if I could come and teach about missions the following Sunday. The church was doing an outreach that afternoon, and he wanted me to encourage the congregation, so I happily agreed. After services were over, he invited our family to join them in the outreach. That is when I discovered Calvary Temple was organizing the "God Loves Arusha" event.

When we arrived, we saw hundreds of people being ministered to and having their practical needs being met. Lawyers had a tent available for counsel, and in another, physical exams were being conducted. A band was playing on a portable stage. Dental exams were taking place in a tent, and food was being served, all free to the public. I was both stunned and amazed at what was taking place!

Later that week, I had lunch with Pastor Philip, and we talked about the event. He said it was the first time the church had ever attempted to do anything like that for the city. The church members did everything, with the doctors, dentists, and lawyers volunteering their time. He told me that before we came and did Global Pathway, the church was involved with missions, but they didn't have a concrete plan, and their involvement was not well organized. After the church implemented Global Pathway, the congregation became excited about doing missions, and their influence expanded. The church continues to grow in how they do missions. They have sent several congregation people to various parts of Tanzania and Burundi as missionaries.

After being married for some time, Veronica and I sensed a change was coming, and we explored our options. We prayed about moving to Mwanza, a city on the edge of Lake Victoria in northern Tanzania. Veronica had attended university and lived there for a few years, and I had assisted in a Global Pathway conference there before I moved to Tanzania. Our Pamoja missionary colleagues planned to extend their influence and impact. One strategy was to open offices in various parts of the country as distribution centers for the materials they produced. Another option we prayed and talked about was moving to Dodoma, which had become the country's capital. We kept those possibilities in prayer and made preliminary plans to visit both regions to scout out the land and put our feet on the ground. But then the Lord opened another door for us to walk through.

Along with the vision to expand the Pamoja ministries' impact and influence, our colleagues, Jacob, Kim, and James Mills, moved to Eldoret, Kenya—a short two-hour drive from the Kenya/Uganda border. They had found a home in a new housing development. The day had come for the family to depart for their new adventure in Kenya. We offered to help and packed our car with their belongings and followed them to Eldoret.

Our plan was a good, solid plan. We talked and prayed about it, and we just needed to execute it. Usually, when a plan is executed is when the fun takes place! We planned to drive straight through to Eldoret, about a thirteen-hour drive from Arusha, unload their belongings, and spent the night there. Then the following day, we would drive back to Limuru, which is just outside of Nairobi, spend the day and night, and then return to Arusha the following day.

Things were going according to plan; we crossed into Kenya with no problem and were making pretty good time. The highway would pass the outskirts of Limuru on our way to Eldoret, and we anticipated arriving there shortly after dark. However, we discovered a hiccup we hadn't accounted for. There was a traffic jam as we neared Limuru, and we couldn't figure out the problem. As we approached, we saw hundreds of cars and trucks sitting still in both directions. I followed Jacob, and he was following other vehicles taking a detour and getting off the freeway. After sitting in the traffic jam for over thirty minutes, we were moving again. We thought the detour would bypass the bottleneck, and we would reconnect with the freeway and continue our journey to Eldoret.

After we passed through Limuru and arrived at the freeway entrance, we saw vehicles in the middle of the road up on blocks. The tires had been taken off and set on fire. Protesters blocked all the freeway entrances and exits in both directions. It was like a movie scene. We later discovered the people were protesting against the government. They would block all freeway entrances and exits in and out of Limuru for the remainder of the day.

As missionaries, we are used to things not going as planned, so we adjusted our schedule. We couldn't complete our travel to Eldoret that day, but the freeway opened back up early the following morning. The next day was extremely long, as it is a six-hour drive to Eldoret from Limuru. We made it to Eldoret, and we saw the home the Mills' would live in. We unloaded our vehicles and then turned around and returned to Limuru and spent a couple of days there before returning to Arusha.

Jacob and Kim Mills had scheduled a furlough to the United States before they moved to Eldoret. They had been living in Eldoret for just a few months when it came time to travel. They asked us if we would temporarily move into their home and also take over the scheduled Global Pathway conferences and keep the ministry running while they were gone. Veronica and I prayed and talked about it, and we both felt peace, so we agreed to move to Eldoret. Grace was just two months old when we moved. We didn't think much about it then, but as I'm writing this, it was crazy for us to make that move with a newborn infant, especially considering we were new parents! It was only supposed to be a four-month stay. That was our plan, but God had a different plan for us.

Kenya: Our Next Assignment

We arrived in Eldoret about a week before the Mills family departed for the United States. They showed us around town and introduced me to the pastors hosting the Global Pathway conferences. That week was a whirlwind of activity, meeting people, receiving final instructions, and getting to know our way around town.

Eldoret is a relatively small town, with a population of about four hundred and fifty thousand people. A new mall had just opened, and we were blessed to see KFC, as well as a well-known Kenyan restaurant chain that served burgers and steaks. I am passionate about burgers, so I was pleased we would have dining options. One main highway cuts through the center of town, which, depending on the direction you are traveling, will either take you to the Uganda/Kenya border or Nairobi. English is widely spoken in Kenya, so communication was easy.

One thing I noticed right away is Eldoret is windy. The wind blew every day, and I didn't like it. It reminded me of my childhood where I grew up with the wind blowing in basically one direction. I didn't like it as a child, and I certainly didn't like it living in Kenya! The wind and dust contributed to my cough over the previous couple of years. Along with the cough, I noticed times of shortness of breath, more so than what I was used to. The cough would linger, then go away, only to return.

The first Global Pathway conference we conducted was in Malaba, on the Kenya/Uganda border. It is a small border town of about seven thousand people, and despite its small size, it was incredibly congested. The highway leading to Malaba is used to transport goods into Uganda. It is the main route for trucks going into Kampala and beyond. Trucks stretched for several kilometers before reaching the border, waiting to go through and clear Customs. They blocked traffic, leaving only the oncoming lane and the dirt beside it for personal vehicles to travel on.

There is a saying we had heard several times since being in Kenya, "When in Kenya, do as the Kenyans do." When we made our first trip to Malaba and encountered the trucks blocking traffic, we sat parked behind that long line of trucks for what seemed like forever. Our turn-off to the church was just about two kilometers ahead, but we were stuck behind what seemed like hundreds of trucks. Cars that came up behind me passed and drove on the lane for oncoming traffic, forcing the oncoming cars to swerve off the road and onto the dirt to let them pass. After a long time of waiting, I boldly got behind a vehicle that passed me and drove slowly until I reached our turnoff. That became a regular practice whenever we visited.

The church was called Maranatha, and we hit it off with the bishop instantly. We both had children named Grace, who coincidentally were born on the same day!

The hotel we stayed at during the conference was "the best" hotel in the city. With the five-star rating system for hotels, I would say it wouldn't even garner one star. The rooms were extremely tight with no ventilation and came with only a mosquito net and fan, which didn't have a regular plug-in as you would expect in the United States. The plug was two wires to insert into each prong in the wall socket!

However, this hotel was the safest one in town, and it included break-fast at ten dollars per night.

The bishop had planted twenty churches in the region. He wanted all his pastors to attend the conference and learn how to implement missions into their congregations. Some Kenyan pastors had already gone through the Global Pathway certification program and were trained to be facilitators.

Veronica and I had a vision to train a team of Kenyan pastors who would teach alongside us with the goal of releasing them to facilitate Global Pathway conferences on their own. We planned to work our-selves out of a job by training the pastors with whom we had relation-ships. We had a connection with two pastors, and at our first confer-ence, we invited one to join us. That week was powerful! All twenty invited pastors attended the conference. Grace was just a few months old and was the star of the show. Veronica and I took turns tending to Grace as the other taught.

After the conference, the bishop and I had a debriefing about what took place. He was so impressed with the potential impact Global Pathway would have in his churches that he wanted to introduce us to the main bishop over all Kenya's Maranatha churches to implement Global Pathway in all the Kenyan churches.

We did another conference in a small nearby town called Turbo. Jacob had befriended a pastor who had just moved to Turbo, plant-ed a church, and agreed to do a conference with his congregation. One pastor certified to teach Global Pathway lived in Eldoret, and we became friends. He and I did the conference together for that small congregation.

Veronica and I were amazed at the open doors the Lord gave us. When we arrived in Eldoret, it was like stepping on an automatic door opener. Without trying or any effort on our part, doors for ministry opened. The wind of the Spirit was blowing on us, and we quickly gained favor with local pastors and leaders. We sensed God was expanding our vision to reach out into Uganda. He gave us several contacts with bishops who asked us to come to their cities to do Global Pathway conferences. We were entering a new ministry season.

While on furlough in the United States, the Mills were asked to move back to Tanzania and step into the role of Director of Pamoja Ministries. The current director had a family health crisis they could not handle in Tanzania because of the sub-par medical care. They went to Nairobi to be near doctors who could monitor the situation. Jacob called and explained the situation and asked what we thought about permanently moving to Eldoret. Although we made no decision, we agreed to pray. Over the next several weeks, as we prayed and talked, we felt peace in our spirits to stay in Eldoret. God was opening doors for us and expanding our vision, and we felt at ease about staying where we were.

When their furlough was complete, the Mills returned to Tanzania and moved into our house, where our furniture and belongings were. We took over the lease on their house in Eldoret. They returned in January, and Veronica and I planned to take our first furlough to the United States as a family the following May.

Veronica and I conducted a Global Pathway conference in Kampala, Uganda, in February of 2019. That opportunity came because of the Malaba conference we did. That bishop connected us with a friend who had a network of Uganda churches. Jacob agreed to come help teach, along with our colleague in Eldoret, who had been assisting us in our conferences. Crossing the border into Uganda was absolutely chaotic. A new road was being constructed, and cars and trucks had to make their way through a ditch on a dirt road. Clearing Immigration was so complicated that we had to hire someone to help us with our passports and the requirements for taking our car out of Kenya and into Uganda. It took us several hours just to cross the border, but we were finally in Uganda!

It was the first time we traveled in Uganda, and we were not familiar with the roads. It took us several hours longer than we anticipated to arrive at our Kampala destination. Several hundred attended the conference. We usually paid our way wherever we went, but the church paid for our hotel and meals this time. Since they knew we were a family, they rented a two-bedroom apartment in a hotel for us, and we were comfortable.

We stayed after the conference was over and preached in the Sunday services. I remember to this day what happened as we walked into service that morning. The pastor was talking, and when we entered, all eyes looked in our direction, and people gasped out loud. It distracted the pastor, who asked why the congregation wasn't paying attention to what he was saying. In unison, they all looked at Veronica and said, "She's so beautiful!" The pastor broke down in laughter, and I stood a little taller in my shoes. Yes, I am married to the most beautiful woman the good Lord ever created!

38

Work Permits and Residency Visas

One of the most challenging issues missionaries face in foreign countries is having the proper work permits and residency visas. Obtaining them is extremely important, and in my experience, the process has never been easy. When I lived in Thailand, I couldn't get my work permit until I first had a residency visa. I couldn't secure my residency visa until I had a sponsoring organization. In most cases, the organization sponsoring a missionary used the work permit and residency visa for control and manipulation, always using the threat of deportation. And the government constantly changed the work permit rules and requirements based upon who ran the government. In Thailand, every new administration changed the requirements for foreigners living there, so we never knew what we would need to renew our visas each year.

When I moved to Tanzania, the process was relatively straightforward. I was granted a work permit and resident visa for two years. Several months before they expired, we submitted the visa renewal applications, theoretically receiving the renewal before the expiration date. In my case, when the paperwork was submitted, the government added policies for granting work permits. I fell under the new rules, which put me in limbo for the next year.

Veronica and I were in between countries then. Our official residence was in Tanzania, but we stayed in Eldoret while the Mills were on furlough. We agreed to move to Kenya but had not yet started the visa application process. We spent Christmas in Arusha and had until the first week of January to exit the country before my work permit expired. Once we left Tanzania, I wouldn't be allowed to return until they approved my work permit. We didn't know it then, but it would be well over a year before the new work permit was issued.

Saying Goodbye

As the time for departure to Kenya arrived, we said our goodbyes to friends, not knowing how long it would be before we would return. Grace was about six months old and a bundle of joy for us. We packed our car as full as possible with things we would need and departed Arusha for the last time. We left early in the morning and drove in silence most of the way to the border, with Veronica and Grace sleeping in the backseat and me lost in my thoughts.

I thought, *what am I doing?* I was taking Veronica away from her family and everything she knew. How is she handling that? We had talked about the instability of missionary life before we were married, but I wondered if this was what she had bargained for. Was she ready to leave her country and family and friends behind? Would she resent me for taking her away?

When we crossed into Kenya, it felt like a door had been closed, never to open again. It was surreal. Being single and moving from nation to nation was one thing, but now I had a family, and my actions didn't just affect me anymore. Was I doing the right thing? We eventually broke the silence, and as we talked about our future together in Kenya, our spirits lightened. We didn't know if we would ever return to Tanzania.

God continued to open doors for us. We spent the next several months in Kenya doing conferences and building relationships. We found a church where we could settle, and we felt like Kenya was our home.

We had taken over the lease from the Mills and were using their furniture. The Mills had taken over our Tanzania house and were using our furniture. We talked about when and how to transfer our belongings, knowing it would be difficult. I hadn't applied for and received my visa and residency permit, so legally, we could not bring our belongings across the border from Tanzania. We had planned our first trip to the United States for later that summer, so we all agreed to switch our furniture after we returned. We were delighted to travel for the first time as a family, and Veronica was especially excited. She had dreamed of visiting the United States ever since she was a little girl.

I continued to struggle with my health. The challenge with the cough had continued, and I noticed the shortness of breath was getting worse. I had been to several Eldoret doctors, but they couldn't find the problem. Each doctor would give me a round of antibiotics which would make the cough go away, but sooner or later, it would return. Veronica was concerned about my health, and I promised her I would get checked out by a doctor when we got to the United States. I told her the health care in the States was the best in the world, and I could get a proper diagnosis. That promise would prove difficult to keep.

We gathered the needed paperwork to apply for my Kenyan work permit and residency visa before leaving for our trip. We thought they could process our application, and my visa would be granted by the time we returned. However, the government added additional requirements for first-time visa applicants the day before I submitted my paperwork. Now, I had to obtain a police clearance certificate from my previous home in Nevada. I had acquired one several years previously for a job, so I knew it wouldn't be a problem. However, when we made our travel plans, we were to visit Nevada at the end of our trip, which would set our application process back by several months. When we got to Nevada, it took just a few minutes to get the necessary certificate, and we sent it to Nairobi. The application had been submitted, and now we would just wait for approval.

Our First Furlough as a Family

The United States trip was wonderful, but not without challenges. Veronica enjoyed every moment of being in the States, a dream come true for her. Grace celebrated her first birthday while we were stateside, and she was the star of the show wherever we went.

We needed to take Grace to see a doctor when we first arrived in Florida, but no doctor would see us without medical insurance, and appointments were booked at least six months out. I wondered what had happened to health care in my country, and I was astounded by how difficult it was to get an appointment. The medical clinics would not see Grace without medical insurance, even after explaining we were missionaries and did not have coverage. Finally, we found one clinic that would see Grace and allow us to pay cash. It was convenient as it was right on the beach, and we played in the sand and water after the visit!

I still hadn't seen a doctor, and I had limited options without insurance. The only place I could get a doctor's appointment was at a California medical clinic with a bad reputation. Comparable to my Kenya experience, the doctor did a chest x-ray and gave me a round of antibiotics. I could not get a medical professional to look deeper into what was going on with my health. Like the previous visits, the antibiotics only helped for a short time before the cough and breathing challenges came back. We ended our trip without discovering the root cause of my medical challenge.

I had broken the promise I made to Veronica, and it affected her as we departed the United States. We realized our travel and appointment schedule was too extensive. We were both exhausted when we returned to Eldoret. Our arrival back in Kenya was on November 1, 2019, and our world would soon come crashing down around us.

39

Crisis of Faith

I don't know why I didn't pursue seeing a doctor in the United States. We weren't in one place for long, but I should have tried to get a thorough check-up. Maybe I didn't want to face the fact something was wrong. I had been relatively healthy during my life, so maybe I thought what I was experiencing would pass. Maybe I was afraid. Whatever the reasons, they were all just excuses. The cough and shortness of breath continued. When I laid down to sleep, I couldn't get enough air.

I checked around and found I could have a complete physical done at a Nairobi hospital. I hadn't had a physical done since I lived in Thailand and had been told I had Hepatitis B and lived through that health crisis. Both Veronica and I were anxious when we got to the hospital, but we hoped to find an answer. When I told the doctor about my breathing, she asked the following questions. Did I smoke? Yes, I had smoked from about age eight until twenty-four, but I hadn't smoked for thirty-two years. Family history of COPD? Yes, my dad possibly died from emphysema. After answering her questions, the doctor suggested I have a breathing test. She said the results would show whether I had asthma or COPD. I looked at her and said in disbelief, "COPD?" She said matter-of-factly, "Yes, COPD." I felt the blood drain from my face at those words as I was escorted out of the office to have blood drawn for lab tests.

After I completed all the tests, we were asked to wait to see the doctor for the results. We were ushered into the doctor's office, and as we sat down, we made small talk. Before I had the physical done, I told Veronica everything would turn out good, and I would be told I needed to lose weight, and maybe my cholesterol would be a little high.

As the doctor went over my results, she confirmed my prognosis. We had just returned from the United States, and I had gained about twenty-five pounds, and sure enough, I needed to lose that added weight! Then she looked at me and said, "Mr. Wheeler, the other test results show you have a mild case of COPD." "You're kidding, right?" I replied, not believing what I had heard. She went over the tests, but I heard little of what she said, as the words *COPD* rolled over and over in my head. I was stunned, and it felt like I had been sucker-punched. I heard my name being spoken, which brought me back to reality. I looked at Veronica, holding Grace, composed, and talking with the doctor. The doctor gave me a prescription for two inhalers and asked me to return for a follow-up consultation in two months. It was December, just about a week before Christmas.

We drove back to the hotel in silence, each of us lost in our thoughts. I spoke little over the next several days as I thought about the ramifications. I knew COPD was not a good diagnosis. Although I knew several people who had died from that disease, I didn't know much about it. I researched on the internet, and what I found shook me to my core. One website showed the disease's different stages, and I went to the stage the doctor diagnosed me with and looked at these words, "The lifespan for this stage is around fourteen years." *Fourteen years. Fourteen years.*

I was fifty-six, had been married for just a little over two years, and Grace was just over a year. My thoughts raced as fear gripped my soul and wouldn't let go. I felt as if I had just been given a death sentence. Would I see my girl grow up? Would I walk her down the aisle or live to see my grandchildren? What would happen to Veronica? Was that what she bargained for when she married me? I tried to control my thoughts, but they crept back again as soon as I pushed them from my mind. I hadn't talked for three days.

A dark heavy cloud replaced the joy and laughter that had filled our home. Veronica asked me one morning what I was thinking about, and I told her I didn't want my thoughts to come out of my mouth. Veronica does not cry much, but as we talked, she shed tears as she said, "I am glad we went to see the doctor. At least now we have an answer. After these past two years, we finally know what is going on, and now we know how to pray."

Pray. How was I supposed to pray? A theological battle was happening inside me that I needed to settle before even thinking about praying. Could I ask God to heal me? I mean, after all, I smoked for several years when I was younger. Even though I hadn't smoked for over thirty-two years, did that excuse me from the consequences of my actions?

The enemy of my soul jumped into my inward conversation with myself, with the thoughts of, *you will reap what you sow, you smoked all those years, you can't ask God to help you now. You don't deserve to be healed.* Yes, I know I don't deserve to be healed. I know I will reap what I have sown. But isn't that the point of salvation and grace? God already did for me what I could not do for myself. I didn't deserve to be forgiven. I did nothing that would warrant my salvation, but

God in His mercy took the punishment for my sin so I could be reconciled, saved, healed, delivered, and made whole.

An Anchor of Hope

I have preached on and believe in healing. I have taught divine healing in our Bible schools. Over the years, I had prayed for many people who needed healing and saw many miracles. I had faith in God and His Word that He would heal others, but did I have faith God would heal me? That was the issue—the *crisis of faith* for me at that moment. Would God heal me? Would God want to heal me? Did I deserve to be healed? As I struggled inwardly with these questions, the Lord impressed upon me to read Philippians 4:6–8 (TPT):

> *Don't be pulled in different directions or worried about a thing. Be saturated in prayer throughout each day, offering your faith-filled requests before God with overflowing gratitude. Tell Him every detail of your life, then God's wonderful peace that transcends human understanding will make the answers known to you through Jesus Christ. Keep your thoughts continually fixed on all that is authentic and real, honorable and admirable, beautiful and respectful, pure and holy, merciful and kind. And fasten your thoughts on every glorious work of God, praising Him always.*

Within these verses, I found hope, an anchor I could hold on to, and instruction. The Lord said to me through these Scriptures not to worry because everything would be okay. I trusted God with my life up to that point, and I could continue to trust Him. I was instructed to fix my thoughts on the reality of God's Word, not on my circumstances, and not let my mind wander into the what-ifs.

Planning for the Future

Over the next several days, weeks, and months, I saw how this diagnosis stripped away Veronica's security. I realized if something happened to me, there was no one to take care of Veronica. Veronica had been facing fears and uncertainties as well. As we talked, Veronica cried as she shared her fears, "If something were to happen to you, I don't know what I would do. I don't know what would happen to Grace. Would we be separated, with her being in the United States and me living in Tanzania? I wouldn't even know how to survive."

It was my responsibility to make sure Veronica and Grace were taken care of if I died, *and I was not prepared.* It was a wake-up call that caused me to panic. I needed to take care of this, and I felt the added stress and burden of knowing I hadn't done what I needed to care for my family. I had accomplished some things. I had updated my will, and when we were in the United States, we added Veronica's name to my bank accounts, but we were lacking in many other vitally important areas.

As we went through pre-marital counseling, we talked about who would handle the finances and be responsible for paying the bills. Veronica didn't want that responsibility, so we decided I would handle the finances. Although we talked about how we spent money, I never actually taught her how we paid our bills with online banking. Veronica said, "I wouldn't know what to do if something were to happen to you. I wouldn't know how to pay bills or get money out of the bank. I would be completely lost with our finances." I thought I had been a good husband and provider, but at that moment, I realized how we had handled our finances contributed to the loss of her security. We did our online banking together, and I taught her how to access our bank account and credit cards, which was a great help to both of us.

I had a ten thousand dollar life insurance policy through Go To Nations, which they required missionaries to have, but we quickly realized that would not be enough to financially care for Veronica and our growing family. I looked around for additional life insurance, but every company I talked with declined to insure me once they discovered I was a missionary. However, we purchased a supplemental life insurance policy through Go To Nations.

We also discussed seeking U.S. citizenship for Veronica. We planned to move to the United States once we got older and could no longer be active on the mission field. In our retirement years, we would obtain citizenship for Veronica. Tanzania's law didn't allow dual citizenship, and we thought the laws would change in the future. Now, we faced a different reality. Grace is a citizen of both Tanzania and the United States. We planned for her to get her college education in the United States. If Veronica hadn't received her U.S. citizenship by that time, she and Grace would be separated, which was something we had not planned for. We discussed the possibility of changing our long-term plans and researched the required steps to obtain a green card for Veronica.

We still needed to work toward goals, but we were making progress, and we both felt better about the future. As 2019 came to a close, we had no idea the COVID pandemic would turn the world upside down in early 2020.

40

Divine Establishment

We realized we needed a Sabbath when we returned from the United States. People sometimes have the misconception that when missionaries come to the United States on furlough, they are on vacation, but that is not the reality. Furlough is often a grueling experience for missionaries.

That first trip we took as a family was especially difficult. We spent five months traveling across America by car, and our schedule was extremely challenging. We lived out of our suitcases, stayed in hotels or in friends' or familys' homes, and ate out almost every meal. Although we saw much of the country, and had the blessing of seeing our friends, family, and ministry partners, we were exhausted when we returned to Eldoret. We needed time to recover, so we took time before stepping back into doing ministry. Our schedule had been cleared before we left Kenya. We were glad not to have ministry scheduled during the Christmas and New Year holidays.

As December rolled into January, we heard the Word of the Lord for the new year. Our pastor did a series of teachings declaring it would be a year of divine establishment. One Scripture reference that spoke to our hearts was Job 22:28: "You will also decide and decree a thing, and it will be established for you" (AMP). Veronica and I talked about what divine establishment meant for us, and we sensed 2020 would be a time for our financial house to be established. I had been working on paying off my credit card debt since 2014 and still owed a large balance, and Veronica had a school loan. We made a list of declarations we would confess over our lives every day during our prayer times. We focused our declarations on four areas: our family, finances, health, and finally, our ministry. We declared and decreed every day we would be debt-free in 2020.

We had submitted our work permit and residency visas for Tanzania and Kenya. We didn't know how long the process would take, and we just needed to wait. We settled into a daily routine, and we recovered from the United States trip. We heard news reports of a virus from China that spread, and while the world was concerned, it didn't affect us much in Kenya at first. We received news my work permit and resident visa for Tanzania had been approved. We were ecstatic, as we had been waiting for well over a year for the approval.

Living in an Upside Down World

By that time, COVID-19 was rapidly spreading worldwide, and countries and borders were closing down. We needed to travel to Tanzania and appear at the Immigration Office in Arusha to have the work permit officially stamped into my passport. We were on our way to Arusha and spent the night in Nairobi when we faced a dilemma.

Kenya had recorded the first case of COVID-19 on March 12, and Tanzania had recorded its first case on March 16. When we got to Nairobi, the border was still open, but there was talk of closing it. Would we get to Arusha and safely return to Kenya? If the border closed while we were in Tanzania, we would be stuck there for who knew how long. Did we want to take a chance on being stranded in Tanzania, not knowing when we would return? One option we discussed was to go to Tanzania and return to Kenya the same day, thinking maybe we could get my passport stamped and cross the border before it closed. That would be too risky, so we stayed in Kenya. The border closed later that day, and we would have been stranded if we would have traveled to Tanzania. The world was shutting down. I had never experienced anything like it in my lifetime.

Suddenly, it seemed there wasn't anywhere safe, and for the next several months, I battled fear. Because of my COPD diagnosis, I was in the high-risk category for contracting COVID-19, which was now classified as a pandemic. It was incredibly stressful for our family. We were dealing with a health crisis, and I had not prepared to take care of my family if something happened to me. That weighed heavily on my heart and kept me awake many nights. I was a man of faith, but fear had gripped my soul and wouldn't let go.

The U.S. embassy sent me notices, urging me to evacuate the country. The notices would state, "There is one flight departing Nairobi in two days. We urge all U.S. citizens to depart Kenya before flights into and out of the country are suspended." Oh, my goodness, I thought, what are we going to do? Veronica didn't have a visa for the United States. Would the U.S. government force me to evacuate, leaving my wife and child stranded in Kenya? I felt trapped with the world closing in on me.

Kenya eventually closed their borders, and we couldn't leave even if we wanted to. I had never felt so out of control in my life. We were trapped and alone with no way out. Who knew how long we would be in this situation? Different scenarios played out in my mind over and over again, adding to my stress. I was fearful both of dying in Kenya and also being forced to evacuate, leaving my wife and child behind. I

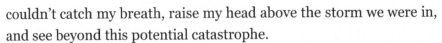

couldn't catch my breath, raise my head above the storm we were in, and see beyond this potential catastrophe.

Slowly, Kenya shut down. The COVID-19 hotspots were Nairobi and Mombasa, which were far away. We paid close attention to the government announcements. A nationwide curfew was put into effect, and facemasks were mandatory in all public areas. Handwashing and sanitizing were compulsory. The disease spread to other parts of the country as people left Nairobi for the villages. The government stopped all people from entering or leaving Nairobi for several months.

Because of my COPD health risk, I was not allowed to go out in public, so Veronica did the grocery shopping while Grace and I stayed in the car. We secluded ourselves and hunkered down, not knowing when things would turn around. The government banned gatherings of people, so churches were not allowed to have in-person services, and everything moved to online streaming. All our ministry plans had been disrupted, canceled, or postponed. It was like the end of the world had come.

After the initial shock wore off, we adjusted to what people were calling *the new normal*. The fear I experienced gave way to hope. While we were cautious whenever we went out in public, we adapted. We learned to trust the Lord more deeply during that unprecedented time. We were limiting our interactions with people by staying home as much as we could. We had been declaring we would be debt-free in 2020, so we paid off as we could each month on our credit cards, and we made progress in our financial goals.

Shifting Our Ministry Focus

We found new avenues to minister to people. Our ministry focus shifted from training large crowds to one-on-one personal ministry. A man paralyzed in his legs sits on a bench along the dirt road outside our housing complex. One day Veronica stated she would witness to him and lead him to the Lord. As she exercised, she would stop and talk with him, and after several weeks, she announced she had led him to the Lord! Veronica discipled him, and we gave him a Bible to read. Grace took a special liking to him and prayed daily that God would bless him and heal his legs. Soon, our hearts were moved with compassion, and we purchased food for him whenever we went shopping.

Another man we ministered to works in our housing development as a landscaper and handyman. We hired him to do extra work for us, and he and I formed a friendship. When we first met, he said his wife and young child had left him, and he wanted them to come home. One thing that touched my heart was his thankful attitude toward us. We gave him money each month as a blessing for doing work for us. Every time we sent him money, I always got three or four voice messages from him saying, "Thank you, sir. Thank you so much." I had never met anyone who exhibited such a thankful heart, and it impressed me, so I enjoyed giving him money for his work.

Grace took to him, and she added him to her prayer list. She prayed his wife and child would come home. Since he worked in our development, we saw him several times throughout the day. Grace would always run to him, say hello, and give him gifts, usually a flower she had picked. I told him she was praying for his wife and child to come home, and often Grace would stop and pray for him as we talked.

After praying for several months, he said his wife and child were coming home! He was so excited God had answered Grace's prayer! We continued to have "teaching" moments throughout the next several weeks. One day he said, "Sir, I want to teach my child how to pray as Grace does." I could see God was reaching in and changing his heart. He asked for a Bible to read with his family when they came home. When he reunited with his wife and child, the first thing he did was invite us to his home to introduce us to his family. It was the first home in Eldoret we had been invited to, and we were excited to meet his wife and daughter. We visited with them and prayed over them as a couple. It was a highlight for God to use us in some small way in this young man's life.

One day we talked, and I could tell something was not right. He said he and his wife had a fight. He said, "I got angry with her, and I slapped her twice on the face." My heart sank as I heard that, and I wondered how I should respond. I said, "It is not right for you to hit your wife." When I saw him the next day, I asked how things were going. He said, "My wife and I talked about everything, and we have decided to adopt your culture, and I have promised my wife I will never hit her again." Wow, I thought, I have influence with this man.

As time went on, we talked about marriage and how the husband and wife should treat each other. We talked one day about work I wanted him to do, and he said, "You don't have to pay me. I do these things for you and don't expect anything from you. You take time to listen to me, and I know you really care. You are not like most mzungus (Kiswahili word for foreigner). You take your time to speak with me." He choked up with emotion and held back tears. We explained we enjoyed paying him for the work he does for us, and I thanked him for telling me it wasn't necessary. I encouraged him to ask God to supply money for him and told him God would always care for his needs. I walked away from that conversation amazed by what God was doing. I had no idea I was having such an impact on his life.

He told me his wife wanted to find a job, and we prayed. Grace prayed every night before bed, "God, give his wife a good job." We continued to pray, and one afternoon, I said, "Grace has been praying every night for your wife to find a good job. It would be good if she found something she could make with her hands to sell." I left it at that, and a couple of weeks later, he came and said, "My wife decided that instead of finding a job working for someone else, she would open a fruit and vegetable stand. She can set her hours and work after our daughter goes to school and is home when school is out." He then said, "After you talked to me about asking God for money, we did that, and since then, we have never been without cash in our pockets." Forming this relationship and seeing how the Lord used us to minister to this man and his family has been one of the greatest joys of our lives throughout 2020!

We discovered a restaurant in town that made chapati and githeri, some of our favorite African food. One morning, we stopped to pick up chapati. We saw a large gathering of homeless people milling around the area. I didn't think much of it; however, God worked in Veronica's heart. A few weeks later, she said, "I want to find out about those homeless people we saw and see if we can do something to help." We asked the restaurant owner what those people were doing there that day, and she replied a business gave bread to eat on Fridays. We talked about what we could do, and the more we talked, I realized God was stirring Veronica's heart to do something. We approached the restaurant owner to see if they would work with us in preparing a healthy meal to give to the homeless on that day as well, and they agreed to partner with us. We didn't want anyone to know where the food was coming from. Because of the pandemic and social distancing regulations, we did the feedings without any fanfare.

For several months, we worked with the restaurant. They provided the meals and handed them out to the homeless while we sat in our car parked alongside the road. We usually fed about fifty to sixty people at each outreach. We felt it was important the local businesses were seen as the ones providing the meals, which worked well for us. We knew this wasn't our primary calling, but we simply saw a need and took what we had in our hands to meet that need.

We both wanted to talk with our pastors about what we were doing and made an appointment with them. As we shared our hearts, we were pleased to hear the church had a ministry to the same homeless people at one time. When the church moved their current location, that ministry ended. They encouraged us to do something more than providing a meal and to feed the people spiritually as well.

A plan was formed to have church services when we provided meals, and the pastors agreed to provide members of their pastoral staff to preach. Veronica and I were so happy after that meeting! We continued to take a back seat and allow the church pastors to lead in ministering to the homeless in our city. We began turning that ministry over to the church, and we felt God was using us as a catalyst for our church to resume the ministry that had been laid down.

The reputation we had quickly spread throughout that area, and other businesses did projects as well. One day, we just happened to be at the restaurant picking up chapatis and saw many homeless people wearing face masks. We asked the restaurant owner what was happening, and she replied, "One business here has been watching you give food away, and they want to do something too. They looked at what they had, and they could provide face masks." We had no idea people were watching what we were doing, and we were blessed others were following our lead.

I remember the first church service we held for that homeless group. We gave the restaurant owner the task of finding a place to have a short church service before giving away the meals. Previously, we gave our meals away by the side of the road, and it was a quick event. Now we needed to find a place where we could have a service. The restaurant owner found an empty grass lot around the corner that the owner agreed to let us use. Our pastor arranged for one of his pastors to lead the service.

When we arrived at the venue, we heard singing in the distance. The homeless were so excited to hear there would be a service that they arrived early and sang praises to the Lord while they waited for us to arrive! We were glad to have help as it was difficult to control the crowds. When we began having services, the number of people who came increased, and we provided meals to over seventy people. We were saddened to see many women living on the streets with infants and toddlers.

Our largest event was the Christmas celebration, the Friday before Christmas. We purchased bottled water, toothpaste and toothbrushes, crackers, and chocolate candy bars. We provided a special meal, while a local grocery store donated bars of soap. The crowd was particularly unruly that day, and we were glad we had a couple of pastors from our church to help with crowd control. That was our last event for 2020. When the new year began, the youth department took over the ministry. We passed the baton and had successfully worked ourselves out of a job. We started a ministry and then handed it over to the nationals to run with it.

Finding Financial Freedom

We declared every day for well over a year that we would be debt-free in 2020. The pandemic postponed our ministry plans for the year, so we focused on getting out from under our credit card debt. We cut back on our spending and put all the funds we could on our credit cards. We took several online classes about financial stewardship and adjusted our priorities. I had accumulated over twenty-six thousand dollars in credit card debt, which I had been paying off since 2014. We learned more about biblical stewardship, and we put our financial house in order. By God's grace and mercy, our hard work, sacrifice, and diligence paid off, and on December 15, 2020, we made our final payment on our credit card! We ended 2020 debt-free and entered 2021 with a clean slate financially! I was free from the financial bondage I had put myself under, and for the first time since 2014, I felt liberated. We acknowledged God's goodness in our lives. It would be a great Christmas.

41

Christmas—The Season of Great Joy and Sorrow

We decorated our Christmas tree early, and we were determined to have a good Christmas. The previous year my COPD diagnosis put a pall over the celebrations. Grace knew more about Christmas in 2020, and she loved singing Christmas carols. "Jingle Bells" was her favorite which she sang everywhere she went.

As a family, we had evolved with our Christmas celebrations. The first Christmas Veronica and I celebrated together, we each bought one present to put under the tree on Christmas Day. The second year, we managed to buy two presents each a couple of days before Christmas. In 2020, we had our tree up and presents for Grace several weeks before Christmas Day, a first for our family! Veronica did not grow up with the tradition of having a Christmas tree or a big celebration, so our Christmas celebration as a married couple changed from year to year.

Communicating with family in the United States has always been difficult on the mission field. When I lived in Thailand, I had an internet telephone, which worked off and on, depending on the internet traffic. I had a phone number people could use to call me, and for a time, it was sufficient. However, when I moved to Africa, the internet wasn't strong enough to use the phone, so Facebook Messenger became the main way I communicated with family and friends.

My brother, Glen, had been slow to join the twenty-first century and disliked cell phones, texting, and all the new technology that came with the evolution of the internet. He eventually got a computer and cell phone, embracing all the benefits available at his fingertips. He used to tease me about my cell phone, computers, and iPad, but when he joined Facebook, we communicated with each other frequently. In late November of 2020, he popped into my mind, so I wrote him a short message. When he replied, he shared he had been diagnosed with Stage 3 kidney disease. He had a good prognosis but needed more tests to determine the right treatment course.

On December 17, he sent me a message saying, "Now I'm positive for COVID-19." He was online, so I made a video call, and we talked. After having a fever for four days, he went to have the COVID test done. He felt fine and seemed in good spirits. The only symptom he had was the fever. I had Grace sitting next to me, and she talked with him for several minutes. We talked about family and how everyone was doing and got caught up. Just before we ended our conversation, Grace and I prayed for him. I saw him wipe a tear from his eye as we said goodbye. I didn't know that would be the last time I talked with Glen.

Glen Eldon Wheeler
1959–2020

The next day, Glen became worse. The other symptoms that accompany COVID-19 hit him hard, and he spent the next several days in bed. His last Facebook post on December 20 stated, "I need help! I can't kick this!" It scared me to read that post. My sister-in-law Carolyn was showing symptoms of COVID-19 as well, and she texted me every day to update me on how they were doing. Suddenly, I felt so far away and powerless. The wonder of the internet had brought our worlds closer, but now I felt the distance of the oceans that separated us. When I woke up on the morning of December 26, I saw Carolyn posted a message telling me Glen had been taken to the hospital during the night. That morning, she said he was resting comfortably and was on oxygen and fluids.

Glen is gone. I stared at that message for what seemed like forever. It was early morning on December 27. *Glen passed away today,* said another message. I didn't want to believe it. There must be some mistake. I didn't have a phone, so the only way my family could contact me was through a Facebook message. This can't be happening, not to our family, not now. My nephew and niece were planning to go to California to be with their mom and would arrive the next morning. I was stuck in Kenya and feeling isolated and trapped by my circumstances.

I had sent Glen a text message to his cell phone that said in part, "You can beat this, and you must fight." It was sent on the morning he died. Did he see it? My grief turned into anger in moments. I was angry at Glen. Why didn't he fight harder? Didn't he realize we needed him? If I were honest, I had moments when I was angry at God. "Why did You allow this to happen?" I questioned whether being a missionary was worth the tragedies and crises I had experienced. In those fleeting moments of doubt and confusion, I found comfort in the Scriptures.

This wasn't how it was supposed to end for Glen. He was supposed to retire, and in his later years, he would enjoy barbeque burgers and have a wonderful time traveling or doing whatever he wanted to. Glen had worked hard all his life, and he deserved time to enjoy the fruits of his labor, but he was robbed of that opportunity. I was robbed of having my brother around when I retired too. I felt cheated.

The Valley of the Shadow of Death

The next few weeks were difficult as our family walked through the valley of the shadow of death. My nephew and niece arrived in California the day after my brother died. Their mother was very sick after contracting COVID-19 while taking care of Glen. I got a message saying an ambulance took her to the hospital. For the next few days, it seemed as if we might lose Carolyn too.

Shortly after receiving that news, I got a message my aunt was also sent to the hospital and diagnosed with COVID-19 and pneumonia. A few weeks before that diagnosis, I talked with her. She was thrilled to hear we were having another baby. She was doing well when we had our last conversation. She passed away on January 10, 2021.

The best man at our wedding had also contracted the virus. It seemed COVID-19 was touching everyone I loved. Carolyn slowly recovered and was sent home from the hospital. When my niece returned to Texas, she contracted the virus and was sick for a time. It was all so sad and tragic and such a heavy loss, not only for us but for our whole family. In hindsight, I praise God we talked with both my brother and my aunt shortly before they passed away.

Sarah Elizabeth Wheeler

In the winter of 2020, which in Kenya is June through September, we talked about adding a baby sister or brother for Grace. We planned to have another baby, but the timing never seemed right. Grace was about to turn two when we discovered Veronica was pregnant!

Although we were ecstatic to add another child to our family, we were concerned about having our baby during the midst of COVID-19. Where would be the safest option for delivery? We wanted to have the baby delivered in Nairobi, where Grace was born, but Nairobi was a virus hotspot, and we were hesitant about exposing ourselves, so we opted to have the baby in Eldoret.

We were thrilled to hear we were having a baby girl, and Grace was excited she would be a big sister! We have heard each pregnancy is different, and we were pleased we didn't have challenges.

Once we found out we would have a girl, we discussed names. Veronica had a dream the baby was named Elizabeth, and we researched the meaning of that name. We discovered Elizabeth meant, *My God is an oath, My God is abundance, God promises, consecrated to God, God is perfection,* and *God gives*[3]. I wanted a name that expressed the joy we felt when we heard we were expecting. I came across the name Sarah, which means *Princess.* In Arabic, Sarah is translated to mean *joy and delight*[4]! One day we asked Grace what she wanted to call the baby, and without thinking, she quickly replied, "Ruthie." To this day, we don't know where she got that name because we don't know anyone named Ruth! When we researched the meaning, we discovered Ruth meant *companion, friend,* and *vision of beauty.*[5]

The *plan* was for me to be with Veronica in the delivery room as Sarah was born. However, because of the pandemic, there was uncertainty about what would happen. We planned for one of our Nairobi colleagues to come stay with Grace while we were at the hospital and help us for a few weeks afterward. The closer we got to the due date, the more intense the Kenya situation became, and our plan unraveled.

Another COVID-19 wave broke out and surged across the country. Just a few days before our colleague was scheduled to come from Nairobi, the government announced five counties, including Nairobi, would be locked down, with no one to enter or exit. *That's just great, now what are we going to do?*

We didn't know what to do, and several questions swirled around our minds. Who would stay with Grace while we were at the hospital? We heard reports the hospital we were scheduled to have our baby in was overrun with COVID-19 cases. Would it be safe to give birth there now? Would Veronica and the baby be at risk? Would I be safe? My COPD diagnosis the previous year changed everything. Now I needed to contemplate risk factors for going out in public.

Veronica suggested she go to the hospital by herself when labor started and give birth to our child alone while I stayed with Grace at the house. *Absolutely not. There is no way I'm going to allow that to happen.* I cannot tell you how stressful those days were for us as we struggled to develop a new plan. We had talked about hiring someone to come help around the house after the baby was born, and our pastor recommended someone they knew. We spent some time with her and asked if she would come and stay with Grace when it came time to have the baby, and she readily agreed.

Veronica was now at forty weeks with no sign of labor. It seemed Sarah Elizabeth was comfortable and not in a hurry to join our world. We had an appointment with our doctor, who suggested we induce labor, and we settled on the date of April 8, 2021. Since the pregnancy began, we had prayed every day that labor and delivery would be quick and without complications. We needed to trust God.

April 8 was a Thursday, and when we awoke in the morning, the air was heavy with apprehension and anxiety. As Veronica and I headed to the clinic for our doctor's appointment, we talked. "How do you feel, honey?" I asked. "I'm scared," she replied and continued, "I didn't sleep last night, and I couldn't eat anything." When I asked her what she was afraid of, she said, "I'm afraid I won't have the strength to push when the contractions start." I tried to comfort her, and we reminded ourselves we had been praying for a quick and easy delivery. We saw the doctor who administered the medicine to induce labor, and then went to the hospital. As we left, the doctor said, "It usually takes about four hours for labor to start, so I will check on you then."

We got to the hospital, and I looked at my watch; it was eight-thirty in the morning. As we filled out paperwork at the maternity ward, Veronica whispered to me, "I think it's starting already." I was handed the paperwork and told I needed to go register and make a payment. I didn't want to leave Veronica, but the nurse insisted. I looked at Veronica and asked her if she was going to be okay, and she said, "I'll be okay, but please hurry."

I wasn't gone too long, and by the time I returned, Veronica was in the last stages of labor. Contractions were one minute apart, and I asked the nurse to check her out, and when she did so, we discovered Veronica was dilated to eight. The baby was coming! A call was made to our doctor to come quickly, and we were not sure he would make it in time. I remember Veronica saying, "The baby is coming!" We soon heard our doctor's voice, and I was relieved he had arrived.

Within five minutes of the doctor arriving and three pushes by Veronica, our precious gift from God arrived. It was 10:15 a.m. that Sarah Elizabeth entered into our world. The worship song by Hillsong, "How Great Your Love Is," was playing when Sarah was born. I heard in the background these words, "Then sings my soul, how great Your love is, how great Your love is." I leaned over Veronica, kissed her, and whispered softly, "She's here! You did it!" Veronica raised her hands in worship as we thanked the Lord.

All the months of anxiety and fear we experienced melted away as we held our little girl in our arms. She was perfect. Our gift from God. We had truly experienced a miracle. It was just one hour and forty-five minutes from inducing labor to delivery, which was unheard of. We marveled at God's goodness. God, You have been so good to us!

We were discharged from the hospital at two o'clock and headed home. We were in the hospital for five hours. Grace met us as we parked the car in the driveway, "Dada, is baby sister here?" she asked as she ran to Veronica. She peeked at Sarah and said, "Hi, baby sister."

It was such a relief to be home. Safe. Secure. Protected. Those first few hours being together as a family was so special. We saw how quickly Grace bonded with her new little sister. We were in the bedroom, and Sarah cried. Grace ran to Mom's side and cried too, jumping up and down, trying to help her sister but not knowing what to do. It was so touching to see her heart being touched by her sister's cries. "She's okay, Grace. Sarah just wants to eat." Grace quickly calmed down and stayed by Mom's side as Veronica fed Sarah.

For months, every night before bed, as we said our prayers, Grace would put her hand on Veronica's stomach and pray, "Jesus, bless baby, give her good sleep, in Jesus' name. Amen." Then she would stoop down and kiss Veronica's stomach and say, "I love you, baby." On our first night together, we said our prayers. It was moving to see Grace lay her hands on Sarah's head and pray, "Jesus, bless sister, give her good sleep. In Jesus' name. Amen." She then kissed her on the cheek.

During a worldwide pandemic, in uncertainty, anxiety, fear, and the tragedy of losing my brother and aunt to COVID-19, we experienced a miracle.

42

Back to the Beginning

I have always had a problem with answering, "Where are you from?" because I am both from everywhere and nowhere. When I'm asked where I grew up, my mind wanders back to the yellow house on Candlelight Street in the Mariana Ranchos subdivision in Apple Valley, California. At the bottom of Mount Ord is my home—the yellow two-bedroom house where my mom, dad, two older brothers, and I lived. When I was a child, the house seemed huge; it was only when I became an adult when I realized how small it really was. Yes, that is where I grew up. That is *home* for me. The place where I lived the longest. My earliest memories are there.

I have been in several nations throughout my life and have lived in many places. But my heart has always longed to return to that place on Candlelight Street—that place called *home*. For it was in *that place*, for that short time, I experienced stability. Our family lived in that yellow house for about seven years of my life. My mom and dad separated when I was about nine or ten, and when that happened, my life turned upside down. I never really knew what stability or consistency was after that and would rarely live in one place for longer than two or three years at a time. I longed for the stability that always seemed just out of reach.

I grew up feeling like I was broken, and no one wanted me. In my teenage years, I constantly heard, "You will never amount to anything. You are worthless," and I lived up to those words spoken over me. I turned to alcohol and drugs to numb the pain and eventually became addicted. I didn't have a vision for my life and never thought I would live to see my twenty-first birthday, and I lived as if I would die. I was shocked when I lived to see twenty-one and remembered thinking, what will I *do now?*

In my early twenties, Jesus came into my life and rescued me. Jesus saw value in me. Jesus *wanted* me. He had created me with a purpose, and I was not an accident but was born on purpose, for a purpose. The moment Jesus came into my heart, I knew I had a reason for *being. I had a reason for living.* For the first time in my life, I had a reason for waking up in the morning. It's been almost thirty-five years since I accepted Jesus as my personal Lord and Savior and about twenty-five years since I first said yes to go wherever He wanted me to. While life has not always turned out as I expected, I never lost that sense of purpose; that *reason for living* awakened inside me on that day in September of 1987 when I first declared Jesus is Lord of my life. It has been an adventure, and for that, I am so very thankful.

EPILOGUE

We have been amazed at God's goodness toward us, as He has kept us safe and healthy. Despite our disrupted ministry plans, we have been incredibly productive. We felt another change and transition was coming and began pressing into the Holy Spirit for direction. We set several goals for ourselves while waiting on the Lord and for ministry to open back up. Once we obtained financial freedom, we prepared for the next step, not knowing what that would entail.

We began hearing about plans to develop our online equipping track for Go To Nations. Our leaders in Jacksonville talked with us about bringing Calvary Bible School to an online platform. We were asked to pray about relocating to the United States to pioneer this project. After praying and seeking the Lord, we felt a peace in our spirits that this was the next thing the Lord had for us. The adventure of faith continues as we plan to relocate to our world headquarters in 2022. While it will be a big adjustment to come off the mission field for a season, we are confident the Lord is guiding our steps, and we will continue to find fulfillment as we put our hand to the plow.

It has been my privilege to travel all over the world to preach the gospel. I had no idea when God got hold of my life in 1987 what would be in store for me. Never in my wildest dreams did I think I would get to do the things I have done, nor go to the places I have had the privilege to go to.

I have had the most rewarding life, and I am thankful to the Lord for all He has done for me. I can truly say it has been such an adventure, and I have enjoyed every minute of it. I wouldn't trade it for anything, as God has taken my brokenness and brought healing.

*"So we are convinced that every detail of our lives
is continually woven together to fit into God's perfect plan
of bringing good into our lives..."*
Romans 8:28 TPT*

*Verse from the 2018 edition, used by permission.

If you desire to know more about how you can be involved in missions and fulfill the Great Commission, please contact our offices.

Go To Nations
P.O. Box 10305
Jacksonville, FL 32247

(904) 398-6559
www.gotonations.org

For more information about our ministry, please visit our website:

www.gotonations.org/wheeler

SOURCES REFERENCED

1. "Pray for Thailand." *Operation World.* https://operationworld. org/locations/thailand/. Accessed November 22, 2021.

2. "Isan Thai in Thailand." *Joshua Project.* https://joshuaproject. net/people_groups/15460/th. Accessed November 22, 2021.

3. "Elizabeth." *Wikipedia.* https://en.wikipedia.org/wiki/Eliza- beth_(given_name), or *She Knows.* https://www.sheknows.com/ba- by-names/name/elizabeth/. Accessed November 22, 2021.

4. "Sarah." *She Knows.* https://www.sheknows.com/baby-names/ name/sarah/, or *Wikipedia.* https://en.wikipedia.org/wiki/Sarah_ (given_name). Accessed November 22, 2021.

5. "Ruth." *She Knows.* https://www.sheknows.com/baby-names/ name/ruth/. Accessed November 22, 2021.

Made in United States
Orlando, FL
15 June 2022

18852400R10232